THIS FISSURED LAND

An Ecological History of India

THIS FISSURED LAND

An Ecological History of India

MADHAV GADGIL
RAMACHANDRA GUHA

DELHI
OXFORD UNIVERSITY PRESS
OXFORD MELBOURNE

Oxford University Press, Walton Street, Oxford OX2 6DP

Oxford   New York
Athens   Auckland   Bangkok   Bombay
Calcutta   Cape Town   Dar es Salaam   Delhi
Florence   Hong Kong   Istanbul   Karachi
Kuala Lumpur   Madras ˌ Madrid   Melbourne
Mexico City   Nairobi   Paris   Singapore
Taipei   Tokyo   Toronto

and associates in
Berlin   Ibadan

ISBN 0 19 563341 5

**Published in association with
The Book Review Literary Trust, New Delhi**

Printed at Rekha Printers Pvt. Ltd., New Delhi 110020
and published by Neil O'Brien, Oxford University Press
YMCA Library Building, Jai Singh Road, New Delhi 110001

To the memory of

Verrier Elwin
Irawati Karve
D.D. Kosambi
Radhakamal Mukerjee

Contents

Acknowledgements   xiii

Prologue : Prudence and Profligacy   1

PART ONE: A THEORY OF ECOLOGICAL HISTORY   9

1 Habitats in Human History   11
  • Modes of Production and Modes of Resource Use   11
  • Four Historical Modes   14
  • Gathering   15
  • Simple Rules of Thumb   23
  • Pastoralism   27
  • Settled Cultivation   30
  • The Industrial Mode   39
  • Conflict Between and Within Modes   53
  • Intra-Modal Conflict   57
  • Recapitulation   64
  • Appendix : Note on Population   67

PART TWO: TOWARDS A CULTURAL ECOLOGY
             OF PRE-MODERN INDIA   69

2 **Forest and Fire**   71
- Geological History   71
- Prudent Predators   72
- Neolithic Revolution   76
- River-valley Civilizations   77
- Social Organization   82
- The Age of Empires   85
- Conservation from Above   87

3 **Caste and Conservation**   91
- Resource Crunch   91
- Conservation from Below   93
- An Eclectic Belief System   103
- The Village and the State   106
- Conclusion   109

PART THREE: ECOLOGICAL CHANGE AND SOCIAL
             CONFLICT IN MODERN INDIA

4 **Conquest and Control**   113
- Colonialism as an Ecological Watershed   116
- The Early Onslaught on Forests   118
- An Early Environment Debate   123
- Forest Policy Upto 1947   134
- The Balance Sheet of Colonial Forestry   140

5 **The Fight for the Forest**   146
- Hunter-gatherers : The Decline Towards
  Extinction   148
- The 'Problem' of Shifting Cultivation   150
- Settled Cultivators and the State   158
- Everyday Forms of Resistance: The Case
  of Jaunsar Bawar   164
- The Decline of the Artisanal Industry   171
- Conclusion: The Social Idiom of Protest   174
- The Mechanisms of Protest   177

6 **Biomass for Business** 181
- Two Versions of Progress : Gandhi and the
  Modernizers 181
- Forests and Industrialization : Four Stages 185
- The Balance Sheet of Industrial Forestry 193
- Sequential Exploitation: A Process Whereby
  a Whole Flock of Geese Laying Golden Eggs
  is Massacred One by One 197
- The Profligacy of Scientific Forestry 207

7 **Competing Claims on the Commons** 215
- Hunter-gatherers 217
- The Continuing 'Problem' of Shifting
  Cultivation 218
- The Changing Ecology of Settled
  Agriculture 221
- Claiming a Share of the Profits 229
- Wild Life Conservation: Animals Versus
  Humans 232

8 **Cultures in Conflict** 239

Bibliography 247

Index 267

TABLES

Table 1.1 Features of technology and economy in a society predominantly following one of the four major modes of resource use   60

Table 1.2 Features of social organization and ideology in a society predominantly following one of the major modes of resource use   62

Table 1.3 The nature of ecological impact in societies predominantly following one of the four major modes of resource use   65

Table 1.4 Features of social organization, ideology and ecological impact of societies in relation to changes in their resource base   66

Table 2.1 Climatic history of the Indian subcontinent   74

Table 3.1 Relative dependence in terms of percentage of reported biomass consumed of the different prey species by the three nomadic castes   99

Table 4.1 Revenue and surplus of Forest Department 1869–1925   136

Table 4.2 India's forests and the second World War   140

Table 6.1 Four stages of industrial forestry   193

Table 6.2 Forest revenue and surplus, selected years (at current prices)   195

Table 6.3 The loss of forest area for various purposes between 1951 and 1976   196

Table 6.4 Species and areas allotted to the

	Indian Plywood Manufacturing Co. Ltd., Dandeli and its allies	205
Table 6.5	Exploitable size of timber under working plans of Ankola high forests	206
Table 7.1	Change in intensity of different forms of resource-related conflict before and after independence	237

FIGURES

Figure 1.1	Material flows in hunter-gatherer society	19
Figure 1.2	Material flows in agrarian society	33
Figure 1.3	Material flows in industrial society	42
Figure 2.1	Paleo-river channels in northern India	80
Figure 3.1	Base villages and operating range of Nandiwallas	101
Figure 6.1	Raw material supply areas of West Coast Paper Mills	202
Figure 6.2	Raw material supply areas of Mysore Paper Mills	203
Figure 6.3	Sequential exploitation of Quilon Forest Division	204

Acknowledgements

A number of colleagues have contributed ideas and information for this book. We would like especially to thank Bill Burch, Anjan Ghosh, S.R.D. Guha, Kailash Malhotra, Juan Martinez Alier, Narendra Prasad, N.H. Ravindranath, C.V. Subbarao, M.D. Subash Chandran and Romila Thapar. Close readings of a draft by Mike Bell and Jim Scott were of great help in revising the manuscript for publication. Geetha Gadagkar typed numerous drafts with care and precision. Nor can we neglect to mention the support of the Indian Institute of Science, an institution which has successfully withstood the moral and intellectual degeneration of our times. This book was largely written at the Institute's Centre for Ecological Sciences, itself founded with the generous assistance of the Department of Environment, Government of India. Finally, we should note that an earlier version of chapter 5 was published in *Past and Present*, number 123, May 1989.

The dedication indicates our debt to an earlier generation of scholars. Verrier Elwin wrote a series of remarkable ethnographies of tribal communities on the margins of survival. His studies of the cultural meanings of the forest, and of the impact of colonial forestry on tribal life, are of abiding interest.

Through her imaginative work on the pastoral communities of Maharashtra, Irawati Karve laid the foundations of ecological anthropology in India. Her interpretation of the Mahabharata stands out for its insights into the ecological basis of social conflict in ancient India. D.D. Kosambi, mathematician and Sanskrit scholar, broke new ground through his materialist interpretations of Indian history. He also highlighted the importance of different modes of resource use in the mosaic of Indian culture. Radhakamal Mukerjee was an early harbinger of the coming together of ecology and the social sciences. His theoretical studies of 'Social Ecology' were fleshed out through detailed investigations of socio-ecological change in the Indo-Gangetic Plain. These four scholars may justly be regarded as the pioneers of human ecological studies in India; it is our privilege to acknowledge their influence on this work.

THIS IS A GOOD EXAMPLE OF CLEAR INTRODUCTION

Prudence and Profligacy

Contemporary India is a fantastic mosaic of fishing boats and trawlers, of cowherds and milk-processing plants, of paddy fields and rubber estates, of village blacksmiths and steel mills, of handlooms and nuclear reactors. Its 850 million people live in tiny fishing hamlets and camps of nomadic entertainers; in long-settled villages and slowly-decaying old towns; in suburban ghettoes and burgeoning metropolitan cities. Some build their shelters with bamboo and mud, others with cement and steel. Some cook with small twigs on a three-stone hearth, or with coconut husks on a mudstove, some with electricity and gas in modern kitchens.

Naturally, the demands of this remarkable mosaic on the country's resources are exceedingly varied. Thus, bamboo is coveted by rural artisans for weaving baskets and to fashion seed drills, by graziers to feed their cattle, and by industry to convert into paper and polyfibre. Landed peasants want the less fertile lands around villages to graze their cattle, the landless to scratch it to produce some grain, the forest departments to produce marketable timber. Peasants want the mountain valleys to grow paddy, power corporations to construct hydro-electric dams.

The resources so varyingly in demand are regulated in equally varying ways. There are sacred ponds which are not fished at all, and beach seiners recognize customary territorial rights of different fishing villages—even though none of this has any formal legal status. Many tribes in north-eastern India own land communally and put it to shifting cultivation, an ownership pattern recognized by law. Village common lands, used as grazing grounds, and wood-lots were once controlled by village communities; they are now government land under the control of revenue or forest departments. There are tenants who cultivate lands that belong to absentee landowners, though much of the land under cultivation is now owned by the tiller. A good bit of the land cultivated by tribals is, however, legally state-owned; this is part of a vast government estate which covers over a quarter of the country's land surface, mostly designated 'Reserved Forest'. Business corporations control large tracts of land, as tea or rubber estates, and there are moves to permit even larger holdings for forest-based industries.

A whole range of these resources, regulated and utilized in many different ways, is under great stress. There are very few deer and antelope left to hunt for hunter-gatherers such as the Phasepardhis of Maharashtra. A majority of the shepherds in peninsular India have given up keeping sheep for want of pastures to graze them. The shifting cultivators of north-eastern India have drastically shortened their fallow periods from a traditional fifteen to a current five years. All over, peasants have been forced to burn dung in their hearths for want of fuelwood, while there is insufficient manure in fields. Ground-water levels are rapidly going down as commercial farmers sink deeper and deeper bore-wells. There are long shutdowns in industry for want of power and raw material, and every urban centre is groaning under acute shortages of housing, fuel, water, power and transport.

In this ancient land, which harbours what is undoubtedly the most heterogeneous of cultures on earth, these resource shortages have given rise to an amazing range of adjustments, collusions and conflicts. However, the country is living on borrowed time. It is eating, at an accelerating rate, into the capital stock of its renewable resources of soil, water, plant and animal life. Does this mean we are headed for disaster? Or is this a temporary phase before we get back on the path of sustainable resource use? Or perhaps before further technological advances open up an undreamt range of resources? It is obviously true that not *all* resources are being decimated everywhere. In the village of Gopeshwar in the Garhwal Himalaya, for example, there is a nice grove of oak and other broad-leaved species. All families in the village carefully observe traditional regulations on the quantum of plant biomass removed from this grove. But this quantum is quite inadequate for their needs, and for the balance they turn to other hill slopes where exploitation is unregulated and denudation at an advanced stage. This was apparently not the case some decades ago, when the grove was larger and fulfilled the demands of a smaller population in a sustainable fashion.

Human history is, as a whole, precisely such a patchwork of prudence and profligacy, of sustainable and exhaustive resource use. In contemporary India the instances of profligacy clearly outnumber (and outweigh) those of prudence, although this book will argue that such was not always the case. In our own times, acute resource shortages have given rise to a host of social conflicts, and these have significant consequences for what is now happening to the life of India's people and to the health of its land.

The implications of the uses and misuses of India's biological resources are only dimly perceived by the rich and the powerful. But we, in common with the majority of Indians who face the burden of this misuse in their daily lives, believe them to be of tremendous significance: hence this book. We have attempted an ecological history of changing human interactions with living resources, using the Indian case illustratively to explore four themes. The significance of these, in our view, is scarcely restricted to one country, nor even to one continent.

- RESOURCE SHORTAGES → SOCIAL CONFLICT.
- THE RICH AND POWERFUL ARE NOT AWARE OF THE MISUSE OF RESOURCES

First we ask: under what conditions may we expect human beings to exercise prudence in their use of natural resources?

Second, we investigate both the 'hardware' and 'software' of natural resource use in different historical periods. 'Hardware' refers to the forces and relations of production—namely the technological infrastructure and the systems of property—open access, family, communal, corporate, or state—governing resource use. 'Software' refers to the belief systems (for example, religion, tradition, or science) which legitimize and validate human interactions with nature.

Third, this book analyses the forms of social conflict between different groups of resource users. Here we are especially interested in changes in the intensity of social conflict over time, and in its escalation as one mode of resource use gains ascendancy over another.

Finally, we are interested in the impact of changing patterns of resource use, as well as of social conflict, on the status of living resources. Beginning with the conditions that favour prudence, we come full circle with our analysis of the conditions under which profligacy predominates.

These four themes—i.e. prudence, profligacy, strategies of resource use, and the conflicts to which they give rise—provide the unifying framework for the three parts of this book. The theoretical framework of the study is outlined in Part I. Here we analyse the different forms of restraint on resource use reported from human societies. We locate these practices of resource use in specific cultural and historical contexts. This link between ecology and history is accomplished by means of our typology, which we designate 'modes of resource use'. We put this forward as a supplement to the 'modes of production' scheme which social scientists have traditionally used as a framework for historical periodization.

Part II presents a new interpretation of how the cultural and ecological mosaic of Indian society came together. Given the fragmentary nature of historical evidence on this, our reconstruction may be viewed as *one* plausible scenario of the ebb and flow of different social systems, as well as of different belief systems of resource use, which existed in the Indian subcontinent before British colonialism. Based on our fieldwork in peninsular India, we advance an ecological interpretation of the caste system, thereby complementing standard economic and ideological interpretations of the persistence of caste as the organizing principle of Indian society.

Part III draws on more abundant source material. It presents a socio-ecological analysis of the new modes of resource use which were introduced by the British, and which have continued to operate, with modifications, after independence in 1947. We argue that British colonial rule marks a crucial watershed in the ecological history of India. The country's encounter with a technologically advanced and dynamic culture gave rise to profound dislocations at various levels of Indian society. While sharply critical of colonialism, Indian historians have, in the main, been indifferent to the ecological consequences of British intervention. Our analysis, in contrast, highlights the essential interdependence of ecological and social changes that came in the wake of colonial rule. Furthermore, our study shows that the socio-ecological consequences of European colonialism in India, while significant in themselves, were quite different from those in the New World.

The British did not merely change Indian history, they also changed the writing of it—by providing historians with an unprecedented level of documentation. Consequently, Part III draws upon a far wider range of sources than the earlier two parts; even so, its focus is only on the most important aspect of the ecological encounter between Britain and India—changes in the ownership and management systems of India's forests. For over a century, India has had the benefits—such as these are—of an extensive system of state forestry. With over one-fifth of the country's land area in its charge, the forest department has been, since the late nineteenth century, by far our biggest landlord. Since students of modern Indian history have shown a surprising unawareness of this fact (cf. Sarkar 1983;

Kumar 1983), and also since every member of India's agrarian society had a direct economic relation to forest produce, a historical assessment of colonial forest management is long overdue. The edifice of colonial forestry has been taken over by the government of independent India. Therefore our analysis will shed light on the links between economic development and ecological change in one important Third World country. Finally, the Indian case, as presented in our history, may illuminate several current debates on tropical deforestation.

In this manner, Part I presents a theory of ecological history; Part II provides a fresh interpretive history of pre-modern India; and Part III contains a socio-ecological history of the forest in modern India.

Although our focus is specifically on interactions between humans and living resources, the business of covering the broad sweep of Indian history is daunting. So we have no illusions about the 'definitiveness' of this enterprise. Our generalizations and data are bound to be modified, altered, even overthrown, in the course of time, as is normal with academic ventures in relatively uncharted terrain. Yet it is undeniable that to date historians of India have been almost completely unaware of the ecological dimensions of social life. Their focus has been more or less exclusively on relations around land and within the workplace, never on the ecological fabric within which both field and factory are embedded, and which these in turn transform. Hence the questions which scaffold this book—the hardware and software of natural resource use, social conflicts around nature, and the cumulative impact on ecological health—are, we believe, asked and partially answered for perhaps the first time in relation to ancient, medieval and modern India.

Ultimately, the ecological history of India must be constructed around detailed regional studies, sharply bounded in time and space. Yet there are periods in the development of scholarship when a new interpretation cannot endlessly await the steady accumulation of certified data. Indeed, to plot the pieces of a jigsaw puzzle one must begin determining the shape and structure of the puzzle. In the circumstances, while this book provides new data and new interpretations of old data, it provides above all a new and alternative framework for understanding Indian society and history.

Here we draw inspiration from Marc Bloch, who prefaced his great study of French agriculture—itself a model of ecological analysis—with these words:

> There are moments in the development of a subject when a synthesis, however premature it may appear, can contribute more than a host of analytical studies; in other words, there are times when for once the formulations of problems is more urgent than their solution . . . I could liken myself to an explorer making a rapid survey of the horizon before plunging into thickets from which the wider view is no longer possible. The gaps in my account are naturally enormous. I have done my best not to conceal any deficiencies, whether in the state of our knowledge in general or in my own documentation, which is based partly on first-hand research but to a much greater extent on soundings taken at random . . . When the time comes for my own work to be superseded by studies of deeper penetration, I shall feel well rewarded if confrontation with my false conjectures has made history learn the truth about herself.

PART ONE

A Theory of Ecological History

CHAPTER ONE

Habitats in Human History

Modes of Production and Modes of Resource Use

Many social scientists have found the Marxist concept of modes of production useful when classifying societies according to their technologies and relations of production. Undoubtedly the original scheme, of primitive communism–slavery–feudalism–capitalism, derived largely from the European experience, has been modified by an increasing sophistication within the writing of the histories of non-western cultures. Notwithstanding the problems in applying European models of feudalism to societies such as India and China, as well as the continuing debates around the so-called Asiatic mode of production, the framework itself remains very much in favour. It is strongest while delineating the features of the capitalist mode of production. With the emergence of capitalism as a 'world system', it is currently enjoying a revival in those far-flung corners of the globe where the clash between pre-capitalist relations of production and the capitalist ethos is only now gathering momentum.

Among several important criticisms made of the mode of production scheme, we single out three. The first, made by

Marxists themselves, relates to the relative lack of emphasis in this scheme on political structures and struggles. In his widely-noticed interventions in the 'transition' debate, Robert Brenner argued that the form and intensity of political conflict, rather than changes in production technology or expansion in trade, better explain the nature of the transition from feudalism to capitalism in different parts of Europe (Brenner 1976 and 1978). Other scholars have suggested a supplementary concept, 'mode of power', to more accurately capture the structure of power and domination in different societies (Chatterjee 1983). Second, there are criticisms which, while accepting the relevance of the scheme to European history, express reservations about its application elsewhere. The European model of feudalism does not, for example, fit the Indian experience, and the Asiatic mode is scarcely of any use either, since the state played by no means as important a part in providing public works and irrigation facilities for agriculture as this notion suggests. Finally, there are the criticisms of non-Marxists (and non-economists). These amount to the view that, whatever the merits of the mode of production concept while explaining differences in economic structure, this concept is of little use when interpreting differences in the religious, cultural and ideological attributes of different societies.

While all these criticisms are compelling, from the perspective of this book they do not go far enough. An ecological approach to such questions suggests that the mode of production concept is not adequately materialistic in the first place. This may seem an ironic accusation against a doctrine as supposedly materialist as Marxism, yet a little reflection bears it out. Marxist analyses usually begin with the economic 'infrastructure'—the so-called relations of production and productive forces—without investigating the ecological context, i.e. the soil, water, animal, mineral and vegetative bases of society in which the infrastructure is embedded. As exemplified by recent political and economic histories of modern India, both Marxist and non-Marxist, the most major lacuna in existing

POLITICAL AND ECONOMIC ANALYSES
AND HISTORIES DO NOT TAKE INTO ACCOUNT THE
ECOLOGICAL INFRASTRUCTURE.

Habitats in Human History • 13

scholarship is an inadequate appreciation of the *ecological* infrastructure of human society. We therefore propose to complement the concept of modes of production with the concept of modes of resource use.

While focusing on spheres of production, such as the field and the factory, most analyses of modes of production have ignored the natural contexts in which the field and factory are embedded—the contexts to which they respond, and which they in turn transform. The concept of modes of resource use extends the realm of production to include flora, fauna, water and minerals. It asks very similar questions. With respect to relations of production, for example, it investigates the forms of property, management and control, and of allocation and distribution, which govern the utilization of natural resources in different societies and historical periods. And with respect to productive forces, it analyses the varying technologies of resource exploitation, conversion and transportation that characterize different social orders.

While complementing the mode of production framework, the mode of resource use scheme incorporates two additional dimensions. First, it examines whether one can identify characteristic ideologies that govern different modes. More importantly, it identifies the ecological impact of various modes, and assesses the consequences of these different modes for the pattern, distribution and availability of natural resources.

Three caveats are in order here. First, the mode of resource use concept, like the mode of production concept, is at bottom an 'ideal type'. Hence, the identification of distinct modes does not preclude the existence of more than one mode in any given social (or, more accurately, socio-ecological) formation. Still, it is usually possible to identify the *dominant* mode within a socio-ecological formation. Second, our treatment is largely restricted to human uses of *living* resources—i.e., flora and fauna—both husbanded and in their natural state. This framework can of course be extended to incorporate other natural resources, such as water and minerals. Finally, one important

DEVELOPMENT PATH OF CAPITALIST
AND SOCIALIST SYSTEMS ARE DIFFERENT,
BUT - FOR ECOLOGY THESE
ARE SIMILAR.

14 • *This Fissured Land*

respect in which our scheme differs from the Marxian mode of production scheme is that the industrial mode of resource use, as defined by us, includes both capitalist and socialist societies. While there are significant differences between socialist and capitalist paths of development—for example with respect to property and the role of the market—from an ecological point of view the similarities in these two developmental paths are more significant than the differences. For instance, there are structural similarities in the scale and direction of natural re-source flows, the technologies of resource exploitation, the patterns of energy use, the ideologies of human–nature interaction, the specific resource-management practices, and, ulti-mately, the cumulative impact of all these on the living environ-ment in capitalist and socialist societies. Consequently, it makes sense to treat industrial socialism and industrial capitalism as being, ecologically speaking, simply two variants of one in-dustrial mode of resource use.

Four Historical Modes

From the long sweep of human history we can distil four distinct modes of resource use: gathering (including shifting cultivation); nomadic pastoralism; settled cultivation; industry. Later we shall examine the distinctive characteristics of each mode across different axes. These shall include:

• aspects of *technology*, such as sources of energy, materials used, and the knowledge base relating to resource use
• aspects of *economy*, such as the spatial scale of resource flows and the modes of resource acquisition
• aspects of *social organization*, such as the size of social group, the division of labour, and mechanisms of control over access to resources
• aspects of *ideology*, including broad perceptions of the man–nature relationship, as well as specific practices promoting resource conservation or destruction
• the nature of the *ecological impact* itself

After presenting the ideal-typical characteristics of different modes of resource use, we outline the characteristic forms of social conflict *between* as well as *within* different modes. The chapter concludes with a recapitulation, while the appendix contains some reflections on the forms of reproductive behaviour typical of different modes.

Gathering

Technology: The largest period of human history has been spent within the gathering mode of resource use, during which the hunting of wild animals and the gathering of vegetable matter were the mainstay of subsistence. Gathering continues to be significant during the phase of shifting cultivation as well (cf. Elwin 1939; von Fürer Haimendorf 1943a), and we may also include societies that practise shifting agriculture under this rubric. In the gathering mode, societies depend almost exclusively on human muscle power and wood fuel as sources of energy, and on naturally available plants, animals and stones to fulfil their material requirements. Their knowledge base is fairly limited, and nature is viewed as almost totally capricious, as something not subject to human control. The ability to store food and other materials is also very limited, as is the ability to transport materials over long distances.

The economy within this mode of resource use is based on resources which are acquired within a small area of, at best, a few hundred square kilometres. Only a very small range of resources, such as shells, peacock feathers and flint tools, may be transported over larger distances. The diversity of plant and animal matter consumed from the social group's immediate surroundings is high; yet, given this restrictive spatial scale as well as the limited ability to process resources, the actual variety of resources used *in toto* is small, while the quantities consumed are restricted to subsistence needs. Societies which pursue the gathering mode of resource use are highly susceptible to variations within resource availability through space and time. They respond to such variations by fine-tuned adaptations to local conditions. In the harsher and more variable environments the people comprising these societies subsist as nomadic bands; in the more productive and stable environments they exist as tribal groups confined to relatively small territories. Such territorial restriction also continues with a swich-over to shifting cultivation.

Social organization: The sizes of social groups among hunter gatherer–shifting cultivators are small: kin groups of the order of a few hundred perhaps, largely in face-to-face communication with each other. There are hardly any transactions outside such social groups; the relationship with aliens is largely one of conflict, often over territorial control (Rappaport 1984). The division of labour within these groups is minimal; what exists is primarily based on age and sex, and to some extent upon knowledge and leadership abilities. The women will principally be found involved in gathering plant foods and small animals, while the men will be found hunting the larger animals. As regards the gender equation, men play a greater role in organizing information and taking decisions relating to resource use on behalf of the group as a whole.

In the gathering mode there is little variation among members of a group in terms of access to resources, and notions of private property are extremely poorly developed. Within a group, here, no individual is in a position to dominate and coerce others to any significant degree. While within-group differences thus tend to be low, the differences between groups may or may not be equally low. Till 10,000 years ago, before plants and animals began to be husbanded by humans, between-group differences were, without doubt, at a low level. The human populations of any region might then have been divided amongst a large number of endogamous groups competing with each other for control over land and water. This competition would have been intense in productive and stable environments, such as tropical rain forests, where inter-tribal warfare over territorial rights was probably a routine occurrence. On the other hand, the limits of territories are likely to have been much fuzzier in harsher, highly variable environments, such as tropical deserts or the coniferous forests of higher latitudes. Here, inter-tribal conflicts would have been correspondingly less acute. With the beginnings of cultivation and animal husbandry, and later the industrial revolution, people who pursued the gathering mode came to be increasingly disadvantaged *vis-à-vis* people with access to advanced levels of technology.

Economy: We may characterize the economy of gatherers as a *natural* economy, in so far as it draws all its resources directly from nature (Dasmann 1988, Worster 1988). Here, the flows of resources are largely closed on spatial scales of a few hundred, or at best a few thousand, square kilometres, over which each endogamous social group of gatherers might range (Fig. 1.1). While there may be some flows of materials, such as shells or stone tools, over longer distances, these are insignificant (in terms of physical mass) when compared to food and the other resources utilized by the human groups concerned. The material flows would, therefore, not only be closed, they would also be balanced, i.e. with inflows matching outflows on a fairly restricted spatial scale. This balance is apt to be disrupted when gatherers come into contact with people practising more advanced modes of resource use. The latter are then likely to organize net resource outflows from regions inhabited by gatherers, and perhaps also affect such regions through inflows of wastes—of materials they discard.

Gatherer societies, as indeed all human societies, encounter three distinct situations with respect to their resource base. First, their demands on the resource base may be small compared to the overall availability. This may be due to their having colonized a new habitat—as must have happened when some groups first crossed over into North America—or on account of a technological innovation such as the bow and arrow, which opened up a new range of species to prey upon. This is a situation analogous to that of r-strategists in ecological literature, i.e. of populations that increase relatively rapidly for most of the time. The r-strategists include weedy species which rapidly colonize disturbed environments, or micro-organisms like influenza which spread in epidemics. Other societies may be in equilibrium with their resource base, as for instance fishing communities in an isolated coral island. These are analogous to the k-strategists of ecological literature, examples of which include shade-tolerant and timber-tree species in rain forests, or micro-organisms like tubercular bacilli. Finally, societies may be confronted with a shrinking resource base, as may have confronted gatherer societies who were displaced by advancing glaciers, or by technologically more advanced human societies. Ecologists have no specific term for this situation. However, given the fact that some twenty times as many biological species have gone extinct as are alive today, many biological populations must be adapted to dealing with a shrinking resource base.

Under conditions approaching equilibrium with their resource base, gatherers exist in kinship-based, small, viscous groups that are more or less tied to specific localities, depending on the variability of the environment. Such an organization might be broken up when gatherers come in contact with people who work within more advanced modes of resource use, and consequently have to adjust to a shrinking resource base. In the former case, the group's members would tend to be involved in a network of co-operative behaviour, and would be very sensitive to group interests. In the latter case, such co-operative behaviour, as also the perception of group interests, may dissolve.

Ideology: To gatherers, with their limited knowledge base, nature follows its own capricious ways, hardly subject to human control. Gatherers typically regard humans as merely part of a community of beings that includes other living creatures, as well as elements of the landscape such as streams and rocks. Especially where gatherers are attached to particular localities, as in productive and stable environments like tropical humid

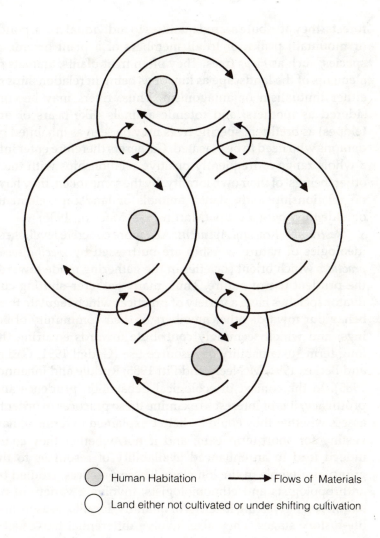

○ Human Habitation   ──▶ Flows of Materials

○ Land either not cultivated or under shifting cultivation

Figure 1.1

In productive, stable environments, hunter-gatherer cum shifting-cultivators maintain well defined territories. Cycles of materials in such environments are largely closed on the spatial scales of territories with flows of materials across territorial boundaries being much less significant. The thickness of an arrow indicates the intensity of the flow.

forests, they attribute sacred qualities to individual trees, ponds or mountain peaks, or to all members of a plant or animal species, such as *Ficus* trees. They often treat plants, animals or elements of the landscape as kin, or as being in relationships of either mutualism or antagonism. Thus, rivers may be considered as mothers, and totemic animals (like bears or antelopes) as brethren; specific trees may be seen as inhabited by demons who need to be placated. Gatherers therefore enter into a whole range of frequently positive relationships with these other 'beings' of their own locality. By the same token, they have no relationship with plants, animals or landscape elements outside their own locality (Martin 1978; Macleod 1936).

Restraint—Real and Apparent: At a more concrete level, these ideologies of nature worship are buttressed by *specific social practices* which orient societies in the gathering mode towards the prudent use of nature. Thus, many gatherer–shifting cultivator societies have a variety of practices which regulate their behaviour towards other members of their community of beings, and which seemingly contribute towards ensuring the long-term sustainability of resource use (Gadgil 1991; Gadgil and Berkes 1991; McNeely and Pitt 1985; Ruddle and Johannes 1985). In the context of ecological debates on prudence and profligacy, it is of interest to examine these practices in order to assess whether they could be better explained in terms of harvesting for short-term gain; and if not, whether they could indeed lead to an enhanced availability of resources to the group as a whole in the long run. These practices, studied by anthropologists and ethnobiologists, involve a variety of restraints on harvesting in terms of quantity, locality, season, and life-history stages. They also involve differential harvests by age, sex, or social class. It is, of course, possible that such apparent restraint may have nothing to do with a long-term conservation of the resource base. A harvester interested in calculating an immediate return may still not use a resource if the net gain obtainable from it is below a certain threshold, which in turn would depend on the net gain obtainable from

alternative resources. We must therefore examine each supposed instance of restraint to assess whether it could involve
such a discontinuation of resource use. This may happen, for
instance, because the cost of harvest increases excessively
(Smith 1983; Borgerhoff Mulder 1988). ✓

The whole range of practices demonstrating the restrained
use of resources by human beings can be classified under ten
broad categories:

• A quantitative restriction on the amount harvested of a given
species, or from a given locality, by harvesters. The imposition
of such quotas implies that the harvest is halted at resource
densities greater than those at which individuals would find
the net gains too low to continue harvesting. As a corollary,
these quotas are likely to enhance total yields over the long-
term, and at the sacrifice of some immediate return. These are
therefore likely to be genuine instances of restraint. NOT NECESSARILY

• Harvesting a certain resource may be abandoned when resource densities fall. In parts of New Guinea, for example, the
hunting of Birds of Paradise is temporarily abandoned if their
populations decline (Eaton 1985). This sort of response is expected from harvesters who are attempting to maximize a
short-term net gain, since a fall in the resource density would
progressively increase the costs of harvesting. It is possible,
though not very probable, that harvesting is abandoned well
before this level is reached in the interest of long-term yields.

• Harvesting from a certain habitat patch may be abandoned
if yields from that patch are reduced. Thus, in the Torres Strait,
fishing may be stopped in regions where fish yields are known
to have declined (Nietschmann 1985). This again is a response
which is to be expected from a forager who is attempting to
maximize immediate net returns. It can be related to long-term
resource conservation only if concrete quantitative evidence is
available to indicate that harvesting is abandoned in advance
of the returns reaching a value low enough to justify abandoning harvests. *Good*

• Harvesting from a certain species may be abandoned in a

certain season. Illustrative here is the taboo, in many Indian villages, on hunting certain animals between July and October (Gadgil 1985a). Possibly this taboo is a consequence of returns which are too low to justify harvesting for immediate gains in that season. Conversely, if in fact net returns in that season are expected to be relatively high, this is likely to be a conservation measure.

• Harvesting from a certain habitat patch may be abandoned in a certain season. Again, this could be a response to an excessively low level of net gain from that habitat patch in that season. This should be verified by a comparison with net gains in other seasons, and if possible by a quantitative assessment.

• Certain stages of life—by age, sex, size or reproductive status —may immunize an animal or bird from being harvested. For example, in the village of Kokre-Bellur in the state of Karnataka, birds in the breeding within a heronary may be left unmolested, though they may be hunted elsewhere and at other seasons (Gadgil 1985b). If such protected stages appear to be critical to population replenishment, and if they are likely to yield as high or higher net returns than the unprotected stages, it is reasonable to assume that this measure is designed specifically to conserve the resource. On the other hand, if these stages are likely to yield lower net returns in comparison with the un-protected stages, then they might be left unharvested simply in the interest of maximizing the immediate net gain.

• Certain species may never be harvested either because of the relative difficulty of procuring them (risk of injury during the hunt) or because they carry parasites that can affect humans. If these conditions do not operate, conservation can indeed serve the long-term interest of human resource use: if the species thus protected enhances the availability of some other species that are harvested. This is likely for a widely protected species, such as trees belonging to the genus *Ficus*, but much less likely for a wide variety of species protected as totemic by certain tribes (Gadgil 1989).

• Certain habitat patches may either never be harvested, or be subject to very low levels of harvest through strict regulation. It is extremely difficult to arrive at workable prescriptions on quantitative quotas, closed seasons, or protected life-history stages that decisively guard against resource decimation. Providing refugia (sacred groves, sacred ponds, etc.) may then be the most easily perceived and most efficient way of guarding against resource depletion (Gadgil and Vartak 1976).

• Certain methods of resource harvest may be wholly prohibited or strictly regulated. Thus, fishing by poisoning river pools is severely regulated by tradition in many parts of India (Gadgil 1985a). If these methods are likely to provide as high, or higher, net returns than the permitted methods, their regulation may serve the interest of long-term resource conservation.

• Certain age/sex categories or social groups may be banned from employing certain sorts of harvesting methods, or from utilizing certain species or habitat patches. Thus in New Guinea adult males are banned from hunting rodents (Rappaport 1984). This could contribute towards long-term resource conservation by moderating the total amount of harvest. It could also assist in long-term conservation by restricting the access to a limited number of individuals who may more readily come to use the resource in a prudent fashion. It is, of course, quite possible that such restrictions merely benefit segments of the community that are in positions of power, without really serving the interest of long-term conservation.

Simple Rules of Thumb

Given the complexity of ecological communities, precise prescriptions for the prudent use of living resources are difficult. Detailed quantitative prescriptions seem impossible, given the present state of knowledge (Clark 1985). This is particularly so if the entire prey population is continually subject to being harvested. But certain simple prescriptions to avert a resource collapse seem easy to formulate and should have a significant effect in enabling sustainable use. These prescriptions are five-fold: provide complete protection to certain habitat patches which represent different ecosystems, so that resource populations are always maintained above some threshold; provide complete protection to certain selected species so that community-level interactions are disrupted minimally; protect such life-history stages as appear critical to the maintenance of the resource population; provide complete protection to resource populations at certain times of the year; and organize resource use in such a way that only relatively small groups of people control or have access to a particular resource population (Johannes 1978).

Modern ecological and evolutionary theory suggests that such prescriptions are likely to assist in avoiding an environmental collapse, although they would by no means ensure harvests at maximum sustainable yield levels. In his classic experiments on prey-predator cycles of protozoans, Gause showed that prey extinction could be effectively avoided only by providing the prey a refugium, an area of the experimental arena inaccessible to the predator where the prey could maintain a minimal population and from which other areas could be colonized by it (Gause 1969). Sacred groves, sacred ponds, and stretches of sea coast from which all fishing is prohibited are examples of such refugia. Modern ecological theory also stresses the significance of certain species which serve as keystone resources or mobile links in maintaining the overall functioning of the community (Terborgh 1986). The tree of the genus *Ficus*— to which belong species such as banyan and peepal (widely protected in Asia and Africa)—is one such keystone resource. Contemporary ecological theory also points to the fact that certain stages in a population are of higher 'reproductive value', and therefore more significant in permitting continued population growth. Pregnant does and nesting birds, again often protected by humans, are such stages (Fisher 1958; Slobodkin, 1968). Finally, recent work on the evolution of co-operative behaviour emphasizes that restraint is progressively more likely to evolve if the number of individuals involved in repeated social interactions gets progressively smaller (Joshi 1987; Feldman and Thomas 1986; Berkes and Kence 1987).

It thus appears plausible that, over the course of human history, there have been human groups whose interests were strongly linked to the prudent use of their resource base, and that such groups did indeed evolve conservation practices. Many of the practices described above have in fact been reported from different gatherer societies. These conservation practices were apparently based on several simple rules of thumb that tended to ensure the long-term sustenance of a resource base. These rules of thumb were necessarily approximate and would have been arrived at by trial and error. Practices which seemed to keep the resource base secure may have gradually become stronger; conversely, there could have been a gradual rejection of those practices which appeared to destroy the resource base (Joshi and Gadgil 1991). Conservation practices observed by various other social groups may also be emulated if they appear successful in resource conservation. Such a process is likely to lead to the persistence of a whole range of practices, some beneficial from the point of view of resource conservation, but also others that are neutral; and perhaps some that might once have been beneficial or neutral but later prove harmful on account of changed circumstances.

Diversity of resources: In conjunction with their various practices of restrained use, gatherer societies are remarkable for the great diversity of biological resources they utilize. Studies on the American Indians of Amazonia have shown that they utilize several hundred different species of plants and animals for food, and as sources of structural materials and drugs. They have distinct names for as many as 500 to 800 biological species (Berlin 1973). For another thing, different tribal groups may be familiar with and utilize a different set of species. As early as 30,000 years ago, for example, two Neanderthal groups of Dordogne in France had apparently specialized in different prey species, one group concentrating on horses and the other on reindeer (Leakey 1981). We may therefore conclude that primitive gatherer-shifting-cultivator societies valued a very wide range of biological diversity, and evolved cultural practices which promoted the persistence of this diversity over long intervals.

Deliberate destruction: While gatherer societies typically have a variety of practices that could help conserve the resource base of their own localities, they may also deliberately destroy the resource bases of aliens. Thus, when New Guinea highlanders defeat and drive away a neighbouring group from its territory, the conquerors do not immediately occupy this territory. They cut valued fruit-yielding trees from the conquered group's territory, thereby rendering it far less desirable for recoloniza-tion by the conquered. The actual territory may be physically occupied only later, if it is not reoccupied by the vanquished group (Rappaport 1984).

Ecological impact: Gatherer societies, with their low popula-tion densities, low per capita resource demands, cycles of ma-terials closed on limited spatial scales, and a number of prac-tices that promote sustainable resource use, necessarily have a low level of impact upon the environment. Over long intervals, however, even this can add up to substantial changes. Such changes are especially likely when the resource base changes relatively rapidly, as might have happened with fluctuations during the ice age; or when a gatherer population encounters an entirely new resource base, as during the initial colonization of the Americas. It has, for instance, been suggested that the widespread extinction of large mammalian species during the Pleistocene was a consequence of human overhunting, and that many of the savanna-grassland formations of East and South Africa are a result of fires lit over tens of thousands of years by human populations (Menant *et. al* 1985). Nevertheless, the pace of such impact would be considerably slower than the pace in populations which possess more advanced modes of resource use, as described later in this chapter. Some writers have claimed that hunter-gatherers possess an ecological wisdom far in advance of that shown by modern man (Shepard 1982). Be that as it may, it is indisputable that the ecological impact of this mode of resource use is minimal.

Pastoralism

Technology: The long period of history when human beings were exclusively gatherers began to come to a close with the domestication of plants and animals. This coincided with the withdrawal of glaciers, ten thousand years ago. It is possible that climatic and vegetational change prompted human populations to intensify resource use, and to initiate agriculture and animal husbandry. These processes began in parallel, and have often gone hand-in-hand. While the cultivation of plants has been of greater significance in tracts of moderate-to-high rainfall and moderate-to-high temperatures, animal husbandry has held pride of place in tracts of low rainfall, and at the higher altitudes and latitudes where temperatures are too low to support agriculture (Grigg 1980). Over large tracts where agriculture is not feasible, it is also difficult to maintain herds of domestic animals within a single locality. Animal husbandry is therefore based, in such tracts, on moving herds from place to place often over several hundred kilometres. This requires taking advantage of the seasonal abundance of grazing resources in different parts of a region. Nomadic pastoralism thus evolved as a distinctive mode of resource use, a mode that held sway for several centuries over large regions, particularly in Central Asia and North and Central Africa (Leeds and Vayda 1965; Forde 1963).

Pastorals have access to animal muscle power, an important additional source of energy, especially for transport. The animals also serve as a source of food which can be tapped as required, thus greatly increasing flexibility in the use of different habitats.

Economy: Nomadic pastorals move over large distances, and with their access to animal energy, have been critical in creating flows of resources over distance scales that are vastly greater than those which prevail in gatherer societies. The resources they moved have been both high-bulk commodities like salt, and high-value, low-bulk luxury items like precious stones and musk. They also served as carriers of information about resources of distant regions and of technologies elaborated by other societies. Consequently, pastorals not only continued some hunting-gathering while on the move, and produced meat, milk, hide and wool from their animals, but also acquired resources, especially from settled agricultural societies, in exchange for material and information. Even more important, nomadic pastorals could effectively deploy force to usurp resources from societies of cultivators, as Chengiz Khan did with great success over the huge regions of Asia and Europe. Indeed, nomadic pastoral societies, in their heyday, may have behaved much like the r-strategists of ecological literature.

Social organization: The social groups of nomadic pastorals remain limited to kin groups of a few thousand; nevertheless, they come in contact with large numbers of other groups over an extensive terrain. Within the social groups of pastorals, the division of labour is fairly limited. It is based on age, sex, and leadership qualities which emerge during inter-group conflict. Women may be more involved in feeding, milking, and tending animals, men in deciding on migration routes and herding animals while on the move.

In the pastoral mode, elements of private property begin to emerge. However, while herds are usually owned by separate households, pastures are invariably common property, with individual herdsmen possessing rights of access and usufruct. However, like gatherer societies, nomadic groups are relatively egalitarian (Khazanov 1984). With this, coercion within groups remains limited; indeed there is considerable premium on cooperation within the group, especially in the context of conflict with other groups, nomadic or otherwise.

Ideology: By surviving successfully in harsh and variable environments, and with little attachment to any particular locality, nomadic pastorals were perhaps the first societies to perceive human communities as separate from nature, and therefore in a position to dominate it. Since the usurpation of resources controlled by alien and settled communities constituted a significant part of their strategy of resource acquisition, they were unlikely to evolve strong traditions of careful or restrained resource use. Indeed, ideologies which rejected the attribution of sacred value to living creatures or to natural objects, e.g. religions like Judaism, Christianity and Islam, arose in tracts that were dominated by nomadic pastorals in the Middle East. In fact, as Lynn White (1967) notes, such religions sometimes prescribed the deliberate destruction of sacred trees and sacred groves.

RELIGION

The ritual life of nomads is quite meagre: no pantheon of gods, as in peasant societies, no system of totemism, as in gatherer societies. Ritual importance may be placed on livestock, but almost never on natural locations or specific fields. Equally striking is the relative unimportance here of witchcraft. In comparison with peasants and gatherers, nomadic pastorals have little need to pacify or placate nature; in the event of resource shortages they remove themselves to more resource-abundant areas—something peasants cannot do (Goldschmidt 1979).

Apart from these broad ideologies, in their day-to-day interaction with nature nomads do have practices which reveal a deliberate restraint on resource use. These practices include the complete exclusion of grazing pressure during certain periods within fodder reserves, and its limited use during other periods in terms of the kind and number of animals permitted for grazing—as for example in the system of *ahmias* around Taif in Saudi Arabia (Draz 1985).

Ecological impact: It is possible that nomadic pastorals contributed to a gradual overgrazing, and to the expansion of arid regions at their margins, all through their history. This they have certainly done across many regions in modern times. They have also contributed to ecological degradation through the organization of trade and the diffusion of technology over large distances and perhaps most importantly by disseminating the belief in man's mastery over nature.

Settled Cultivation

Technology: Human societies learnt to cultivate plants and domesticate animals around the same time, beginning some 10,000 years ago. In some regions the two developed hand-in-hand, with the traction power of animals and the manurial value of their dung being vital to agricultural operations. This, for instance, was the case in the Middle East, from where the use of cattle and the plough, and the cultivation of wheat and barley, gradually spread over parts of Asia, Europe and Africa. In other areas, domesticated animals played a much less significant part in cultivation, as in the paddy-growing tracts of Asia—or had no role at all—as in the case of maize cultivation in pre-Columbian America (Grigg 1980).

Cultivation involves an intensified production of certain species of plants, and the removal of plant material from a relatively restricted area of land. The plant material so removed, for instance cereal grains, are particularly rich in certain elements, such as nitrogen and phosphorus, and contain a number of micronutrients, like boron and molybdenum, in smaller quantities. The continuation of cultivation on a piece of land therefore depends on returning to the earth what is taken away from it. This happens either through long periods of fallow, as in shifting cultivation, or by the application of river silt, organic manure, or mineral fertilizers if the same piece of land is tilled year after year. Shifting cultivation is, of course, the option followed so long as the amount of land available is large relative to the population. As this ratio declines, the same piece of land has to be used more and more intensively. Almost everywhere, this has called for the extensive use of organic manure derived from natural vegetation in the surrounding areas, gathered either through grazing domestic animals or directly by human effort. This has changed radically only in recent times, when fossil fuel energy began to be used to efficiently mine, transport and synthesize mineral fertilizers to augment agricultural production (Pimentel and Pimentel 1979).

Through most of its history, settled cultivation has thus depended on human muscle power, supplemented in some regions by animal muscle power. In the industrialized world, it has come to depend increasingly on fossil-fuel energy. However, pre-industrial agriculture depends primarily on plant and animal-based materials, along with some control of natural flowing water for irrigation. Consequently, pre-industrial agricultural societies (more properly, peasant societies) have a fairly substantial knowledge base in relation to husbanded plants and animals; they also view nature as being subject to human control to a very significant extent.

Economy: In peasant societies, cereal grains can be stored and moved around, especially on the backs of animals or in carts, over long distances. Resources can here flow over much larger distances than in gatherer societies, enabling the concentration in towns of human populations not directly involved in gathering or the production of food. Changes in settlement patterns also correspond to shifts in consumption. Of course, a majority of the agrarian population consumes natural resources largely for subsistence—e.g. for food, clothing, shelter, implements, fodder and manure. However, a small but powerful segment of the population is involved in the large-scale consumption and use of materials not directly related to subsistence—both luxury items such as silk and wine, and instruments of coercion such as the horse and elephant, metal swords and shields. Fig. 1.2 shows the resulting structure of material flows in such a system. There are large-scale exports of materials out of intensively cultivated patches of lands, both to nearby villages and to more distant urban centres. The volume, range of items and distance-scale of such flows steadily increase with technical improvements, especially in animal-based transport. These outflows from agricultural land are balanced by inflows from surrounding non-cultivated lands. In peasant societies there are no counterflows from urban centres back to cultivated lands. However, as Fig. 1.3 shows, in industrial societies there are large flows, back to the land, of materials such as farm machinery and synthetic fertilizers.

Characterized by fairly extensive resource flows, especially of foodgrains and livestock, peasant societies are much less subject to environmental variation in space and time. Nevertheless, the techniques of cultivation and animal husbandry, the choice of plant and animal varieties, and the way that resources of non-cultivated lands are gathered and put to use are all greatly dependent on the local environment. There is therefore a substantial degree of locality-dependent adaptive variation in patterns of resource use within peasant societies. This begins to disappear only with large-scale inputs of fossil-fuel energy and advanced technology into agriculture.

Social organization: Cultivation requires intensive inputs of human energy in relatively restricted areas of land—a few hectares per person in the pre-industrial stage. Therefore a small kin group rather than a large band can most effectively organize such inputs; hence the family becomes the basic unit of an agricultural society. Family groups need to co-operate with each other in a variety of ways, including defence against the usurpation of their production (apart from what is surrendered as tax to the state). Several families thus remain banded together in a village, which becomes a social group of a few hundred to a few thousand individuals. This social group also tends to control and manage a territory of non-cultivated land surrounding the cultivated areas, from which come a variety of inputs such as fuel-wood, fodder and leaf manure.

Sex-based division of labour is quite pronounced in the peasant mode. Typically, men confine themselves to operations such as ploughing, which require higher power output. Women take on the burden of more tedious work, such as weeding and transplanting, and, outside cultivation, the collection of fuel, fodder and water.

While cultivated plots are usually (though not always) con-

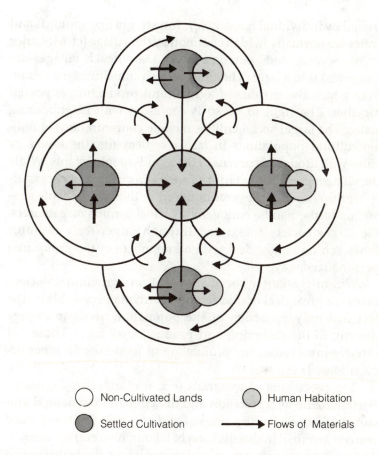

○ Non-Cultivated Lands   ◓ Human Habitation

● Settled Cultivation   ➤ Flows of Materials

Figure 1.2

Material flows in an agrarian society. Settled agriculture makes possible
generation of surplus grain and livestock production which can support
concentration of non-agricultural populations in towns and cities. This
material export from cultivated lands has to be made good by flows from
surrounding non-cultivated lands. Material cycles thus become much more
open in comparison with the hunter-gatherer shifting cultivator stage.
Settlements adjacent to cultivated land represent villages, the larger
habitation in the centre, towns. The thickness of the arrow indicates the
intensity of the flow.

trolled by individual households, forests, grazing grounds and water are normally held in common by the village (cf. Mukerjee 1926). Several, and sometimes very many, such villages are integrated into a larger chiefdom, which constitutes the terrain over which the surplus of agricultural production is pooled together. The right to do so is contested with neighbouring states. The larger social entities include concentrations of non-agricultural populations in larger settlements, the towns or cities with thousands or tens of thousands of inhabitants. While the villages constitute a face-to-face social group (not necessarily kinship based) of several hundred or thousand people analogous to the bands/endogamous tribal groups of gatherers, the larger society integrated through larger-scale resource flows can no longer deal with all members of the group in a personalized way.

Within the larger social group of an agricultural society there is a great deal of division of labour, made possible by the fact that only a fraction of the population needs to engage directly in the gathering and production of food. Those not directly involved in the production of food take on other occupations. These are—

The processing of materials (e.g. textiles, oilseeds), transportation, the interpretation and dissemination of natural and cultural knowledge (by priests) and coercion (by specialized warrior groups). In this division of labour, men end up monopolizing the more prestigious and skilled jobs, passing on the less skilled and tedious work to the women. There is now a substantial differentiation of coercive abilities within the social group— from peasants who receive very little in return for the surplus production they yield to others, to priests and warriors who provide others little in return for the surplus they manage to get hold of (Service 1975).

In comparison with the gatherer mode, the peasant mode shows a sharp separation between cultivated and non-cultivated land. This separation is significant in directing resource flows (Fig. 1.2), and equally so with regard to differing forms of property and control. At the lowest spatial scale agricultural land may be controlled by a family. Such control may be subject to regulation by the village community, which could reassign plots of land and, further, treat land as a community resource, perhaps for grazing purposes, outside the cropping season (Bloch 1978). The non-cultivated land within village boundaries, typically a few square kilometres in extent, serves to supply fuel, grazing, manure, etc. for the community as a whole. These large chunks of land, different portions of which may be used at different seasons, may be most effectively controlled as community, rather than family, property. (This also applies to water sources such as tanks, rivulets, lakes and springs, typically held in common.) However, with technological advance and the concentration of powers of coercion, village communities may lose control over cultivated lands and become tenant-cultivators. Access to non-cultivated lands may be lost too, for instance with the enclosure of commons by powerful landlords or by the state. In addition to land in the vicinity of villages, the state may lay claim to larger uninhabited tracts, constituted as princely hunting preserves or forests from which the army derives its supply of elephants (Thompson 1975; Trautmann 1982).

The large-scale resource flows of agricultural societies are accompanied by imbalances involving net outflows from rural areas and inflows into urban centres. These imbalances become progressively more acute as technological advances in storage, transport and processing create an effective demand for a larger range of produce from both cultivated and non-cultivated lands, and as the coercive power of the non-agricultural sector increases *vis-à-vis* the agricultural sector. The overall imbalances decrease with large-scale inflows of synthetic chemicals, fertilizers and machinery to agricultural lands in industrial societies; however, it is very likely that, given the larger inflows and outflows, the imbalances pertaining to specific elements such as micro-nutrients, or to larger organic molecules like humic acids, may become all the more acute (Pimentel and Pimentel 1978; Stanhill 1984).

Agricultural societies might be at equilibrium with their resource base; or they might encounter either expanding or shrinking resource bases. Agriculturists who newly colonize lands earlier held by gatherer societies, or who newly benefit from a major resource input such as irrigation, would find themselves with an expanding resource base, analogous to the r-strategists of ecology. On the other hand the base may be shrinking because of an adverse climatic change, or if access is cut off from important inputs like leaf manure and fodder from forests newly taken over by the state. Their resource base may also shrink if agricultural productivity remains stagnant in the face of human population growth. An approximate equilibrium may be maintained if the population grows slowly, if the external demands on agricultural production remain stable, and if technological progress keeps pace with the need to continue increases in agricultural production in consonance with population change.

In the last case—that of approximate equilibrium as with the k-strategists of ecology—the social groups are likely to be highly viscous, with related individuals tending to stay together and tied, perhaps generation after generation, to a given locality. Under these conditions they may exhibit high levels of co-operative behaviour among themselves, as also behaviour which favours long-term group interests. The peasant societies of India, China and South East Asia, in the period before European colonization, perhaps fall into this category. On the other hand, when the resource base is rapidly expanding, especially with new land being brought under cultivation, social groups are likely to be much more fluid and far less tied to any locality. Their level of co-operative behaviour, and especially their willingness to sacrifice individual interests to long-term group interests, would consequently be much lower. This would seem to have been the case with European pioneers in seventeenth and eighteenth century North America. Finally, peasant cultures faced with a shrinking resource base may also lose group coherence and the attachment to a particular locality, as has been reported from several parts of India in recent times (Guha, 1989a).

Ideology: In comparison with hunter-gatherer societies, agricultural societies have established substantial control over natural processes; nevertheless, they are still very subject to nature's caprices in the form of droughts, floods, frost, and plagues of locusts. Indeed, certain life-history stages of agricultural crops are themselves especially sensitive to the environment. Hence, agricultural societies continue, in part, to perceive man as one among a community of beings. At the same time, the image of man as a steward of natural resources acquires influence. The restrained use of natural resources could thereby be expected to form one part of the ideology of agricultural societies, especially when they are in a state of near equilibrium with their resource base. On the other hand agricultural societies in the process of encountering an expanding resource base—either through new technologies or, especially, while colonizing lands earlier held by gatherers—are much more likely to view man as separate from nature and with a right to exploit resources as he wishes (cf. Cronon 1983).

In stable peasant societies, practices of restrained use relate to cultivation itself, and are linked to a philosophy of minimizing risk rather than maximizing immediate profit (Scott 1976). The use of a whole variety of different crops and crop rotations, and the careful community-based maintenance of irrigation ponds, may be part of such an approach. This approach would also encompass the non-cultivated lands from which the villagers gather fuel, fodder, small timber, leaf manure, and so on. A variety of practices of restrained resource use with respect to non-cultivated lands have been reported from peasant societies which are at equilibrium with their resource base. For example:

• A quantitative restriction on the amount of harvest from a given locality, e.g. on the amount of wood or grass harvested by a family or their livestock from community lands.

• Restrictions on the harvest in certain seasons. Thus, lopping the green leaves of trees may be permitted only after the rainy season, i.e. after the trees have ceased to put on growth.
• Certain species, e.g. trees belonging to the genus *Ficus*, may be wholly protected.
• Certain habitat patches may never be harvested. In the state of Mizoram, in north-eastern India, the community wood-lots from which regulated harvests are permitted, called supply forests, are complemented by sacred groves, aptly called 'safety forests', from which no harvests are permitted.
• Certain methods of harvest may be completely prohibited. In the Aravalli hills of Rajasthan there are patches of forests called *oraons* where harvesting by using metal tools is prohibited, though wood may be removed by breaking twigs by the hand (Brara 1987).
• Specific age-sex classes or social groups may be banned from employing certain harvesting methods, or from utilizing certain species or habitat patches.

These practices all depend on a high degree of co-operation between the members of a village community. One could say that, in the peasant mode, *custom* and *tradition* provide the overarching framework within which human–nature interactions are carried out. While religion continues to permeate social life, in the realm of resource use it is supplemented to a significant degree by custom. In other words, customary and time-honoured networks govern relationships of reciprocity within peasant society—as, for example between different castes in a village (cf. Chapter 3), between nomadic pastorals and peasant cultivators, or between the village and the state. Clearly, such relations (with respect to resource use, as elsewhere) are often asymmetrical: but they normally fluctuate only within the limits defined by custom.

Ecological impact: The ecological impact of the peasant mode may be characterized as *intermediate*. With the march of agriculture a significant proportion of land begins to be converted into artificial grasslands or cropfields, which replace forests, mar-

shes or natural grasslands. Fire, stone axes and metal axes aid
in this process of conversion. Cultivation also imposes increasing demands on natural vegetation and a greater removal of
forest produce, to be used as fuel, fodder, manure, building-
timber and implements. The discovery of iron, which in many
areas led to the colonization of the forest by agriculturists, also
facilitates the continued felling of individual trees in a forest. In
villages where such felling takes place, natural regeneration is
relied upon to restore tree cover. At the same time, improvements in weapon technology enable a more flexible hunting
strategy. The cumulative impact of these interventions is a
striking change in the landscape, which very likely becomes
heterogeneous, manifesting a variety of successive stages within a mosaic. It could also result in the local extinction of some
species of plants and animals.

Of course, agricultural societies which newly colonize lands
held by gatherers have had a dramatic ecological impact even
in the short run—transforming the landscape, exterminating
certain species and depleting others, introducing weedy
species, and so on (Cronon 1983; Crosby 1986). This would also
be the case with agricultural societies expanding their resource
base through technological innovations such as large-scale irrigation and the use of pesticides. On the other hand, agricultural societies in approximate equilibrium with their environment—dominated by 'local production for local use'—have
only moderate levels of impact in transforming landscapes and
bringing about gradual changes in the composition of biological communities.

The Industrial Mode

Technology: The latest mode of resource use to appear in human
history, large-scale industry, has been with us for just about two
hundred years. This is only one-fiftieth of the time that *Homo
sapiens* has spent husbanding plants and animals, and one-two
hundredths of the time since when hunter-gatherers painted

grand hunting scenes in the caves of Lescaux and Altamira. But its ecological impact has been profound, far surpassing all that preceded this revolution. The main reason for this is the quantum jump in the use of energy, with heavy demands on non-renewable sources (coal, oil), coupled with the use of entirely novel sources such as nuclear energy.

If the pattern of energy use in the gatherer mode may be characterized as *passive* (relying only on human-muscle and wood-fuel power) and that of the agricultural mode as *active* (augmenting human power with animal power, wood-fuel and water power), in the industrial mode energy use follows an *extractive* path, wherein natural resources are both *harnessed* (hydro power) and *mined* (fossil fuels) for human consumption. The industrial mode has also brought into use a whole new range of man-made materials; e.g. metals, plastics, silicon chips and synthetic pesticides. These newly-fashioned materials can now be preserved to be used for long periods, and transported for consumption elsewhere. Great improvements in transportation within the industrial mode mean that even bulky, heavy goods—e.g. timber or rocks, can be transported with ease over large distances (Ayers, 1978). 'The windmill gives you the feudal lord, the steam engine the capitalist', says Marx when distinguishing between different modes of production. Distinguishing between different modes of resource use according to their technological infrastructure, we may likewise say: 'the axe and bullock cart give you the peasant mode, the chain-saw and locomotive the industrial mode'.

These abilities *vis-à-vis* materials processing, storage and transport have revolutionized flows of resources, these having now become truly global. Any material, be it animal, vegetable, or mineral, natural or man-made, can now be rapidly transported anywhere, and whenever desired. With this a significant fraction of humanity, albeit still very much a minority, has come to consume vast quantities of a very wide range of resources (IIED and WRI 1987). Consumers in the high centres of industrial civilization can draw upon the natural resources of most parts of the globe, taking for granted the continued supply of teakwood from India, ivory from Africa, and mink from the Arctic. This elite is now scarcely affected by the natural variations within resource availability in space and time; it has developed a lifestyle which could truthfully be called global. In the process it has wiped out myriad locally-adapted lifestyles in different parts of the world.

Economy: Over the last three centuries, industrial societies have steadily expanded their resource base. This has been achieved by a growing knowledge about the working of nature—through the hypothetico-deductive method of modern science and by the links established between scientific discovery and practical application—in order to tap additional sources of energy, process materials, and transport goods faster, more economically, and over ever-longer distances. This process of the intensification of resource use has led to the continual over-use and exhaustion of many resources. The typical response to such exhaustion has been to find a substitute, though initially, when the resource being substituted was abundant, the use of the substitute would have involved more effort in terms of energy, material, and labour. In the classic case, when wood became scarce in Europe, coal came to substitute for wood charcoal in the manufacture of iron, while locomotives were invented to replace horse-drawn carts even as there developed serious scarcities of fodder for horses. Industrial societies have gone on to consume resources at an accelerating rate, exhausting them one by one in sequence, going from the economically desirable resource of the moment to less and less desirable resources as the more desirable resources become exhausted. And, alongside, technological innovations now continually extract better and better results from what were once the less desired resources (Wilkinson 1988).

The expansion of the resource base in industrial societies has rested upon access to land and natural resources which were earlier controlled by gatherer and peasant societies. Reeling under an energy and transport crisis brought about by the

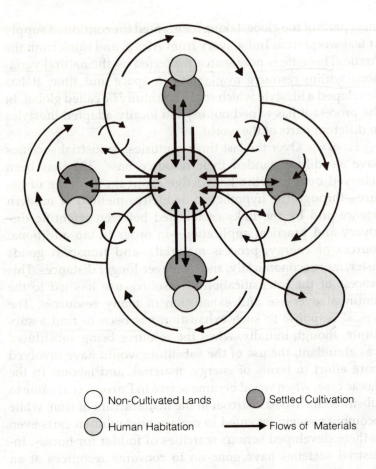

Figure 1.3

Material flows characterizing modern Indian society. Such societies not only tap surplus agricultural production, but also a great deal of the produce of non-cultivated lands to meet the requirements of the urban-industrial sector. Thereby the material cycles become totally open, with large outflows from rural hinterlands. These are partially compensated for by the organization of flows of materials such as fertilizers from the urban-industrial sector to the cultivated lands. The large central human habitiation represents an Indian city such as Bombay; the separated habitation in the upper right hand corner, the industrialized countries. The thickness of an arrow indicates the intensity of the flow.

exhaustion of their forests, European colonists laid claim to vast terrains the world over. Wherever the 'portmanteau biota' of these Europeans—wheat and cattle, their weeds and diseases—could establish itself comfortably—as in North America and Argentina, South Africa, Australia and New Zealand—it created neo-Europes (Crosby 1986). Where the ecological setting did not permit such a takeover, as in the older civilizations of the Middle East and Asia, or in the humid tropical forests of the Amazon, the Congo and Malaysia, these Europeans nevertheless established a firm hold on the resources of these regions and organized outflows of what they most desired to their own lands and people. Thus, India became an exporter of teak, cotton, jute, tea, indigo and precious metals; Burma of rice and teak; the West Indies of sugar; Brazil of rubber and coffee; and so on. Although colonialism has formally ended, this process vigorously continues, and India now exports prawns and trained manpower along with tea, rather than teak or cotton; and Brazil exports beef and forest produce instead of rubber.

These flows are highly asymmetric, with industrial societies receiving large volumes of unprocessed resources at low prices and exporting small volumes of processed resources at much higher prices. Simultaneously, this process also implies the production in industrial societies of high volumes of wastes; these are then sought to be disposed of elsewhere, either in the global commons of the oceans and the atmosphere, or through their sale to Third World societies plagued by foreign debt.

Social organization: The greatly enhanced scale of resource flows in industrial society goes together with a substantial increase in the number of humans involved in this network. Face-to-face contact is obviously impossible among such large numbers, and they tend to interact through the medium of formally codified transactions. Within such large social groups there is, of course, a rather elaborate division of labour. In modern industrial societies this division largely hinges upon skills in processing, transporting and exchanging materials and information. Smaller social groups based on such division of labour—for instance, car mechanics or teachers—and corporate groups banded together to carry out a task—for instance, car manufacture or schoolteaching—become important. Among these exist relations involving face-to-face communication equivalent to those in hunter-gatherer bands or peasant villages. In these societies, too, men have tended to monopolize the more skilled and prestigious jobs, leaving the bulk of the unskilled and tedious work to women. Such discrimination has persisted despite the rhetoric of sexual equality and the development of technologies which tend to discount the advantages of greater physical strength.

Whereas kinship, locality and region define the forms of association in the pre-industrial world, in industrial societies the impersonal criteria of structural location *vis-à-vis* the means of production define the ways in which individuals come together for collective action. These corporate groups, based on the division of labour, are extremely fluid, the membership being in great flux. Again, the continual expansion of the resource base, both in terms of new extractive techniques and new territories to draw upon, has enhanced the fluidity of social groupings. There is therefore a much greater stress on pursuit of individual interest in these greatly atomized societies (Hawley 1986).

The rise of individualism is also accompanied by a tremendous expansion in the role of the state in regulating individual transactions. In most spheres of social life, the personalized and flexible systems of customary law—typical of agricultural societies—are replaced by impersonal and relatively rigid systems of codified law. The forest codes of modern society are amazingly detailed, often running into several hundred sections and subsections (cf. Guha, R. 1983; Merriman 1975; Linebaugh 1976). While safeguarding private property over land and in the workplace, and taking over the ownership of what was hitherto common property, the modern industrial state completely delegitimizes *community*-based systems of access and control.

Forest management provides a good illustration of how the industrial mode admits only the polarity of individual and state control. In the process of industrialization in Western Europe and the United States, an early phase of anarchic capitalist exploitation was followed by the assertion of state control, wherein the government stepped in to assume responsibility for forest protection and production (Hays 1958; Heske 1937). However, when the situation stabilizes with respect to the supply of raw material for industry, the state may withdraw control over certain forest areas by handing over 'captive plantations' to private industry. Simultaneously, the expansion of the market may encourage the widespread planting of commercially valued trees by individual farmers. Thus, forests in the industrial mode are primarily *state*-owned, supplemented in capitalist societies by a small but often growing *private* sector. The victim in this process is, inevitably, village-based systems of *community* forests and pasture management: the lands in these systems are either sequestered by the state or parcelled out among individuals.

Ideology: Developed in a mileu of r-strategists, the ideological underpinnings of industrial society involve the total rejection of the gatherer view of man as part of a community of beings, or even of the agriculturist view of man as a steward of nature. Instead it is emphatically asserted that man is separate from nature, with every right to exploit natural resources to further his own well being. Nature is now desacralized. What has come to be venerated instead is the marketplace; the market is supposed to rationally allocate the use of resources so efficiently that all individuals are as well off as they could possibly be. Among socialists this veneration is transferred to a Central Plan: it is regarded by them as a more efficient allocator than the market.

While the ideology of conquest over nature as well as modern lifestyles have resulted in a radical alteration of the landscape of the globe, industrial societies have, to be fair, made systematic attempts to safeguard their own environments. Such

attempts were triggered off by deforestation and the consequent landslides in the Swiss Alps in the 1860s, and further
strengthened when the western frontier of the United States
was officially declared closed by the 1890 census. Since then
Western conservationists have gradually brought back part of
the forest cover of Europe and North America, set in motion an
effective programme of soil conservation, and set apart wilderness areas (cf. Hays 1958 and 1987; Nash 1982). The problems
of chemical pollution which surfaced after the Second World
War are also being tackled—with the successful cleaning of the
Thames, for instance. But pollution proceeds apace with such
efforts; new environmental issues come up, such as acid rain
and global warming. These require global solutions, so that it
now appears as if industrial societies can no longer restrict
environmental degradation to areas outside their own borders
(WCED 1987).

Despite the increasing scale of environmental problems, the
ideology of industrialism even today rejects as invalid any
concern with physical 'limits to growth', trusting technical
innovation to take care of problems as they arise. It puts its faith
in the efficacy of the marketplace (or of the Central Plan) to
stimulate the discovery of substitutes, and to enhance the efficiency of resource use (Beckerman 1972; Laptev 1977). A variety
of scientifically-based prescriptions on sustainable use of soils,
forests, fisheries and other renewable resources, generated over
the last century, have been interpreted as examples of efficient
resource use, and one of the aims of this book is to examine
whether this is actually so.

Scientific prescriptions for resource use: Just as religion and
custom legitimized patterns of resource use in pre-industrial
societies, in the industrial mode science provides the organizing principle for human interactions with nature. However,
scientific prescriptions for the preservation, the sustainable use
and the deliberate destruction of different species and habitats
parallel, in many ways, the pre-scientific prescriptions typical
of earlier modes. For example:

• Just as there were quantitative restrictions on the amount of fuelwood extracted by a family from a community wood-lot, or on the number of animals to be grazed on a fodder reserve, there are now quantitative prescriptions on the amount of timber to be removed during the course of selection felling from a designated patch of forest, or on the number of deer that may be shot by a licence-holder in a given year.

• Just as New Guinea hunter-gatherers stop hunting a particular species—say the Bird of Paradise, when its population density falls below a certain level—the International Whaling Commission has banned the hunting of certain species of whales whose populations have been severely depleted.

• Just as fishing from certain coastal areas is traditionally stopped if the yields become very low, there have been prescriptions to 'rest' certain forest areas, for instance in India after the excessive harvests of the Second World War.

• Just as there is a traditional ban on hunting in certain seasons, there are closed seasons for mechanized fishing, or for timber extraction.

• Just as certain life-history stages are traditionally given protection—for instance, breeding birds at heronries in many villages in peninsular India—the younger, growing stock in a forest is supposed to be spared all extraction pressure.

• Just as certain methods of harvest, e.g. the poisoning of streams, may be traditionally forbidden, there are regulations forbidding fishing with nets of excessively small mesh size.

• Just as certain habitat patches—for instance, sacred groves or sacred ponds—may be fully protected from harvest, there are prescriptions for keeping certain forest areas totally free from human interference, either for watershed conservation or for the maintenance of biological diversity.

• Just as certain species are totally exempt from being hunted or felled, e.g. monkeys or *Ficus* trees in Indian villages, complete protection may be extended to certain endangered species, such as the California condor or the whooping crane.

In parallel, of course, there exist a whole range of supposedly scientific prescriptions for deliberately destroying certain resources. Thus, just as the entire Khandava forest near present-day New Delhi was supposedly burnt in the time of the Maha-bharata (cf. Chapter 2) as an offering to the fire god, massive forest areas in the Narmada valley in Central India are now being destroyed to create reservoirs for hydro-electric power generation and irrigation. And one cannot forget that the large-scale defoliation of forests during the Vietnam war was sup-ported by considerable inputs from the American scientific commuity.

In this manner, scientific prescriptions in the industrial mode closely parallel traditional, 'pre-scientific' prescriptions based on a large but informal base of knowledge and on simple rules of thumb. In part, modern prescriptions are based on a more detailed knowledge of the behaviour of the system, and on a more explicit definition of what is sought to be achieved. With many tree or fish populations, this aim is defined as achieving maximum sustainable yield, i.e. a yield that will not decline in the long run.

However, deciding upon a harvesting regime that would lead to maximum sustainable yields is beset with manifold difficulties (Clark 1985; Beddington and May 1982). First, every plant or animal population is involved in a number of interac-tions with other members of its community. Thus, harvesting a deer population may, through a change in the composition of the herb layer, affect another resource such as wild cattle. Or harvesting a plant species may result in a change in the avail-ability of honey. In fact, some years ago, biologists warned the fishing industry on the east coast of Canada that scallop fisheries were being over-exploited and were likely to crash. It so happened that just after this there was an outbreak of an epidemic disease among sea urchin populations which prey heavily upon the scallop. With predation pressures reduced, scallop populations increased rather than collapsed, as had been feared by fishery biologists (cf. Berkes 1989). Similar-ly, wild-life biologists concerned with enhancing the carrying capacity of wetlands within the Bharatpur bird sanctuary in north India recommended the banning of buffalo-grazing in the sanctuary. Following the imposition of this ban it was found that, in the absence of grazing, a grass, *Paspalum*, grew so rapidly that it choked the wetland and reduced its carrying capacity for water fowl (Vijayan 1987).

Because of such complex community interactions, the simultaneous harvesting of more than one resource population from a specific locality can have a variety of unexpected consequences. Theoretical investigations suggest that in some cases the natural tendency of a population to fluctuate might be exaggerated by the simultaneous harvesting of another species, and expose it to the danger of extinction (Pimm 1986; May 1984).

But, aside from such complications which arise out of community interactions, it is difficult to understand the behaviour of harvested populations and to assess whether they run the risk of being over-harvested and becoming extinct. For example, the Elk populations of British Columbia are being simultaneously harvested—for subsistence by Amerindians and for sport by European settlers. Wildlife biologists primarily interested in deciding on regulations for sport hunting contend that the Elk populations are declining on account of subsistence hunting. On the other hand anthropologists looking at the same population data suggest that there is no good evidence of a decline in Elk populations (Freeman 1989). It is even more difficult to assess the fate of fish or whale populations for which the only available information is based on harvests themselves. The level of such harvests is a complex function of the number, age and sex composition of the prey population, its distribution in space and time, and the extent and distribution of the harvesting effort. The parameters which characterize the prey population also depend on the extent of the exploitation to which it has been subjected in the past. It is difficult to predict the responses of such populations to different levels of harvests even on the basis of sophisticated mathematical models because our knowledge of many parameters in the model remains limited. Indeed the International Whaling Commission finds it very difficult to arrive at a consensus on what is actually happening to many whale populations (May 1984).

Given all these difficulties, even today successful prescriptions of how to obtain maximum sustainable yields are possible only in very limited contexts. They work only when community interactions, as well as the population structure, are drastically simplified. This is the case with single-species even-aged populations of forest-tree species such as pines, planted for harvest in temperate latitudes. Here all other plant, insect, and microbial species that might enter the forest naturally are sought to be eliminated. Intra-specific competition is regulated by permiting reproduction only through artificial regeneration, by controlling inter-plant distance, and by harvesting the individual plants which are being suppressed through intra-specific competition. It would not be incorrect to say that scientific prescriptions on maximum sustainable yields have largely failed to work, except in such limited contexts. Even in these contexts, the suspicion is that a gradual exhaustion of soil nutrients is now leading to the decline of forests which have been long invoked as exemplars of sustained-yield management. We shall later see, in much greater detail (Chapter 6), how modern attempts to apply such concepts to the tropical forests in India have led to serious over-harvests (see also FAO 1984).

The prescriptions on giving total protection to certain species and localities, such as those embedded in the US Endangered Species Act or CITES (Convention on International Trade in Endangered Species), or to certain localities—as in programmes setting apart national parks or biosphere reserves—also have rather uncertain scientific foundations. This is inevitable, given our very limited understanding of the extent and distribution of biological diversity, and of the ecosystem processes which govern the survival of the species which make up different biological communities. Heated debates on whether to aim for a few large, several small, or even plentifully patchy nature reserves, as well as the debates on minimum viable population size, show that scientists are still far from finding definitive answers on the appropriate ways of conserving natural populations of living organisms (Soule 1986). Indeed one could argue that scientific prescriptions in industrial societies show little evidence of progress over the simple rule-of-thumb prescriptions for sustainable resource use and the conservation of diversity which characterized gatherer and peasant societies. Equally, the legal and codified procedures which are supposed to ensure the enforcement of scientific prescriptions work little better than earlier procedures based on religion or social convention.

Ecological impact: Industrial societies, unlike gatherer or agricultural societies, are no longer directly dependent on the natural resources of their immediate vicinity. At first glance this may suggest that they could effectively conserve their resource base, whereas societies that follow more primitive modes of resource use would perforce suffer a much more adverse impact. This seems borne out by the fact that Japan, the most industrialized Asian country, has the best-preserved forest cover, while the forests of countries like Malaysia and Indonesia —which have large populations dependent on primitive agriculture—are being devastated. But a second look shows that Japan maintains its forest cover, in spite of its enormous per capita consumption of timber, only by shifting the pressure on to Malaysia and Indonesia, precisely the countries which suffer devastation. The Japanese also exploit their coastal fisheries very conservatively, while refusing to give up whaling in international waters. This discrepancy between prudence at home and profligacy abroad also characterizes the behaviour of other industrially advanced countries such as the USA and the (former) USSR.

If one looks at the overall picture, therefore, it is obvious that the enormous resource demands and waste production of industrial nations, and of the industrial segments in less industrialized nations, have the most profound impact on the world's environment (cf. Bahro 1984). This impact includes radical modifications of the landscape, as with the laying of the Alaskan pipeline, or cattle ranching in Amazonian forests; a gradual depletion of forests, as with acid rain in Europe or over-extraction in Malaysia and Kalimantan; drastic reductions in, or extinctions of, populations, as with the passenger pigeon and the bison in the last century, or the African elephant and myriad other species in Amazonia in this century; a wholesale poisoning of the biosphere, as with wide-spectrum pesticides and nuclear waste; a modification of bio-geochemical cycles, as with the increased production of carbon dioxide; and perhaps a long-term adverse modification of the climate as well (cf. Richards 1986).

In assessing the ecological impact of different modes, one is struck by two paradoxes, which we illustrate here with respect to forest use. Spatially, hunter-gatherers live *in* the forest, agriculturists live adjacent to but within *striking distance* of the forest, and urban-industrial men live *away* from the forest. Paradoxically, the more the spatial separation from the forest, the greater the impact on its ecology, and the further removed the actors from the consequences of this impact! The same conditions operate with regard to other resources, such as water.

Second, the faster the development of formal, scientific knowledge about the composition and functioning of forest types, the faster the rate of deforestation. One important reason here is undeniably higher levels of economic activity, but another though less obvious factor is the *idiom* of resource use itself. While enormously enlarging our knowledge about specific physical and chemical processes, modern science has not always displayed the same understanding of the ecological consequences of human interventions which follow the development of scientific knowledge. However, the *belief* that science provides an infallible guide has nonetheless encouraged major interventions in natural ecosystems, and these have had unanticipated and usually unfortunate consequences. The history of both fisheries and forest management are replete with illustrations of the failure of sustained-yield methods to forestall ecological collapse (McEvoy 1988; FAO 1984). While there no longer exist social constraints on levels of intervention, scientists are also inadequately informed on the ecological processes in operation. Ironically, therefore, religion and custom as ideologies of resource use are perhaps better adapted to deal with a situation of imperfect knowledge than a supposedly 'scientific' resource management.

Conflict Between and Within Modes

Inter-modal conflict: As one mode of resource use comes into contact with another mode organized on very different social and ecological principles, we expect the occurrence of substantial social strife. In fact, the clash of two modes has invariably resulted in massive bursts of violent and sometimes genocidal conflict. One of the best documented of such conflicts is the clash between the indigenous hunter-gatherer/shifting-cultivator populations of the New World on the one hand, and the advance guard of European colonists practising an altogether different system of agriculture on the other. Historians of the victorious white race have in recent years depicted, with marked sensitivity, the ecological bases of a conflict that resulted in the extermination of the bulk of the native population and the traumatization of the segment which escaped annihilation (Cronon 1983; Crosby 1986). Yet, as Chapter 2 of this book argues, such episodes are not exactly foreign to the histories of the Old World. For the brutal conflict between the American Indians and the English colonists was anticipated several millenia before—in the conquest of indigenous hunter-gatherer populations within India by invading agriculturists, a clash vividly captured in the sacred text of the conquerors, the Hindu epic Mahabharata.

The environmental and social costs of the encounter between agrarian and industrial modes in Europe have been ably chronicled by a long line of distinguished historians. The rise of industrial capitalism radically altered relations not merely in land and the workplace, but also around the utilization of nature. The conflicts over the enclosure of what was previously common land, and the assertion of state control over forests, while perhaps not as brutal as the clash between hunter-gatherers and the neolithic vanguard, also exacted a heavy human cost (cf. Agulhon 1982). As one American forester, documenting the enclosure of the forests by the state and lords in Germany, laconically put it:

> All these changes from the original communal property conditions did not, of course, take place without friction, the opposition often taking place in peasants' revolts; hundreds of thousands of these being killed in their attempts to preserve their commons, forests and waters free to all, to re-establish their liberty to hunt, fish and cut wood, and to abolish titles, serfdom and duties (Fernow 1907, p. 34).

Even where there was no open revolt, peasants resorted to poaching and the theft of forest produce. These forest 'crimes' were very widespread. In Prussia in 1850, 265,000 wood thefts were reported, as against only 35,000 cases of ordinary theft. In this class struggle over nature, between the peasants on one side and landlords and the state on the other, the wood thieves were 'defending their entire economic system—the family economy which was based on collective usage rights' (Mooser 1986). Indeed until well into the present century, European foresters were unable to fully extinguish the customary rights of user granted as a consequence of the peasant opposition to state forest management (cf. Heske 1937). In the American South too, common rights of hunting and grazing on non-cultivated land withstood landlord and state pressures until the early decades of this century (Hahn 1982).

The European experience is directly comparable to the Indian (detailed in chapters 5 and 7), where the encounter between peasant and industrial modes, mediated partly by colonialism, has also greatly intensified social conflicts over forest resources. In the colonial societies of South East Asia and Africa as well, the takeover of forest land for strategic and commercial purposes fuelled bitter conflicts between the state and the peasantry (Scott 1976; Grove 1990). Here we must note that colonial methods of ecological control also intensified conflicts within the agrarian sector. Two examples come to mind. One is the clash over forests, lands and water in colonial and semi-colonial societies, between large cash-crop plantations and the traditional peasantry (Womack 1969; Pandian 1985). The other is the restrictions placed on subsistence hunting-gathering and grazing by the setting up of game reserves by white colonists (cf. Kjekshus 1977).

While gatherer–peasant and peasant–industrial conflicts are both vividly represented in myth and history, a third inter-modal conflict dominated medieval Europe and medieval Asia, namely between the peasant and pastoral modes. Despite the many instances of nomad–peasant symbiosis, for example the pasturing of livestock on fallow fields in return for manure, this relationship has historically been fraught with friction. Medieval sources in the Near East talk of nomads driving their livestock to graze on *sown* fields—a practice beneficial to the pastoralists but disastrous for cultivators. Conflicts have also arisen when agriculturists shift to crops (e.g. cotton) which do not provide stubble during the dry seasons. In this conflict between two modes of resource use that have, for the most part, overlapped in time and space, the nomads have on occasion greatly expanded their resource base—as with the Mongols of Central Asia in the medieval period—while at other times their own niche has steadily shrunk—as with the reservation of forests and the expansion of irrigated agriculture in modern India (Khazanov 1984; Gadgil and Malhotra 1982).

Our final example of inter-modal conflict comes from the contemporary West. In recent years a distinctively new form of ecological conflict has surfaced, between votaries of the industrial mode of resource use and a mode struggling to be born. Thus, while scientific foresters and industrial users continue to look upon the forest primarily as a resource to be harvested, in the perspective of the Western environmental movement forests are to be preserved as a haven from the workaday world and as a reservoir of biological diversity. Although this conflict has by no means been as violent as those between earlier modes of resource use, the ideological differences between the industrial mode and what environmentalists call the 'post-industrial' mode can hardly be minimized (Nash 1982; Hays 1987).

Two aspects of inter-modal conflicts need to be highlighted. First, apart from massive bursts of social conflict, the encounter between the different modes also signals a spurt in rates of ecological destruction. The deforestation of the Indo-Gangetic plain in the first and second millennium BC, the draining of the fens in eighteenth-century Europe, and the destruction of forest cover in colonial India—all these testify to the enormous environmental costs associated with the advent of a new mode of resource use. (Of course the emergence of a 'post-industrial' mode, if it occurs, may reverse this trend.) As one mode wins out, there is a slow but perceptible diminution in the levels of social conflict and ecological disturbance.

Second, while the conflict between different modes of resource use is, at the most elemental level, a struggle for control over productive resources, it is invariably accompanied by an ideological debate legitimizing the claims of the various modes. Agrarian societies have typically justified their takeover of the lands and resources of gatherer societies in terms of the latters' low productivity and 'wasteful' use of nature, a distinction used by colonists in America for their conquest of Indian territories (Cronon 1983; Prucha 1985). Likewise, votaries of the industrial mode have used the rhetoric of scientific conservation when legitimizing their claims. The scientific model of natural resource management, it is claimed, is a distinctively modern innovation, and inherently superior to the idioms of religion and custom which legitimized human interactions with nature in earlier epochs. And, as the widespread disaffection with excesses within the industrial mode finds expression in modern environmental movements, it is no accident that religion and custom are upheld as being, after all is said and done, more prudent in their use of nature than modern 'scientific' methods.

Intra-modal Conflict

The ebb and flow of social conflict *within* different modes of resource use is perhaps not as visible in history and myth as the violent struggles *between* modes. Yet such conflict is by no means absent. Most of the primate relatives of human beings are engaged in struggles to hold on to and expand group territories, and it is very likely that hominids were similarly engaged ever since their origins. There is little fossil evidence of violent death in the period before 30,000 b.p., when modern *Homo sapiens*, with its capacity for symbolic communication, finally came into its own. Since that time, conflicts relating to territorial control have undoubtedly been a feature of most hunter-gatherer societies, as documented by anthropologists in such far-flung areas as New Guinea, New Zealand, and the Amazon (cf. Rappaport 1984; Vayda 1974).

Such intra-modal conflicts become more complex as one passess on to more advanced modes of resource use. They become especially acute when the ideal-typical characteristics of a mode, as outlined earlier in this chapter, are perceived as being distorted to subserve the ends of a particular social group. When feudal lords fail to honour the customary codes of the moral economy, for example, or when the workings of forest law and science are seen to be class-specific rather than class-neutral, the ideological basis of the mode of resource use begins to crumble. At such times an idiom of conflict, rather than collaboration, characterizes intra-modal relations.

Coming to the peasant mode, in many periods conflicts between the peasantry and overlords over natural resources has been endemic. In England, for example, conflicts over rights in forests were especially acute in the thirteenth and fourteenth centuries, a period of rising demographic pressure and the expansion of arable land. There were growing numbers of prosecutions for timber theft, with peasants also occasionally invading woodland enclosed by lords and abbots (Faith 1984; Birrel 1987). Conflicts over forest and pasture were an important element in one of the greatest ever anti-feudal revolts, the German Peasant War of 1525 (cf. Engels 1956). And in France from the sixteenth to the eighteenth centuries, peasants repeatedly rose in revolt against attempts by landlords to usurp forests, swamps and grazing grounds earlier held in common (Ladurie 1980; Bloch 1978). Finally, resistance to the enclosure of community pastures by plantations was widespread in early-twentieth-century Mexico (Lewis 1964; Womack 1969).

Another form of intra-modal conflict, characteristic of mature feudalism in Europe, related to peasant rights over pasturage and timber in forests which were reserved exclusively for hunting by the nobility (Thompson 1975; Hay *et al.* 1975). While in normal times peasants were unable to challenge this monopoly (though they continued to breach it on the sly), when the state was vulnerable they quickly and forcefully asserted their rights. Thus, in the rural revolts that accompanied the French Revolution, groups of peasants broke into the hunting preserves of the nobility and 'determinedly hunted the game' (Lefebvre 1982, p. 44 and *passim*). Similar invasions of forests controlled by the nobility were also reported in the wave of peasant strikes during the Russian Revolution of 1905 (Shanin 1986).

With the shift from the peasant to the industrial mode, conflicts within the peasant mode intensify as one class within agrarian society is quicker to adapt to the socio-ecological orientation of the coming mode (e.g. landlords, in the case of the enclosure movement). But the internal conflicts characteristic of the industrial mode—particularly its capitalist variant—are quite different. These are, first, the continuing struggles of individual capitalists with each other, and against the state, for formal proprietorial control of non-cultivated areas, as well as the terms of disposal of living resources. Second, the industrialization of forest usage itself creates a new class of workers whose interests are not always in harmony with those of capitalists in the timber harvesting and processing sectors (Vail 1987).

These forms of intra-modal conflict, and the ways in which they are resolved, shed light on the interlinkages between modes of production (defined in the Marxian sense) and their corresponding modes of resource use (as defined here). In the natural economy of hunter-gatherers, of course, the mode of production is simultaneously the mode of resource use. In the peasant and industrial modes the links are more complex. In the former case, even where relations around land are accepted (however grudgingly) as asymmetrical, peasants insist that they have full access to the 'free gifts' of nature. And when enclosure-minded landlords and hunting monarchs violate this tacit agreement by restricting the exercise of common rights, peasants resist and the levels of conflict escalate. For the *stable* functioning of the mode of production, therefore, there must exist some discrepancy between the rights of the overlord to land (and a portion of its produce), and to living resources, respectively.

The stable functioning of the industrial-capitalist mode likewise requires a discrepancy between property relations in the field/factory, and in the forest. While private ownership predominates in the former case, forests are, to a much greater extent, owned and controlled by the state. However, the underlying rationale of government intervention is precisely to safeguard the stability of the industrial mode, by taking the long-term view available only to the state, thereby harmonizing conflicts between individual capitalists.

TABLE 1.1

FEATURES OF TECHNOLOGY AND ECONOMY IN A SOCIETY
PREDOMINANTLY FOLLOWING ONE OF THE FOUR MAJOR
MODES OF RESOURCE USE

	Gathering (including shifting cultivation)	*Nomadic pastoralism*	*Settled cultivation*	*Industry (including fossil-fuel-based agriculture)*
Energy resources used	Human muscle power, fuelwood	Human and animal muscle power, fuelwood	Human and animal muscle power, fuelwood; coal, water power to some extent	Fossil fuels, hydro-electricity, nuclear power; fuelwood, human and animal muscle power much less important
Material resources utilized	Stone	Plant and animal material	Stone, plant and animal material, some uses of metals	Extensive use of metals and synthetic materials
Abilities to store resources	Very rudimentary	Domestic animals serve as meat supply on hooves	Grain and domestic animals make long-term storage of food possible	Even highly perishable materials like fleshy fruit and meat can be stored over long periods
Abilities to transport resources	Very rudimentary	Domestic animals like horses make long distance transport possible	Domestic animals make long distance transport possible	Fossil-fuel based vehicles render transport over great distances easy

	Gathering (including shifting cultivation)	Nomadic pastoralism	Settled cultivation	Industry (including fossil-fuel-based agriculture)
Abilities to transform resources	Very rudimentary	Rudimentary	Low, including metal making, weaving	Very extensive
Spatial scale of resource catchments	Small, mostly of order of a few hundred or thousand km^2	Could be quite extensive	Moderate	Global
Quantities of resources consumed	Very moderate	Moderate for most	Moderate for most, a small elite may consume large quantities of commodities	Large numbers consume enormous quantities

TABLE 1.2

FEATURES OF SOCIAL ORGANIZATION AND IDEOLOGY IN A
SOCIETY PREDOMINANTLY FOLLOWING ONE OF THE FOUR
MAJOR MODES OF RESOURCE USE

	Gathering (including shifting cultivation)	Nomadic pastoralism	Settled cultivation	Industry (including fossil-fuel-based agriculture)
Size of social groups	Small, a few thousand people	Moderate, several thousand people	Moderate, several thousand people	Very large, in hundreds of thousands
Extent of kinship within social groups	Very strong	Strong	Strong, but interactions with non-kin increasing	Very weak
Extent of attachment of social groups to particular localities	Often strong	Weak	Often strong	Very weak
Division of labour	Rudimentary	Sex-age based	Rudimentary sex-age based	Considerable, based on specialized skills and knowledge
Role of division of labour in formation of social groups	Very weak	Very weak	Moderate to strong	Strong

	Gathering (including shifting cultivation)	Nomadic pastoralism	Settled cultivation	Industry (including fossil-fuel-based agriculture)
Idiom of social transactions	Totally informal, based on face-to-face contact	Informal, primarily based on face-to-face contacts	Social conventions and codified transactions	Codified transactions with legal sanctions very important
Within group differentiation of access of resources	Weak	Weak	Considerable	Very extensive
Mechanisms governing access to resources	Community-based decisions	Community-based decisions	Private control of farmland, community and state control of non-cultivated lands	Private, state and corporate ownerships predominant; community ownership delegitimized
Perception of working of nature	Nature viewed as autonomous, capricious	Nature largely seen as capricious	Nature viewed as partially law-bound, controllable	Nature viewed largely as lawful
Idiom of man-nature relationship	Man part of community of beings	Man potentially conqueror of nature	Man a steward of nature	Man above and apart from nature, fully capable of controlling it

good

Recapitulation

The salient features of the four modes of resource use are reproduced in Tables 1.1 to 1.4. To recapitulate, as human societies move temporally from hunting and gathering through pastoralism, agriculture, and finally into industrialization, five distinct but closely interrelated processes occur. First, there is an increasing intensity of resource use and exploitation. Second, there is a secular increase in the level of resource flows across different geographical regions and across different levels of any economic/political system. Third, there is an integration of larger and larger areas into the domain of any given political/economic system. Fourth, there is, at the global level, a secular increase in population densities and in the extent of stratification and inequality with respect to the access, control and use of different natural resources. Finally, there is an intensification of rates of ecological change and ecological disturbance.

Of our four modes of resource use, in the Indian context nomadic pastoralism is best treated not as a separate mode but as being integrated with the peasant mode of resource use, within whose ecological zone it occupied a special niche. In Parts II and III we shall move from the ideal-typical to the historical, narrating the rise, decline and fall of different modes of resource use in the Indian subcontient.

TABLE 1.3

THE NATURE OF THE ECOLOGICAL IMPACT IN SOCIETIES
PREDOMINANTLY FOLLOWING ONE OF THE FOUR MAJOR MODES
OF RESOURCE USE

	Gathering (including shifting cultivation)	Nomadic pastoralism	Settled cultivation	Industry (including fossil-fuel-based agriculture)
Land transformation	Little, some regression of patches of forest to successional stages or grassland	Some extension of grasslands, deserts	Forests, grasslands extensively converted to fields	Large-scale deforestation, desertification, built-up habitats
Habitat diversity	Enhanced	Somewhat reduced	Reduced	Substantially reduced
Bio-diversity	Little affected	Some effect	Moderate effect	Considerable impact
Resource populations	Occasionally over-harvested	May over-graze some grasslands and over-harvest some prey populations	May over-graze some grasslands and over-harvest some prey populations	Many resource populations overharvested
Substances poisonous to life	Nil	Nil	Nil	A large range of synthetic chemicals
Modification of biogeochemical cycles	Very little	Very little	Little	Substantial
Modification of climate	Highly unlikely	Highly unlikely	Unlikely	Quite likely

TABLE 1.4

FEATURES OF SOCIAL ORGANIZATION, IDEOLOGY AND ECOLOGICAL IMPACT IN SOCIETIES IN RELATION TO CHANGES IN THEIR RESOURCE BASE

	In equilibrium with resource base	Resource base expanding	Resource base shrinking
Fluidity of social groups	Low	High	Often considerable
Extent to which group interests prevail over individual interests	Group interests quite significant	Individual interests more important	Group interests may crumble
Perception of man-nature relationship	Man as steward of nature	Man as conqueror of nature	Man helpless
Extent to which sustainable resource use prevails	Quite often	Rarely	Rarely
Level of ecological impact	Low to moderate	High	High

APPENDIX TO CHAPTER I

Note on Population

In our analysis of modes of resource use, we have classified these modes according to technology, pattern of resource flows, social structure, dominant ideologies, and systems of conservation. In this appendix we deal briefly with another dimension which has an important bearing on ecological history—namely the density of human population. The reflections which follow are prompted by the question—under what conditions will human populations regulate rates of reproduction in individual or group interests?

In utilizing the resources of their environment at very low intensities, gatherers also maintain low population densities. As suggested above, in stable environments they are likely to maintain fixed territories, with high levels of conflict with neighbouring groups over territorial control. Under these conditions their interests lie in maintaining the population density at a level which ensures that the territorial group does not have to face occasional resource shortages—shortages that may weaken it in a conflict with neighbouring groups. It is possible that the variety of population-control mechanisms noted among gatherers may serve the function of maintaining their population densities in the group's interest. Such mechanisms may, of course, break down when gatherers lose control over their resource base—upon coming into contact with people practising more advanced modes of resource use.

Coming next to pastorals, their population densities tend to be low because they inhabit the more arid and unproductive regions. Very likely, these levels are maintained by natural checks; it is unlikely that the inhabitants of such variable environments, who have no fixed territories, would have evolved cultural practices to deliberately maintain their populations at low levels.

Characterized by a substantial intensification of resource

use, agricultural societies maintain population densities far higher than those of either gatherer or nomadic pastoral societies. However, most members make rather low-level demands on the resource base, though members of the non-agricultural elite may have high levels of demand for many non-essential commodities. Given these low levels of resource demand, and the possibilities of gradually improving yields from cultivated lands through technical change, agricultural communities are likely to be characterized by slow population growth. Further, the larger states of which they are a part generally ensure that there are no serious territorial conflicts within their limits—conflicts in which overpopulation may be a serious handicap. Yet the military strength of agricultural states may depend on their overall population; therefore the state apparatus would tend to encourage population growth. One therefore expects neither individual nor group-level pressures to deliberately check population growth in agricultural societies; *natural* checks and balances, such as diseases and disasters, may take a periodic and heavy toll of peasant populations.

The population history of the industrial mode is captured in the phrase 'demographic transition'. While in the initial phase of industrialization the population of European stock (both within Europe and in newly-colonized lands) expanded rapidly, over the last century it has grown much more slowly, stabilized, and in some places even declined. This transition seems related to the fact that the attempts of each individual in enhancing his/her resource consumption limits the quantity of resources available to raise offspring. Further, parents try to endow each offspring with a high level of ability to garner resources for itself. The need to invest in the *quality* of children again implies a severe limitation on the *quantity* of children produced. Industrial societies have thus generally stabilized their populations. At the same time, their *per capita* resource consumption remains high and on the increase.

PART TWO

Towards a Cultural Ecology of Pre-modern India

CHAPTER TWO

Forest and Fire

Geological History

When mammals made their appearance on earth 180 million years ago, the Indian subcontinent had recently broken off from the great southern land mass which earlier included South America, Antarctica and Africa. The land mass which is now India was crossing the equator when the age of dinosaurs came to an end, sixty-five million years ago. Fifty-four million years ago its northern tip bumped into the Asian plate; in another four million years it had established contact along the remaining boundary. The aftermath of this collision has been the Himalaya, rising at a rate of two centimetres a century to produce the tallest mountains in the world (Coward *et al.* 1988; Meher-Homji 1989). This barrier has been continually going up over the last fifty million years, so that most mammals have come to India through passes to the west, and some to the east of this mountain chain. Hominid fossils first appeared on the subcontinent in the Himalayan foothills thirteen million years ago; they continued till seven million years BP (before present) as a part of the mammalian communities of wooded habitats. Then they disappeared, presumably victims of habitat changes brought about by the continuing upward movement of the Himalaya (Badgeley *et al.* 1984).

Much later, members of our own genus, *Homo*, moved onto the subcontinent, probably from their place of origin in the savannas of East and South Africa. Tool-using hominids arose in Africa around two million years ago; by one million years BP they had reached Java. Most likely, they colonized India around this time; but firm evidence of human occupation appears in the form of artefacts such as hand-axes somewhat later, between 700,000 to 400,000 BP (Rendel and Dennell 1985). By this time the lifting up of the Himalaya was done and over, and a seasonal monsoon climate had become established (Rajaguru *et al.* 1984).

The hunter-gatherer populations of our own species, *Homo sapiens*, came to cover, in a thin way, much of the country through the remaining part of the late Pleistocene. At this time the climate fluctuated between periods of weak, moderate and strong monsoon. However, the wet and hilly tracts of the Western Ghats, the west coast, and the north-eastern hill regions as well as the Gangetic plain remained unoccupied until the terminal Pleistocene of 20,000 years BP, when the monsoons became distinctly weak at the height of glaciation in the northern latitudes (Rajaguru *et al.* 1984; Pant and Maliekel 1987; see table 2.1).

Prudent Predators

We can only speculate on the ecological-niche relationships of these hunter-gatherer populations. In the productive, stable, tropical environments that they inhabited, most would have been organized in the form of bands with strong bonds to their territories, often in conflict over land- and water-use with neighbouring groups. Each endogamous tribe would have adapted itself culturally to its biological and physical environment, having learnt by trial and error what to eat and what to avoid, how to look for food and how to keep away from predators. Each such tribe may then be thought of as occupying a distinctive, spatially disjunct, niche. As discussed in Chapter 1, such human communities would be expected to develop cultural traditions of sustainable utilization of their resource base (Gadgil 1987).

There is naturally no guarantee that such conservation practices would have led to the long-term persistence of all the elements of their biological environment. But so long as the total demand on resources remained limited, the human populations would tend to reach an equilibrium with their resource base after the elimination of elements that were over-utilized. Even at the hunting-gathering stage, the demand on some resources used as commodities, for instance ivory, could increase without limit and lead to their over-utilization. Drastic environmental changes could also result in a disturbance of the equilibrium that human populations may have reached. Climatic changes attendant on the withdrawal of Pleistocene glaciation 10,000 years ago seem to have resulted in the extinction of many species all over the world; this could in part have been due to the over-extension of human hunting after major changes had taken place in the prey populations. The baboon and hippopotamus became extinct in India at this time, perhaps as a result of such processes (Rajaguru *et al.* 1984; Badam 1978).

While more advanced agricultural societies have replaced hunter-gatherer societies over large parts of the moist tropical forest tracts of India, there are, even today, extensive areas where hunter-gathering shifting-cultivator societies persist. These include the humid forest tracts to the north-east of the Brahmaputra valley, and parts of central India where the eastern end of the Vindhya ranges join the north-eastern tracts of the Eastern Ghats. The difficulties of settled cultivation in this hilly terrain, its poor access from major centres of human populations, and low population densities resulting from malaria and inter-tribal wars—all these have contributed to the persistence of hunter-gatherer shifting-cultivator populations in these regions. Some of these populations have converted to Chris-

TABLE 2.1
CLIMATIC HISTORY OF THE INDIAN SUBCONTINENT

Geological period	Years BP	Climate	Geomorphic data	Human population
Late Holocene	< 4,000	Moderate monsoons	Saline lakes in western India	Agricultural settlements cover the subcontinent
Early Holocene	10,000–4,000	Strong monsoons	Fresh-water lakes, entrenched streams, stable dunes	Beginning of agriculture, denser populations
Terminal Pleistocene	20,000–10,000	Distinctly weak monsoons	Hypersaline lakes, choked rivers, active dunes	Human population spread throughout the subcontinent at low densities
Late Pleistocene	70,000–20,000	Weak to moderate monsoons	Entrenched streams, stable dunes	Hunter-gatherers in small groups, wetter tracts not colonized
Early-Late Pleistocene	125,000–70,000	Strong monsoons	Reddish soils (dating doubtful)	Hunter-gatherers in small groups, nomadic
Middle Pleistocene	700,000–125,000	Monsoonic seasonal climate	—	First evidence of human occupation

Geological period	Years BP	Climate	Geomorphic data	Human population
Lower Pleistocene	2.0 million-0.7 million	Relatively dry seasonal climate	Volcanic ashes, streams aggrading	Hominids found in both Africa and Java; but no definite evidence of human occupation in India
Pliocene	8 million-2.0 million	Tropical equatorial to strongly monsoonic(?)	Volcanic ashes	—
Miocene	25 million-8 million	Tropical equatorial (?)	—	—

SOURCE : S.N. Rajaguru (personal communication), R.K. Pant (personal communication) tianity, drastically changing traditional resource use practices in the process. In the non-Christian tracts, however, we see the persistence of social practices favouring prudent resource use. For example, in Meghalaya, Mizoram and the tribal belts of Orissa, we have evidence of sacred groves and quotas on wood extracted from fuel-woodlots, as well as practices with incidental conservation consequences such as protection given to totemic animals and plants (Fernandes and Menon 1987; Fernandes *et al.* 1988).

Neolithic Revolution

Historians have argued that climatic change at the time of the withdrawal of glaciers 10,000 years BP led to a creeping back of the forest cover and, in time, to a food crisis. This crisis, very likely, prompted hunter-gatherer societies to domesticate animals and cultivate plants. The crisis was not equally acute everywhere; it was perhaps most serious in the Middle East, where the domestication of animals and the cultivation of plants began to gather momentum some 10,000 years ago (Hutchinson *et al.* 1977). Plants such as wheat, barley and lentils, and animals such as cattle, sheep and goats, were first domesticated here. This process undoubtedly provided the stimulus for the beginnings of agriculture and animal husbandry in the Indian subcontinent. The earliest evidence of this comes from Mehrgarh, in what is now the Pakistani state of Baluchistan, around 8000 years BP (Jarrige and Meadow 1980). There is a disputed claim for the origin of rice cultivation in the Gangetic valley of as early as 7000 BP (Sharma 1980); but it is more likely that rice was domesticated in India some 3000 years later, or diffused here from outside (Chaudhuri 1977). It is, however, certain that a number of pulses like horse gram, hyacinth bean, green gram and black gram were indigenously brought under cultivation in India around 4000 years ago. The humped cattle, zebu, is also likely to have been independently domesticated in the Indian subcontinent. These cattle and pulses give Indian agriculture and animal husbandry its special character (Kajale 1988).

Agricultural-pastoral people spread over the Indian subcontinent in many phases. Without metal tools they could not readily penetrate the moister forests, such as those of the Gangetic plains or the west coast. The habitat most favourable to them for cultivation was along the smaller water courses in the relatively drier tracts of north-western India, the Indus plains, and the Deccan peninsula. This is where agricultural settlements developed over the period 6000 to 1000 BC (Possehl 1982; Dhavalikar 1988; Allchin and Allchin 1968). There was also animal husbandry, including nomadic cattle-herding, and this mode of resource use has left traces—such as the ash mounds of the Deccan. It has been suggested that there was a gradual deforestation in parts of the Deccan over this period, with timber fences slowly giving way to stone walls surrounding pastoral camps (Allchin 1963). In the moister tracts over the rest of the country there would have been some shifting cultivation, but this has left no trace. Hunting-gathering, along with shifting cultivation, might then have continued to dominate all the moister tracts of the subcontinent (Misra 1973).

River-valley Civilizations

The first urban civilization of the Indian subcontinent embraced a very wide region of the north-west. Archaeological evidence suggests that this culture was familiar with the use of the plough. They had also begun to add indigenous rainy-season crops, such as rice and pulses, to winter-season crops—wheat, barley and lentils—that were of West Asian origin (Mehra and Arora 1985). The agricultural surpluses thus produced permitted the establishment of many towns where the surplus served to promote further processing and exchange of materials—i.e. artisanal and trade activities. Exchange over long distances, as opposed to barter on a small scale, called for the maintenance of records, and the Indus Valley civilization offers the first evidence of literacy in Indian history (Possehl 1982). The gradual weakening and disappearance of the urban centres of this civilization have been attributed to a variety of possible causes. The explanation with the best documented evidence relates to the shifting of river courses, on account of geological changes associated with the continuing lifting up of the Himalaya. Satellite imagery clearly shows the palaeo-channels of the river Saraswati, which dried up when the Sutlej shifted its course westward to join the Indus, and the Yamuna eastward to join the Ganges (Fig. 2.1). There have also been suggestions of climatic change, as evident from palaeobotany, the flooding of the Indus, and of the salination of agricultural soils on account of irrigation (Agarwal and Sood 1982).

Iron was introduced to India by about 1000 BC, being associated with the Painted Grey Ware pottery culture of the north-west, the Black and Red Ware pottery culture of central India, and the megalithic cultures covering much of the peninsula. Iron, along with fire, made it possible to bring the middle Gangetic plains under intensive agricultural-pastoral colonization, with wet paddy cultivation as a key element (Kosambi 1970).

With the pattern of resource use becoming grounded in a continual march of agriculture and pastoralism over territory held by food gatherers, the belief system of the colonizers would naturally take a form very different from that appropriate to food gatherers, who had a great stake in the conservation of the resource base of their territories. Since the forest, with its wild animal populations, served as a resource base for the enemy, its destruction, rather than its conservation, would now have assumed priority. Supernatural power would now no longer reside in specific trees, groves or ponds, but would be the more abstract forces of nature: earth, fire, wind, water, and sky, whose assistance could be invoked in the task of subordinating hunter-gatherers and colonizing their resource base. Fire to clear the forest, and water to nourish crops in the fields, would be the most valuable of these forces; therefore Agni and

Varuna were the major deities. The main ritual was fire worship, the Yajna, a ritual in which huge quantities of wood and
animal fat were consumed.

The burning of the Khandava forest, as depicted in the
Mahabharata, beautifully illustrates the operation of this belief
system. In this episode Krishna and Arjuna are at a picnic in the
great Khandava forest which lies on the banks of the Yamuna,
where the city of Delhi stands today. A poor Brahman appears
begging for alms. On being granted his desire, the Brahman
reveals himself as Agni, the fire god. He then asks that his
hunger be satiated by the burning of the Khandava forest, along
with every creature within it. Krishna and Arjuna agree to this,
whereupon Agni gives them a fine chariot, and bows and
arrows, to perform the task. The forest is set on fire, and Krishna
and Arjuna patrol its perimeter, driving back all the creatures
who attempt escape. This includes *nagas* (cobras)—probably
the appellation for food-gathering tribes which venerated
snakes.

Arjuna evidently wants to clear the Khandava forest to
provide land for his agricultural/pastoral clan, and to build
their capital city, Indraprashtha. The burning of the forest, and
the killing of wild animals and tribal food gatherers is couched
in the terminology of a great ritual sacrifice to please Agni.
Agni's appearance as a Brahman begging alms is significant,
because Brahmans, who presided over fire sacrifices (Yajnas)
played an important role in the process of colonization. They
served as pioneers, establishing their outposts in forests and
initiating rituals which consumed large quantities of wood and
animal fat. Thus provoked, the native food gatherers, termed
demons or Rakshasas, would attempt to disrupt the holocaust
and save their resource base in order to retain control over their
territories. Specialist warriors, Kshatriyas, would then rush to
the rescue of the Brahmans who had furnished them with
appropriate provocation to invade these territories. This process is represented in the Mahabharata, in Dushyanta's visit to
the abode of the Brahman sage Kanva. Dushyanta combs the

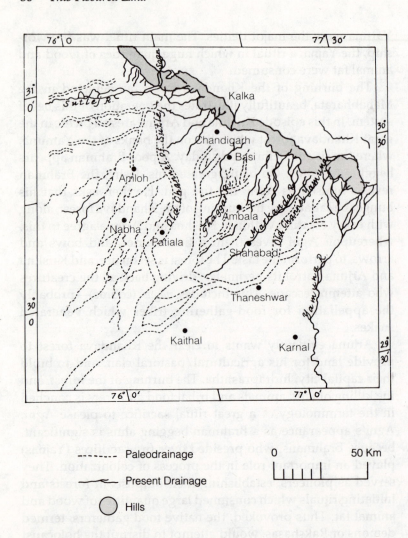

Figure 2.1
The Indo-Gangetic divide showing paleo-river channels.

forest with the help of hundreds of assistants, killing wild animals with complete abandon. It appears reasonable to conclude that the purpose of this slaughter was to destroy the resource base of hunting and gathering tribals who lived in the forest (Karve 1974).

The archaeological evidence that becomes available from this period also makes it possible to make more definite statements about human population changes, and to relate these changes to the ecological setting. The land-to-man ratio would have been high in the phase of expansion—the phase analogous to that of r-strategists of ecology. For instance, Lal (1984) suggests a density of 0.75 persons per km^2 for Kanpur district in the Ganga-Yamuna divide for the Black and Red Ware period around 1350 BC; this would also have been accompanied by a high livestock-to-man ratio. Meanwhile, more forests would have to be burnt and colonized as older lands were over-used and exhausted. An ethic of exhaustive resource use, with the Yajna as its cornerstone, is likely to have been the ruling belief system in this period. If the human population did indeed quadruple over the next eight centuries of agricultural growth, as Lal (1984) has argued, then much of the fertile land would have come under the plough, resulting in a lower livestock-to-man ratio and a declining availability of forest land for further colonization. Now, with the society moving into a phase analogous to the k-strategists of ecology, people would have required a new belief system, stressing more careful and sustainable patterns of resource use. Such a belief system is likely to have appealed to the agricultural-pastoral component of the population, but to have been opposed by the Brahmans, votaries of the Yajna system. Buddhism and Jainism, sects often described as heterodox, i.e. in opposition to the Brahmanic religion, appear to have been responses to this need. Both these religions are known to have protested against the hegemony of Brahmans and the wasteful burning of endless quantities of clarified butter and wood, and the slaughter of animals in sacrificial rituals (Thapar 1984).

As we noted in Chapter 1, the belief system of food gatherers, with its conservation orientation, saw spirits that were respected in trees, groves, ponds, rivers, and mountain peaks. In contrast, in the belief system of food producers conquering new territories, worship focussed on elemental forces such as fire and water, and the great god of war, Indra. As the frontier receded and there were no longer large fertile tracts to move towards, there emerged the belief systems of Buddhism and Jainism, which rejected the supernatural and advocated a rational arrangement of human affairs. These belief systems included an important element of conservation: they advocated that resources should not be used wastefully.

Social Organization

By the time of Gautam Buddha, some 2500 years BP, settled agriculture and pastoralism had covered wide tracts of the country. These continued into the drier tracts of western India, from where they made their way into the peninsula. The central parts of peninsular India are semi-arid, like much of western India, and here too small-scale cultivation and pastoralism took root along the tributaries of major rivers. The highest concentration of agricultural/pastoral populations were of course along the Gangetic plain. In all these tracts chiefdoms would have sprung up, their scale depending on the scale of cultivation and the extent of expropriable surplus. Food gatherers continued in the hilly tracts of the Himalaya and north-eastern India, on the Central Indian plateau, and on the Eastern and Western Ghats.

In the tracts brought under settled agriculture, the original territorial boundaries of food-gathering tribes would necessarily have broken down in this period. Food producers, whose populations must have undergone substantial expansion, moved into these lands, as might have other food gatherers displaced from their territories. An important question arises here—what would happen to the barriers of endogamy and culture which earlier existed in populations that were now thrown together within the larger territories of chiefdoms? One possibility is that these barriers of endogamy and cultural differentiation may have broken down, either partially or completely, producing a more or less homogeneous population. However, an agricultural/pastoral society, with its specialized crafts, trade, administration and fighting forces, is far more heterogeneous than a society of food gatherers because it involves a substantial division of labour and differentiation of status. A more likely possibility therefore is that, instead of merging, the different endogamous groups remain distinct and are assigned different tasks and status within the society. While there has undoubtedly been some merging of earlier endogamous groups and some redifferentiation in Indian society, barriers of endogamy among different tribal groups seem to have been largely retained, being converted into barriers of endogamy among caste groups (Karve 1961).

This transition from tribe to caste probably permitted the elites, which were involved in spreading food production and mopping up the surplus, to assign tedious and low-status tasks to various food-gathering tribes. The process itself was rationalized in the *varna* system, which divided the society into Brahmans or priests, Kshatriyas or warriors, Vaishyas or traders, Sudras or peasants and higher-status artisans, and Panchamas (Untouchables) or lower-status artisans and labourers. The conquered food gatherers were then assigned to the Sudra and Panchama categories, both to till the land and to perform lower-status artisanal and service tasks. However, these categories were by no means genetically homogeneous entities, and in any region a very large number of endogamous caste groups made up any one varna. Thus in western Maharashtra today the Sudra varna is made up of many endogamous groups of peasant cultivators such as Kunbis, of artisans such as Kumbhars, of pastorals such as Dhangars, and so on. Further, the potter Kumbhars or pastoral Dhangars are themselves a cluster of many distinct endogamous groups. Among the pastoral Dhangars of western Maharashtra, for example, we find the Gavli Dhangars who maintain buffaloes in hill forests, the Hatkar Dhangars who maintain sheep in the semi-arid tracts, the Khatik Dhangars who are butchers, the Sangar Dhangars who are weavers of wool, and the Zende Dhangars who used to maintain ponies (Malhotra and Gadgil 1981). It is therefore appropriate to focus on individual endogamous groups as the primary unit of Indian society, and reserve for them the term 'caste' (*jati*) (Karve 1961). A set of castes with similar occupations and with some cultural affinity may then be characterized as a caste cluster. Endogamous castes that make up a caste cluster such as the Dhangars may often be genetically as well as culturally quite varied. Varna itself is a largely artificial construct, with member castes or caste clusters being extremely varied, both genetically and culturally. Even the two higher varnas, Brahman and Kshatriya, who have some cultural affinity among their member castes, have been shown to be genetically quite heterogeneous. For instance, in western Maharashtra the Rigvedic Deshastha Brahmans are genetically closer to the local Shudra Kunbi castes than to the Chitpavan Konkanastha Brahmans (Karve and Malhotra 1968).

This process of forcing the newly-assimilated groups into lower-status tasks was rationalized by the elite in two ways. It was justified first on the grounds that these groups were, at least in some ways, biologically distinctive, and second by attributing birth in lower-status groups to sins committed in a previous birth. A very interesting dialogue of the Buddha addresses this issue. When a questioner equates the different endogamous groups to different species of plants, the Buddha's rejoinder is to point out that the different biological species are separated by barriers to reproduction, with hybrids being either sterile or impossible to produce. Different human groups, on the other hand, are clearly inter-fertile, and, in keeping with his rationalist approach, the Buddha advocates their merger. Buddhism and Jainism, however, did not succeed in destroying the social hierarchy of Indian society.

The Age of Empires

The eight centuries from 500 BC to AD 300, which followed the colonization of the fertile lands of northern India, seem to have been characterized by the availability of large surpluses of agricultural production for activities outside food production. The river valleys of peninsular India—for example of the Krishna, Godavari, Kaveri, and Vaigai—were also being brought under the plough at this time. The larger the surplus available, the larger the scale controlled by the elite which organized the usurpation of this surplus. Large surpluses would also have promoted large-scale resource exchange—i.e. trade. The chiefdoms of earlier times therefore gave way to larger states—to those of the Mauryas and the Kushanas in the north, and to the Chalukyas and Sangam Cholas in the peninsula (Thapar 1966). These states indulged in a vigorous trade, both internal and overseas.

Sustained by the surplus thus garnered, the primary interest of these states would be to generate ever-larger surpluses within their own territory, and to acquire as much surplus as possible from the territories of other states. The first aim can be achieved through an extension of the area under cultivation, and by enhancing the productivity of agriculture through the provision of irrigation facilities; the latter objective is carried out through external trade and warfare. These preoccupations are reflected in the activities of the Mauryan state, as recorded especially in Kautilya's *Arthasastra* (Kangle 1969). Based within the large tracts of fertile and cultivated lands in the Gangetic plain, the Mauryan state was keenly interested in pushing the frontiers of cultivated tracts further and further back, for instance by colonizing Kalinga (modern Orissa). This, of course, represented a continuation of the conflict between food gatherers and food producers which accompanied the colonization of the Gangetic plain itself. As observed earlier, that effort was pushed forward by smaller chiefdoms, with Brahmans and their Yajnas serving as forward probes. The continuation of such expansion under the Mauryan state was a more organized effort in the deliberate colonization of river valleys of the hilly tracts that now bounded the empire. The domesticated elephant probably played a significant role in the invasion of these tracts; a temple frieze in Orissa shows an elephant picking up in its trunk and flinging to death a man with the physical features characteristic of a tribal. At the same time, by providing irrigation works the Mauryan state attempted to boost the productivity of land already under cultivation.

By this time the elephant was established as an important component of the war machine, and Kautilya's *Arthasastra* discusses in some detail the quality of elephants, their capture and care, as well as the conservation of elephant forests. It remarks that every king should attempt to have in the army as large a number of these beasts as possible. Since elephants were never bred in captivity, the *Arthasastra* advocates setting aside, under strict protection, elephant forests on the borders of the state (Trautmann 1982). Such forests were undoubtedly inhabited by food-gathering tribals, and, since the killing of elephants attracted the death penalty, these tribals would be forced to give up the consumption of elephant meat. It is noteworthy that while elephants are hunted for meat in the north-eastern provinces of Mizoram, Nagaland and Arunachal Pradesh—areas that never came under the sway of any Indian state till British times—tribals in the rest of the country do not consume elephant meat. Since these tribals readily consume Gaur, a wild relative of the sacred cow, it is likely that the taboo on elephant meat in peninsular India was a consequence of other taboos enforced by early states such as the Mauryan.

The Mauryan kings also maintained some forested areas as hunting preserves. Parks close to their capitals contained dangerous animals; these seem to have been shorn of their teeth and claws before being released for the hunting pleasures of the nobility. Further away there existed natural forest areas where no one except the nobles was allowed to hunt. This might, in part, have been a strategy to dominate food-gathering tribals by cutting off a major resource. The demarcation of these areas for exclusive use also provided practice in warfare and the pleasures of high life for the warrior classes.

Elephant forests and hunting preserves brought in a new form of territorial control over living resources—control by the state. As noted earlier, to the territorial control exercised by food-gathering tribes, peasants added control of individual fields by families, of forests and pastures by village communities, and of a much larger territorial entity by the chiefdom. Notwithstanding the large claims of the chiefdom, the actual control over cultivated and non-cultivated land vested with villagers. In contrast, elephant forests and hunting preserves were carved out of non-cultivated lands over which the state now claimed direct control, very likely by de-recognizing some of the rights of local food-gathering tribals and/or peasant communities. The latter were perhaps permitted to continue gathering plant material, and to hunt animals which were not explicitly protected. At the same time, the state attempted to regulate the clearing of forests to establish new agricultural settlements.

Conservation from Above

This radical transformation led on the one hand to a considerable breakdown of local autonomy at the food-gathering stage, and on the other to the organized outflows of agricultural produce as well as commodities such as elephants, musk and sandal. Both processes must have profoundly affected man–nature interactions, chiefly through the breakdown of local traditions of resource conservation and a gradual over-harvesting and erosion of the resource base. As the frontiers closed, and as the resource crunch mounted, there would very likely have been an increasing social awareness of the need for readjustment through the more efficient and conservative use of resources. It was argued earlier that Buddhism and Jainism represented such a response, with the abandonment of Yajnas being another way of adapting to the changed circumstances. By loosening the hold of Brahmanism, these religions especially attracted the support of traders who flourished in the heyday of high surpluses. Buddhist and Jain monasteries then helped in the opening up of trade routes and the organization of trade, just as the camps of Brahman sages had earlier catalysed the opening up of forests for cultivation (Kosambi 1970).

Buddhism and Jainism then began to play a role in once again designing social conventions which promoted the prudent use of resources. In part, such conservation practices would have been founded on earlier ones, inherited from food-gathering societies. Apart from their appeal to traders, these religions perhaps appealed most to the lower social strata, composed largely out of food gatherers. In fact the leader of the erstwhile Untouchable castes, the late B.R. Ambedkar, believed that the bulk of the Untouchables were adherents of the Buddhist faith in this historical period (Ambedkar 1948). Buddhism and Jainism may thus have played a role for these people by bolstering traditions by which protection was given to various plants, animal species, and various elements of the landscape, such as groves and ponds. In fact the Buddha himself is said to have been born in a sacred grove full of stately sal trees dedicated to the goddess Lumbini.

The best-known ancient state-sponsored conservation campaign was undertaken by the Mauryan emperor Ashoka, following his conversion to Buddhism. The Ashokan edicts advocate both restraint in the killing of animals and the planting and protection of trees. One such edict, from the third century BC, in Dhauli (in present-day Orissa), goes in translation as follows:

> The king with charming appearance, the beloved of the gods, in his conquered territories and in the neighbouring countries, thus enjoins that: medical attendance should be made available to both man and animal; the medicinal herbs, the fruit trees, the roots and tubers, are to be transplanted in those places where they are not presently available, after being collected from those places where they usually grow; wells should be dug and

shadowy trees should be planted by the roadside for enjoyment both by man and animal.

In the heyday of Buddhism and Jainism, therefore, there appears to have been a widespread perception of the need to moderate the harvesting of plant and animal resources. But, as pointed out earlier, it is difficult to arrive at precise prescriptions that work in any given local situation, and even more difficult to arrive at prescriptions that work under a variety of conditions. Buddhism and Jainism did not attempt to prescribe practices applicable to each given local situation any more than did the religious beliefs of food-gathering tribes. These religions had perforce to suggest broad principles, such as compassion towards all living creatures, a ban on killing animals, and planting as well as protecting trees. Jainism, especially in its Digambara branch, carried this to its extreme logical conclusion. Digambara Jains are against the killing of any organism, plant or animal. They permit the consumption of biological products only so long as this does not involve 'killing': for instance grain and milk can be consumed, but meat is completely taboo. Digambara Jain monks wear no clothes: these may trap and kill insects and other small living organisms. The monks sweep the ground as they walk, to eliminate stepping on living things that normally escape notice.

This extreme ethic of non-violence has had a pervasive influence on Indian society. It has led towards the complete ban on the slaughter of cattle at ritual sacrifices, and to the taboo against beef by all the upper and most of the lower castes. Protection to cattle has undoubtedly been important in shaping the practices of mixed agriculture and animal husbandry so characteristic of India. A significant proportion of India's caste population has also come to assume vegetarianism. Notably, this proportion is relatively high in the drier, less productive tracts, such as Rajasthan, Gujarat and northern Karnataka, where animal power is more critical to agriculture and where deforestation is likely to have been always ahead of that in other, wetter regions. This ethic must have been important in the continuation of old, and in the development of new, traditions of protection *vis-à-vis* wild animals and plants. Traditions such as these have played a significant role in influencing the pattern of utilization of biological resources in India over the last several centuries, especially until the arrival of European colonial power.

CHAPTER THREE

Caste and Conservation

Resource Crunch

The 'ecological' implications of Buddhism and Jainism not-withstanding, the Indian subcontinent entered a period of decline in trade and urban centres in the fourth century of the Christian era, the Gupta period (Sharma 1987). This decline very likely related to a lowering of surpluses from agriculture, which in turn could have been on account of three kinds of changes, operating singly or in conjunction. First, there may have been climatic changes that resulted in a decline in rainfall. This is plausible, for we do know that there have been significant changes in patterns of rainfall over the historical and geological time-scale. There is, however, no definite evidence of rainfall decline over the Indian subcontinent in this specific period. Second, there may have been a fall in agricultural production due to a depletion of soil fertility, occasioned by the failure to adequately replace soil nutrients removed by the harvest of crops. These nutrients need to be replaced by a natural deposition of silt during river floods, or by adding leaf manure, cattle dung or fish to the fields. It is possible that such replenishment was inadequate, perhaps because the sources of organic manure were overharvested or because dung had to be increasingly used as fuel. Again, while this is a distinct possibility, there is no direct evidence to confirm that this was indeed the case. Last, the decline in available surplus may have been a direct consequence of growth in human population resulting in a lower land–man ratio. For instance, Lal (1984) estimates that the population in the Kanpur district grew from densities of 2.35 / km^2 in the Painted Grey Ware period to 12.82 / km^2 by the early historical period, i.e. over the course of about 1000 years. Demographic changes such as these could obviously make a major difference to the available surplus.

Whatever be the reason(s), there is little doubt that the Indian subcontinent experienced a major resource crunch over the fourth to tenth centuries of the Christian era. In this period, there existed few possibilities for the expansion of productive agriculture, except through the provision of irrigation facilities. Some expansion of such irrigation facilities did indeed occur in this period, for example in the Kaveri delta of southern India. However, there remained many regions with little cultivation, while even the cultivated tracts had large areas of non-cultivated land. The reasons for this were several: in north-western India and the centre of the Indian peninsula the rainfall was too scanty and variable; in the terai at the foot of the Himalaya the conditions were swampy and malarial; on the banks of the Ganges there was an excessive fury of annual floods; and in the Eastern and Western Ghats the topography was too steep. These non-cultivated tracts of land nevertheless provided resources of value to humans, as did lakes, rivers, estuaries and the sea. These resources could be tapped in many different ways, by hunting or fishing, by the maintenance of flocks of sheep grazed over a large area with regular seasonal movements, by grazing cattle that provided motive power and dung for agriculture, and by the harvest of leaf manure, fuelwood and timber. The need to ensure the sustainability of agriculture by providing adequate replenishment of soil nutrients, and the importance of sustainable harvests from non-cultivated tracts, would have become increasingly evident as the resource crunch progressed.

Conservation from Below

In these conditions the problems of ensuring the prudent use of renewable resources would be faced by a society very differently organized from the territorial groups of hunter-gatherer-shifting cultivators. This society was an agglomeration of tens of thousands of endogamous groups, the different castes. These endogamous groups resembled tribal groups in being largely self-governing, with all intra-group regulation in the hands of the council of group leaders. Like tribal groups, caste groups were distributed over restricted geographical ranges. However, unlike tribal groups, which tended to occupy exclusive territories, caste groups overlapped with many others. Finally, unlike tribal groups, which were largely self-sufficient and carried out a broad range of activities, caste groups tended to pursue a relatively specialized and hereditary mode of subsistence. With their overlapping distributions and occupational specializations, the different caste groups were linked together in a web of mutually supportive relationships. This is not to claim that caste society was at all egalitarian. It was in fact a sharply stratified society, with the terms of exchange between different caste groups weighted strongly in favour of the higher status castes (Karve 1961; Srinivas 1962; Dumont 1970).

The subcontinent retained tribal hunter-gatherer-shifting cultivator groups in several pockets of hilly and often malarial country. Many of these tribes, too, interacted with caste society, exchanging forest produce such as ivory or honey for commodities like metal tools and salt. Caste society, the Indian variant of the peasant mode of resource use, was further divided into sedentary, nomadic and semi-nomadic caste groups. Nomads were either pastorals who moved around with their animal herds, taking advantage of the seasonal availability of grazing grounds, or non-pastoral communities such as traders,

entertainers, mendicants and specialist artisans. Sedentary villages were, then as now, populated by groups practising mixed
agriculture and animal husbandry, and by service and artisan
castes. Along rivers or on the coast, there were specialized
fishing castes as well.

The basic unit of social organization, the village, most often
included populations of several endogamous caste groups.
These village communities were in many ways self-sufficient
and dealt with the machinery of the state as a unit. Thus, taxes
in the form of surplus production of grain were usually paid to
the state by the village community as a whole, and not by
individual householders. Governed by a council of leaders
from the different caste groups, in many areas the community
also retained the rights of reassigning cultivable land among
different cultivator families, although the cultivated land was
ordinarily never alienated from the group of tillers. Just as caste
councils regulated most intra-caste affairs, village councils
regulated most inter-caste matters, with recourse to any outside
authority a most infrequent occurrence. Each sedentary village
was regularly visited by certain nomadic lineages which had
established a customary relationship with it.

The caste-based village society had developed a variety of
institutions to regulate the use of living resources. Each settlement had a few families whose hereditary caste occupation was
to serve as village guards. These guards were responsible for
monitoring the visits of all aliens, as well as for maintaining
information on the property rights of different families within
the village. In Maharashtra, this function was generally served
by members of the Mahar caste. In a fascinating record of
pre-British Maharashtra, Aatre (1915) mentions that the Mahars
also had the function of preventing any unauthorized wood-
cutting in village common land. Additionally, they had to
harvest and deliver all wood needed by village households.
Since a Mahar family expected to be part of the village community and carry on its hereditary occupation, its interests
would obviously lie in maintaining harvests from the village

common lands at a sustainable level. Elsewhere, too, there are records of the harvests from village common lands being governed by a variety of regulations, notably quotas on the amount harvested by different families and in different seasons (Gadgil and Iyer, 1989; Guha, Ramachandra 1989a).

A resource from common lands such as fuelwood would of course be required by all village households. However, many other types of produce would not necessarily be required by all households. Here, caste society had developed an elaborate system of the diversified use of living resources that greatly reduced inter-caste competition, and very often ensured that a single caste group had a monopoly over the use of any specific resource from a given locale. We might exemplify this remarkable system of ecological adaptation with the help of two case studies, one of a relatively simple two-caste society, the second of a much more complex multi-caste village.

In the high rainfall tracts near the crest of the hill range of the Western Ghats of Maharashtra, the population density is low and the villages often made up of just two caste groups, the Kunbis and Gavlis. Here the Kunbis lived, and still do, in the lower valleys, while the Gavlis lived—they still do—on the upper hill terraces. The major occupation of the Gavlis was keeping large herds of buffaloes and cattle. They curdled the milk, consuming the buttermilk at home and bartering the butter for cereal grains (produced by the Kunbis) and for their other necessities. The protein requirements of the Gavlis were met from buttermilk, and they almost never hunted. They also practised a little shifting cultivation on the upper hill terraces.

The Kunbis, on the other hand, practised paddy cultivation in the river valleys and shifting cultivation on the lower hill slopes. They kept only a few cattle for draught purposes; these produced very little milk. To meet their protein requirements the Kunbis hunted a great deal. Thus cultivation in the valleys and lower hill slopes was restricted to the Kunbis, and that in the hill terraces to the Gavlis; the maintenance of livestock and the use of fodder and grazing resources were largely with the

Gavlis, while the Kunbis had the monopoly of hunting wild animals (Gadgil and Malhotra 1982).

Our second example comes from a village, Masur-Lukkeri, situated on an island in the estuary of the river Aghanashini, close to the town of Kumta in the state of Karnataka (14° 25′ N lat. and 24° E long.). Spurs of the hill ranges of the Western Ghats run all the way to the sea in this region, creating a rich mosaic of territorial, riparian and coastal habitats, supporting a great diversity of natural resources. Populations of as many as thirteen different endogamous groups live on this island of 4 km². There are, even today, hardly any marriages outside the endogamous groups, whose members continue largely to follow their traditional, hereditary occupations. Some of the hereditary occupations are no longer viable—e.g. toddy tapping or temple dancing—while a number of new ones have been introduced, such as rice milling, truck transport and white-collar jobs. Nevertheless, a fairly accurate reconstruction of the traditional subsistence patterns of the groups is possible on the basis of Gazetteers prepared in the nineteenth century, as well as the folk traditions collected over the period 1984-8 (Campbell 1883, Gadgil and Iyer 1989). The thirteen endogamous groups may be placed in seven categories based on their primary traditional occupations.

1. Fishing communities: This island has a population of one community of specialized river fishermen, the Ambigas.

2. Agriculturists: The traditional agricultural communities include the Halakkis, the Patgars and the Naiks. Of these, the Naiks were traditionally soldiers and petty chieftains as well.

3. Horticulturists: The Haviks, a priestly Brahman caste, are the only endogamous group of this region who specialize in horticulture. They are strict vegetarians but consume milk and milk products in substantial quantities.

4. Entertainers: Two endogamous groups: the Bhan-

daris and the Deshbhandaris, traditionally served as musicians and dancers, usually attached to the temples. The Bhandaris also used to tap toddy from coconut palms. Both the groups are now mainly dependent on agriculture.

5. Service castes: There are two service castes, the Kodeyas (barbers) and the Madivals (washermen).

6. Artisans: These include Shet (goldsmith), Achari (carpenter and blacksmith) and Mukhri (stone-workers).

7. Traders: The Brahman caste of the Gowd Saraswats are the chief traders in the region. Unlike most other Brahman castes, they eat fish and seafood.

Apart from the Haviks, the other twelve castes relish fish and meat, a great deal of which are still acquired by hunting and fishing from natural populations. The Gowd Saraswat traders, the Shet goldsmiths and the Kodeya barbers do not hunt or fish themselves, but acquire animal food through barter or purchase. The other nine groups actively hunt or fish, the Ambiga males as their full-time activity, the others as a part-time activity. For this purpose they employ as many as thirty-three different methods, each of which tends to concentrate on a somewhat different habitat and a somewhat different mix of prey species. Interestingly enough, different endogamous caste groups prefer different methods of hunting and fishing, and thereby tap a different segment of the animal prey community. Thus deep water fishing, conducted from a craft and with more elaborate nets, is a monopoly of the Ambigas, the specialized fishing caste. Hunting larger mammals such as deer is a monopoly of the Halakkis, while trapping fruit bats is restricted to the Patgars and the Madivals. The Naiks are the only group to regularly trap bandicoot rats, while the Acharis, the smiths, are the only group to have taken to attracting fish with gaslights. Apart from hunting and fishing, the caste groups also exhibit an interesting diversification in the use of plant material for special purposes, such as mat weaving. Two of the caste groups engage in such activities; but while the Halakkis weave mats from the spiny leaves of *Pandanus*, the Patgars use *Cyperus* reeds.

Thus, sedentary endogamous groups living together, or sympatrically, to use a biological term, display a remarkable diversification of resource use. This pattern of adaptation is also exhibited by nomadic groups that largely tap resources away from village limits. Thus the Tirumal Nandiwallas, the Vaidus and the Phasepardhis are the three major nomadic castes hunting in the uncultivated tracts away from villages in the semi-arid region of Western Maharashtra (19° 5′ N lat. and 74° 45′ E long.). The Phasepardhis were primarily hunter-gatherers, bartering some of the game for other goods. The Tirumal Nandiwallas and the Vaidus had other primary occupations, such as displaying performing bulls, dispensing herbal medicines, selling trinkets, midwifery, etc., but hunted extensively for their own consumption.

We initiated an investigation of the hunting practices of these three castes with the presumption that they hunted much the same animals in the same tract.

However, our investigations showed that the three groups differed markedly in the hunting techniques used. The Tirumal Nandiwallas specialized in hunting with dogs, the average number of dogs per household being five. These dogs are used in locating, chasing and killing much of their prey, which includes the hyena, the leopard cat, the wild pig, the hare and the porcupine. The Vaidus kept a smaller number of dogs, an average of 1.5 per household in contemporary times. By contrast, they specialized in catching smaller carnivores such as the mongoose, the toddy cat, and the domestic cat, using traps often baited with squirrels. In the past they also specialized in catching fresh-water animals such as crabs, turtles and crocodiles (Avchat 1981). The Phasepardhis never used dogs, but instead used a trained cow to infiltrate a herd of blackbuck or deer, laying snares as they moved behind the cow. They also snared birds, particularly partridges, quails and peafowl, on a large scale.

TABLE 3.1

RELATIVE DEPENDENCE IN TERMS OF PERCENTAGE OF REPORTED
BIOMASS CONSUMED OF THE DIFFERENT
PREY SPECIES BY THE THREE NOMADIC CASTES

	Hunted animal species	*Tirumal Nandiwallas*	*Vaidus*	*Phase-pardhis*
I	Small carnivorous mammals (e.g. toddy cat, mongoose)	8.94	41.09	0.28
II	Large carnivorous mammals (e.g. leopard cat, hyena, fox)	24.99	7.86	0.07
III	Small herbivorous mammals (e.g. hare, porcupine)	15.53	5.14	0.01
IV	Blackbuck	1.19	0.00	70.43
V	Wild pigs	29.85	4.14	14.67
VI	Birds (e.g. doves, quails, partridges, peafowl)	2.09	3.59	14.21
VII	Monitor lizards	1.49	12.43	0.24
VIII	Aquatic animals (e.g. fish, crab, turtle)	15.92	25.75	0.00

SOURCE: Malhotra, Khomne and Gadgil (1983).

Table 3.1 provides present-day estimates of the relative
importance of different prey species for the three castes (Malhotra, Khomne and Gadgil 1983). Admittedly, the exact quantitative estimates in this table are not to be taken literally, since
our samples are small (2, 3 and 36 households for the three
castes) and the abundance of prey has drastically declined in
recent years. Nevertheless, the differences reflected in this table
are very real, being a direct consequence of the employment of
very distinctive hunting techniques. What is striking is that
while the hunting techniques employed differ in this fashion,
none of them are sophisticated enough to preclude their adoption by another caste. Thus the Phasepardhis could have easily

added the Vaidus' baited traps to their own snares. The fact that they do not do so points to a genuine cultural adjustment to reduce competition with other castes hunting in the same region.

Notably enough, while sympatric caste groups exhibit resource-use diversification, groups that are identical in their resource-use patterns tend to have a non-overlapping geographical distribution in what may be thought of as an analogue of Gause's principle of competitive exclusion (Hardin 1968).

The operation of this principle is nicely illustrated by two castes of Nandiwallas which had, and largely continue to have, an identical mode of subsistence. These two castes, the Tirumal Nandiwallas and the Phulmali Nandiwallas, are both non-pastoral nomads, making a living by the display of the sacred bull, by selling trinkets and by hunting. They both originated from common ancestral stock in Andhra Pradesh. The Tirumal Nandiwallas migrated into Maharashtra about 800 years ago, while the Phulmali Nandiwallas did so only 300 years ago. While they have developed complete reproductive isolation, their way of making a living and their culture have remained essentially identical (Malhotra 1974; Malhotra and Khomne 1978). They thus exemplify castes with completely identical ecological niches.

It is notable, therefore, that the Tirumal Nandiwallas and the Phulmali Nandiwallas show no geographical overlap whatsoever, i.e. they are completely allopatric. The base village of the Tirumal Nandiwallas is Wadapuri in Pune district, while the thirty-nine base villages of the Phulmali Nandiwallas are distributed over the districts of Ahmednagar, Bhir, Aurangabad and Nasik (Malhotra, *et al.* 1983). Both these Nandiwalla castes traditionally spend the rainy season in their base camps, and then spread out over the dry-season territory to display bulls and sell trinkets in sedentary villages. There was, and there is even now, a complete absence of overlap in the dry-season migratory range of the two Nandiwalla castes (see Fig. 3.1).

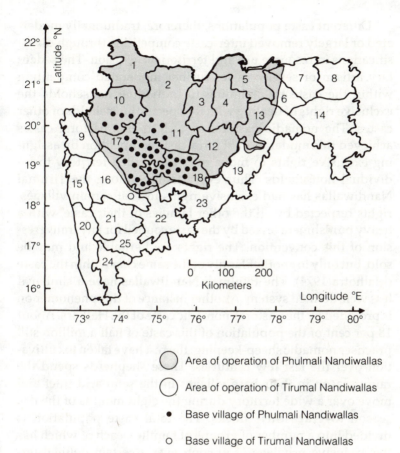

● Area of operation of Phulmali Nandiwallas

◯ Area of operation of Tirumal Nandiwallas

• Base village of Phulmali Nandiwallas

○ Base village of Tirumal Nandiwallas

Names of districts of Maharashtra: 1. Dhulia, 2. Jalgaon, 3. Buldhana, 4. Akola, 5. Amravati, 6. Wardha, 7.Nagpur, 8. Bhandara, 9. Thana, 10. Nasik, 11. Aurangabad, 12. Parbhani, 13. Yeotmal, 14. Chanda, 15. Kolaba, 16. Pune, 17. Ahmednagar, 18. Bhir, 19. Nanded, 20. Ratnagiri, 21. Satara, 22. Sholapur, 23. Osmanabad, 24. Kolhapur, 25. Sangli.

Figure 3.1
The administrative districts of Maharashtra and other localities referred to in the text, base villages and dry season operating ranges of the two castes of Nandiwallas.

Different caste populations, therefore, traditionally moderated or largely removed inter-caste competition through diversifications in resource use and territorial exclusion. The sedentary artisan or service castes further moderated competition within the caste by assigning to individual households the exclusive rights of dealing with the specific households of other castes. The nomadic pastoral as well as non-pastoral castes achieved this moderation of intra-caste competition by assigning exclusive rights to move over a specified territory to individual households. Thus every family among the Tirumal Nandiwallas has had exclusive rights to visit certain villages, rights respected by all the other families of their caste, with a heavy punishment levied by the caste council for any transgression of this convention. The rights are heritable and may be sold, but only to another family of the same clan within the caste (Malhotra 1974). The Phulmali Nandiwallas have a similar if less well-defined system. Another instance of this phenomenon is provided by the pastoral-nomadic caste of the Hatkars. About 18 per cent of the population of this caste of half a million still practises nomadic sheep-keeping; the rest have taken to cultivation over the last few centuries. These shepherds spend the rainy season in their base villages in the semi-arid tract and move over a wide territory during the eight months of the dry season to graze their flocks. The total caste population is divided into a number of groups of families, each of which has the exclusive privilege of grazing over a certain defined territory. This pattern is illustrated for the village of Dhawalpuri in Ahmednagar district in Fig. 3.1. This village comprises four different settlements within a kilometre of each other. While setting out on the migration after the rains, each settlement leaves as a single band, moving in a direction predetermined by tradition. As the band moves, it continues to split along kinship lines into progressively smaller groups, each moving in its own specific direction, till the group of families constituting the ultimate unit of the flock reaches its own territory. This composite territory of the small group of families is hereditarily handed down from generation to generation, and may be encroached upon by other shepherd families only with special permission in times of serious distress (Malhotra 1982).

An Eclectic Belief System

In this manner, diversification and territorial exclusion helped minimize inter- and intra-caste competition over living resources. We believe that this unique system of cultural adaptation to the natural environment was devised by Indian society in response to the resource crunch which it faced in the Gupta and post-Gupta periods, i.e. between the fourth and ninth centuries AD. It was then that social organization crystallized in the form of caste society, defined by its hereditarily prescribed modes of subsistence. Over this same period, Buddhism and Jainism lost the sway they held in earlier periods, with Buddhism being pushed out of India. The belief system that developed then was also distinct from the worship of fire and the rain gods that prevailed while the Indo-Gangetic plains were being colonized. The new system drew on beliefs in the sanctity of individual plants and animals, as well as of elements in the landscape, which the thousands of endogamous groups had inherited from their food-gathering days. The retention of these beliefs was probably aided by the continuity of culture facilitated by the barriers of endogamy. At the same time, these beliefs were, in part, turned into rituals meant to ensure the fertility of fields.

These distinctive local belief systems were now woven together into a composite fabric by identifying many of the spirits with a few key gods in the Hindu pantheon. Predominant among these were Shiva or Ishwara (male phallic worship), and the mother goddess, Parvati, (female fertility worship). A good proportion of local spirits was identified with these two. Others were then associated with them; thus, elephant worship became the worship of Ganesha, one of the sons of Shiva and Parvati. Shiva is also Pasupati—Lord of Beasts. He rides a male bull, Nandi, and around his neck are entwined

cobras—both being creatures associated with fertility. The sacrifice of animals, and sometimes even of humans, continued,
though the fire ritual now largely lost its central place. However, an important element added was devotion or *bhakti*. The
communal pursuit of devotion to deities, synchronized on specific days, now played the role of cementing different endogamous groups together.

This belief system had a clear role in regulating and moderating the use of natural resources. It legitimized in a new
framework the protection accorded to certain elements of the
landscape—for instance groves or ponds near temples, and
protection to certain species such as *Ficus religiosa* (peepal) or
Presbytis entellus (the Hanuman langur)—as sacred to a variety
of deities. Some of these prescriptions may have been functional
in resource conservation, others neutral or even malfunctional.
However, identifying them with deities from the Hindu pantheon was an effective way of continuing these practices.

Even more important than religious sanctions, in this regard, were social conventions. Thus the basket-weaving community of the Kaikadis in Maharashtra did not use the palmyra
palm as a raw material simply because it violated *jatidharma*,
the social duty enjoined on the endogamous group of the
Kaikadis. And the Baigas, a group of slash-and-burn cultivators
in Central India, believed that it was a sin to lacerate the breast
of mother earth by plough cultivation (Elwin 1939). Similarly,
the Agarias, whose hereditary occupation was charcoal iron-
making, held all cultivation to be against their own jatidharma
(Elwin 1942). Violations of caste duty were punished by the
displeasure of other group members in the village, and much
more effectively by social sanctions such as excommunication,
enforced by the council of their own endogamous group.

Many of these social conventions helped resource conservation. We may cite here the case of the Phasepardhis, the hunter-
gatherer group in Western Maharashtra discussed earlier. The
Phaseparadhis had a monopoly on deer hunting in their territory, yet they let loose any pregnant does or young deer

caught in their snares. The Phasepardhis are aware that this convention may facilitate better prey availability in the future. However, the practice was enjoined on all group members as jatidharma, as the right thing to do, and enforced through caste sanctions against any member who violated it.

The endogamous caste groups of Indian society might with profit be compared to biological species, although of course, as Gautam Buddha pointed out, they are all fully interfertile and in no way genetically differentiated from each other. Nevertheless, like biological species, they have been largely, though not absolutely, isolated reproductively through cultural barriers. Like the species within a biological community, the different caste groups also have characteristic modes of subsistence, and often tend to occupy distinct habitats. It is therefore appropriate to talk of the ecological niches of these various caste groups in terms of the habitats they occupy, the natural resources they utilize, and the relationship they bear to the other caste groups with whom they interact. Two interesting statements follow from this perspective, namely that the castes seem by and large to have narrow niches, and that the caste groups that live together have so diversified that they tend to have low niche overlaps.

We have already discussed the concept of a low niche overlap. This is a consequence of the low niche widths of individual caste groups. This narrowness of niches in a human community, developed in a tropical setting, offers very interesting parallels to the narrow niches of biological species in such an environment. Such narrow niches within biological species are considered a result of the high levels of productivity and low levels of variability with time, thus permitting high levels of specialization. The fact that there developed, and for centuries persisted, groups which are so specialized that their entire economy depends on tapping palms for toddy or making baskets from bamboo, suggests that there are genuine parallels. The fairly high levels of productivity, and the relative constancy from year to year, coupled to the low level of resources necessary to subsist in a tropical environment, have permitted high levels of specialization in the various modes of subsistence within Indian caste society. With such levels of specialization, the overlap of niches among caste groups living side by side has been kept at a low level. This has ensured that small numbers of people linked together by bonds of kinship, and by a common culture, have had a monopoly over specified resources in specified localities. As we argued in Chapter 1, this is expected to promote practices of prudent resource use. Indeed many such traditions—including sacred groves and sacred ponds as refugia, the protection to keystone species and to critical life-history stages, and the moderation of harvests from village wood-lots—have persisted in Indian society over the historical period, sometimes down to the present day.

The Village and the State

The Gupta and post-Gupta pre-Muslim period in Indian history, from the fourth to the tenth centuries, was by and large a period of low trade, low levels of urbanization, and many small kingdoms. A change could be wrought in this situation in one of several ways. It could come about through an improvement in climate, or by the introduction of new technologies, such as irrigation tanks, which would lead to a rise in agricultural productivity and production. It could also be brought about by a great improvement in modes of transport, communication and coercion, enabling the accumulation of low levels of surplus, but from over broad areas, to support an extensive state. Again, there is no definite evidence for any climatic change. However, we know that new technologies and vastly improved modes of transport, communication and coercion did come into play in the period following the tenth century.

An example of improved technology is the tank irrigation system with its sluice gates, as well as the social organization of irrigation management, centred on the temple, that permitted the agricultural colonization of large areas of Tamilnadu under the Cholas, from AD 900 to 1200. Interestingly, the priestly castes of Hinduism again spearheaded the spread of this new technology, with land grants to Brahmans accompanying the establishment of new tanks.

Six thousand years after domesticated crops and animals revolutionized that subcontinent's economy, certain specific military techniques and technologies—skilled horseriding, the co-ordination of attack by cavalry, and the use of gunpowder— all came to India from the same north-western route and rev-olutionized political organization (Digby 1971). The period beyond AD 900–1000, indeed, shows the re-emergence of larger states, such as the Chola state, and the Vijayanagar and Mughal empires. Their emergence might in part have been made pos-sible by an improvement in productivity, in part by an ability to better mobilize the surplus over larger areas. Questions on what surplus the state claimed, and what fraction of the produc-tion this constituted, are of some importance to our enquiry. They can be answered with a degree of certainty for Mughal India, for which excellent records exist.

In Mughal India the state essentially claimed only the sur-plus from grain production in agriculture. It also claimed some tax on the animals maintained by farmers above a threshold number. The Mughals did not tax horticulture, sheep-raising or fisheries. Nor did they tax forest holdings. In fact when the Mughal governor in Kashmir attempted to tax sheep-rearing and fishery, there were strong protests, leading to the removal of the governor. The emperor Shahjahan then promulgated an edict stating that the tax on sheep and fishing was cancelled as being against the custom. One can see, to this day, this edict carved upon a mosque in Srinagar. The proportion of surplus expropriated from the peasants might have been as large as 50 per cent; this would have been shared at several levels, begin-ning with the village headman. The peasants could not be dis-possessed of land, and the state had no direct claims over lands other than hunting preserves. Fairly extensive tracts were, in fact, claimed as the emperor's property, wherein the general hunting of game was prohibited, the local population being only permitted to gather other materials (Moosvi 1987).

It has been claimed that outside Mughal India, for instance in Tamilnadu, the proportion of agricultural produce expropriated from the cultivator was much smaller (Dharampal 1986). Be that as it may, there is no doubt that the control and management of local resources did all this time vest in local communities who designed a variety of practices for effective resource conservation. There were, of course, some commodities that the state was interested in acquiring from non-cultivated land. Elephants were one such important element, and the ever-growing demand for elephants did indeed lead to their gradual elimination from one forest area after another. At the time of Kautilya's *Arthasastra*, elephants were noted from parts of Punjab and Saurashtra; by the time of the Mughals, some 1000 to 1500 years later, these areas no longer held elephants.

The demands for timber by the state were not very heavy, except perhaps where shipbuilding was concerned. But there is the memorable story of a sect, founded in the Rajasthan desert some five hundred years ago, that gave absolute protection to Khejadi (*Prosopis cinerarea*), a multi-purpose leguminous tree of great utility to the villagers. Followers of this sect, the Bishnois, never uproot or kill, nor suffer to be uprooted or killed, any Khejadi tree in their villages. Some 350 years ago the prince of Jodhpur needed wood to fuel his lime kilns, which were being deployed to build a new palace, and for this purpose he attempted to fell a grove of Khejadi trees in a nearby village. It is narrated that several Bishnois laid down their lives to prevent these trees being cut. It is quite clear that the growth of Khejadi trees in these desert areas is of much value to the local people. They harvest its pods, leaves and thorny branches as food, fodder, manure and fencing material. Such conservation practices, cast in a religious idiom, were continually arising and were not merely a carry-over from the food-gathering phase (Sankhala and Jackson, 1985).

Conclusion

Our interpretation of the caste system as a form of ecological adaptation may also be used to illustrate the two different paths by which conflicts between different modes of resource use are resolved. The first path, which we call the *path of extermination*, explains both the victory of the neolithic revolution in Europe and the successful establishment of neo-Europes in the colonized territories of the New World. In this scenario, the earlier modes are more or less wiped out. While Eskimoes continued their hunting and trapping in the harsh environments of the Arctic, and fishermen were allowed to occupy niches in marine ecosystems, over the most part of Europe the victory of agriculture and pastoralism was complete. In more recent times the indigenous population of the Americas and Oceania have succumbed to the cultural and ecological expansion of European civilization. In parts of South America the last acts of this eco-drama are being played out now, with utterly predictable results. For the eventual fate of the indigenous population of the Amazonian rain forest is not likely to be any different from that of their counterparts in other areas of the New World.

The alternative pattern, which we call the *path of selective incorporation*, better fits the history of the Indian subcontinent prior to its colonization by the British. Insofar as the history of India exhibits the far greater *overlap* and *coexistence* of different modes of resource use, one can qualitatively distinguish the Indian experience from the European and New World paradigms of eco-cultural change. These differences in the forms of modal competition and co-operation are explicable only through a combination of ecological and cultural factors. The geographical diversity of the subcontinent, and the productivity of hilly and forested areas, enabled the continuance of hunting-gathering and shifting agriculture in large expanses where the plough could not penetrate. The persistence of earlier modes was also helped by patterns of disease which kept population densities at sufficiently low levels, allowing hunters sole possession of tracts of forest such as the malarial Terai. However, one must not underestimate the role of cultural factors in the maintenance of this diversity. As opposed to the exclusivist approach favoured by monotheistic religions such as Islam and Christianity, Hinduism has (at least until recently) relied more heavily on an *inclusive* framework that tries to incorporate rather than reject or convert apparently hostile sects and worldviews. The institutional mechanism for this process of incorporation is, of course, the caste system. And by accepting a distinctive if subordinate position within the caste hierarchy, hunters and gatherers could forestall extinction by continuing their traditional mode of resource use, though only at the cost of a larger subordination to the victorious peasant mode. These two complementary strategies, of leaving some ecological niches (hills, malarial forests) outside the purview of the peasant mode, and reserving certain niches within it for hunter-gatherers and pastorals, helped track a distinctive path of inter-modal co-operation and coexistence.

PART THREE

Ecological Change and Social Conflict in Modern India

CHAPTER FOUR

Conquest and Control

Despite the grave inequalities of caste and class, then, pre-colonial Indian society had a considerable degree of coherence and stability. This permitted a rapid turnover of ruling dynasties without major upheavals at the level of the village. On the one hand, cultural traditions of prudence ensured the long-term viability of the system of production, and of the institution of caste which was its central underpinning. On the other hand, remarkably strong communal institutions—existing at caste and supra-caste levels—oversaw the political, economic and juridical spheres of everyday existence. The agrarian system was well integrated with the highly sophisticated system of artisanal production, operating for local consumption and for trade. Relations between agriculture and industry, and between state and peasant, operated between loosely defined limits that defined the scope of each party.

Even the Mughals, whose religion was Islam, were unable, or perhaps unwilling, to radically alter the existing patterns of resource use and the social structures in which they were embedded. It was an entirely different story *vis-à-vis* India's contacts with Christian Europe. When this contact began in the sixteenth century, Europe was on the threshold of the momentous process of social change known as the Industrial Revolution. While the economic, political and social changes that came in the wake of the Industrial Revolution have been the staple of scholarly work for decades, it is only now that the ecological implications of this process are being unravelled.[1] The revolution in the mode of resource use brought about by industrialization enormously enlarged the possibilities of transforming resources from one form to another, and of transporting them over large distances. With these technological advances, a great range of objects became commodities, objects for which the demand could go on increasing indefinitely, almost limitlessly. Wood, for instance, would be consumed in a subsistence economy on a limited scale as domestic fuel, in the construction of implements, and for shelter. It could now be converted into paper, or burnt as fuel for the steam engines of trains and ships. While there can be a definite limit on the per capita demand for domestic fuel or agricultural implements, there can be no such limit on the consumption of paper, or on fuel for transport.

This conversion into commodities of a whole range of objects also radically transformed the flow of energy and materials. As outlined in Chapter 1, at the food-gathering stage such flows are largely confined to the territory of each group. With settled agriculture starts an outflow of grain from the countryside to the towns, where the non-food producers are concentrated. The advances in technology brought about by the industrial mode, however, prompt an outflow of a much greater range of resources from both cultivated and non-cultivated lands, and from water bodies.

These changes in the patterns of material flows had, of course, profound implications for patterns of resource use. Non-cultivated lands and waters were no longer dedicated

---

[1] Karl Polanyi's *The Great Transformation*, first published in 1944, has some remarkable passages on the ecological implications of the Industrial Revolution. Polanyi's insights have for the most part remained undeveloped.

exclusively to providing for flows within the local region. Communal control by food producers, the peasants, over these lands became a bone of contention, with the elite attempting to usurp rights over these lands and put them to other uses. Such territories were now capable of generating resources of high value, and their control by the elite became attractive because of technological advances in transport, transformation and coercion. The benefit : cost ratio thus changed, making possible the conversion of large tracts of non-cultivated lands and waters into private or state property. This process is well known in European history as the movement for the enclosure of commons by landlords and the state. Over a period of several centuries, forests, fens and waters controlled and used by local peasant communities were converted into the property of landlords and the state. At the ideological level too, private and state property was being upheld, and the validity of communal control questioned.

At the time the Europeans came to India, therefore, they were experiencing at home a far-reaching revolution in patterns of natural resource use. Three elements of that revolution are of particular importance to our story. First, it lowered the emphasis on resource gathering and food production for subsistence, focusing instead on the gathering, production, transport and transformation of resources for use as commodities. The proportion of the population engaged in subsistence gathering and the production of food declined; that of people engaged in manufacturing, transporting or using resources as commodities increased. Second, co-operation with neighbours of long standing, characteristic among people engaged in subsistence gathering and food production, became less and less important. With this came the breakdown of cohesive local communities. Human societies became atomized, with individuals acting largely on their own. This was relatively easy in Christian Europe, where the different human groups were loosely organized, with broad niches and large niche overlaps.

Finally, and perhaps most importantly, the changing 'hardware' of resource use was accompanied by equally dramatic changes in its 'software'. In the now atomized societies, with their possibilities of unlimited expansion in the consumption of resources, the capacity of individuals to command access to resources was at a premium. With manufacture and commerce the dominant activities, markets became the focal point for organizing access to resources. The new belief-system that developed therefore transferred to the institution of the market the veneration reserved for spirits resident in trees by food-gatherers, and in an abstract God by Christian food-producers. Success and status were now clearly measured in terms of money, the currency of the market.

These three characteristics of the industrial mode of resource use are central to a proper understanding of the ecological encounter between India and Britain. For the elevation of commercial over subsistence uses, the delegitimization of the community, and the abandoning of restraints on resource exploitation—all ran counter to the experience of the vast majority of the Indian population over which the British were to exercise their rule. This was a clash, in more ways than one, of cultures, of ways of life.

Colonialism as an Ecological Watershed

The ecological history of British India is of special interest in view of the intimate connection that recent research has established between western imperialism and environmental degradation. World ecology has been profoundly altered by western capitalism, in whose dynamic expansion other ecosystems were disrupted, first through trade and later by colonialism. Not only did such interventions virtually reshape the social, ecological and demographic characteristics of the habitats they intruded upon, they also ensured that the ensuing changes would primarily benefit Europe. Colonialism's most tangible outcome (one whose effects persist to this day) related to its global control of resources. The conquest of new areas meant that the twenty-four acres of land available to each European at the time of Columbus' voyage soon increased to 120 acres per European. Large-scale settlement was only one way in which Europeans augmented their 'ghost acreage'. For the world-wide control they exercised over mineral, plant and animal resources also contributed to industrial growth in the metropolis. In turn, political hegemony enabled these manufactured products to capture non-European markets. Finally, colonialism introduced Old World diseases among vulnerable populations, often with fatal consequences (Webb 1964; Wallerstein 1974; Tucker and Richards 1983).

One of the finest studies of this process of 'ecological imperialism' is Alfred Crosby's monograph of that name (Crosby 1986). The firepower of the European vanguard, and the complex of weeds, animals and diseases it brought, devastated the flora, fauna and human societies of the New World. However, the extermination of native ecosystems and populations only paved the way for the creation of 'Neo-Europes', the extensive and enormously productive agricultural systems that dominate the New World today. In this process, suggests Crosby, the plants, animals and diseases that accompanied the migrating Europeans were as important in ensuring their success as superior weaponry.

In his fascinating yet chilling account of the biological expansion of Europe, Crosby pauses briefly to investigate the areas that he believes were 'within reach' but 'beyond grasp'— the complex Old World civilizations in the Middle East, China and India. He argues that population densities, resistance to disease, agricultural technology and sophisticated socio-political organizations—all made these areas more resistant to the ecological imperialism of Europe. Thus 'the rule (not the law) is that although Europeans may conquer the tropics, they do not Europeanize the tropics, not even countrysides with European temperatures' (Crosby 1986, p. 134).

As Crosby so skilfully demonstrates, their 'portmanteau biota' (his collective term for the organisms the colonizing whites brought with them) enabled the European powers to easily overrun the temperate regions of North and South America, as well as the continent of Oceania. They had to perforce adopt a different strategy in older—and more ecologically resistant—civilizations like India and China. Here they set up initially as traders and military advisers, later making the transition to rulership, either directly or by proxy. This does not mean, however, that European colonialism had an insignificant impact on these ecosystems, as Crosby's account seems to suggest. In India, the Europeans could not create neo-Europes by decimating the indigenous populations and their natural resource base; but they did intervene and radically alter existing food-production systems and their ecological basis. If in the neo-Europes, ecological imperialism paved the way for political consolidation, in India the causation ran the other way, their political victory equipping the British for an unprecedented intervention in the ecological and social fabric of Indian society. Moreover, by exposing their subjects to the seductions of the industrial economy and consumer society, the British ensured that the process of ecological change they initiated would continue, and indeed intensify, after they left India's shores.

This and the following chapter focus on possibly the most important aspect of the ecological encounter between Britain and India—the management and utilization of forest resources.

The Early Onslaught on Forests

By around 1860, Britain had emerged as the world leader in deforestation, devastating its own woods and the forests of Ireland, South Africa and north-eastern United States to draw timber for shipbuilding, iron-smelting and farming. Upon occasion, the destruction of forests was used by the British to symbolize political victory. Thus in the early nineteenth century, and following its defeat of the Marathas, the East India Company razed to the ground teak plantations in Ratnagiri nurtured and grown by the legendary Maratha admiral Kanhoji

Angre (Campbell 1883). 'Of all European nations', one of the early conservators of forests in India, Henry Cleghorn, observed—

> the English have been most regardless of the value of the forests, partly owing to their climate, but chiefly because England has been so highly favoured by vast supplies of coal; and the emigrants to the United States have shown their indifference to this subject by needless destruction of forests in that country of which they now feel the want (Cleghorn 1860, p. ix).

Their early treatment of the Indian forests also reinforces the claim that 'the destructive energy of the British race all over the world' was rapidly converting forests into deserts (Webber 1902, p. 338). Until the later decades of the nineteenth century, the Raj carried out a 'fierce onslaught' on the subcontinent's forests (Smythies 1925, p. 6). With oak forests vanishing in England, a permanent supply of durable timber was required for the Royal Navy as 'the safety of the empire depended on its wooden walls' (Stebbing I, p. 63). In a period of fierce competition between the colonial powers, Indian teak, the most durable of shipbuilding timbers, saved England during the war with Napolean and the later maritime expansion. To tap the likely sources of supply, search parties were sent to the teak forests of India's west coast (Edye 1835). Ships were built in dockyards in Surat and on the Malabar coast, as well as from teak imported into England (Albion 1926). An indication of the escalating demand is provided by the increase in tonnage of British merchant ships (i.e. excluding the Royal Navy) from 1,278,000 tonnes in 1778 to 4,937,000 tonnes in 1860 (Leathart 1982). A large proportion of the wood required came from Britain's newly-acquired colonies. As late as the 1880s, the Indian forest department was entertaining repeated requests from the British admiralty for the supply of Madras and Burma teak.[2]

The revenue orientation of colonial land policy also worked

[2] See National Archives of India (hereafter NAI), Department of Rev. & Agrl. (Forests), (hereafter Forests).

towards the denudation of forests. As their removal added to the class of land assessed for revenue, forests were considered 'an obstruction to agriculture and consequently a bar to the prosperity of the Empire' (Ribbentrop 1900, p.60). The dominant thrust of agrarian policy was to extend cultivation and 'the watchword of the time was to destroy the forests with this end in view' (Stebbing I, pp. 61-2).

This process greatly intensified in the early years of the building of the railway network after about 1853. While great chunks of forest were destroyed to meet the demand for railway sleepers, no supervision was exercised over the felling operations; a large number of trees was felled and lay rotting on the ground (Stebbing I, pp. 298-9). The sub-Himalayan forests of Garhwal and Kumaon, for example, were all 'felled in even to desolation', and 'thousands of trees were felled which were never removed, nor was their removal possible' (Pearson, 1869, pp.132-3). Private contractors, both Indian and European, were chiefly responsible for this destruction, the forests of Indian chiefs not escaping their hands (Paul 1871). Before the coal mines of Raniganj became fully operative, the railway companies drew upon the forests for fuel as well. The fuelwood requirements of the railways in the North Western Provinces, at a high level into the 1880s, caused considerable deforestation in the Doab (Whitcombe 1971) Meanwhile, in Madras, as a member of the Indian Famine Commission noted, the demand for fuel of locomotives was 'large enough to cause a heavy drain, if not an utter exhaustion, of the particular forests, from which the supplies are drawn'. 'It appears certain', predicted a Madras official in 1876, 'that for a considerable time to come the main supply of railway fuel must come from the natural jungles'. In the districts of North Arcot and Chingleput the alternating cycles of flood and drought, which such destruction had caused, seriously affected irrigation, and thereby food production.[3]

[3] NAI, Forests, progs no. 134–35, March 1878, minute by Richard Temple, 18 April 1877; NAI, legislature dept, progs 43-142, March 1878, appendix KK,

One of the most vivid descriptions of the transformation in the ecological landscape wrought by the railways is found in Cleghorn's work, *The Forests and Gardens of South India*. The Melghat and North Arcot hills, formerly crowned with timber, were 'now to a considerable degree laid bare' by the insatiable demand of the railways. All around the tracks, where once there was forest, there now lay wide swathes of cleared land stripped bare of cover, and consequently of protection to wild animals. Thus the progress of the railway 'produced marvellous changes on the face of the country as regards tree vegetation'. In the Madras Presidency over 250,000 sleepers (or 35,000 trees) were required annually from indigenous sources. To meet this demand contractors resorted more and more to *sequential over-exploitation*. On the one hand they cleared jungles further and further away from the railway lines, while on the other they utilized more and more unsuitable species as those less favoured were rapidly exhausted. Although only half a dozen species were considered suitable for use as railway sleepers, more than fifty were tried out. Not surprisingly, sleepers expected to last five or six years only lasted a third of the time. In one consignment, out of 487 sleepers supplied, 458 (or 92 per cent) were found to be of unauthorized woods (Cleghorn 1860, pp. 2-3, 33, 63, 77-8, 253-4).

The pace of railway expansion—from 1349 kms of track in 1860 to 51,658 kms in 1910 (GOI 1964)—and the trail of destruction left in its wake brought home forcefully the fact that India's forests were not inexhaustible. Railway requirements were 'the first and by far the most formidable' of the forces thinning Indian forests (Cleghorn 1860, p. 60). Dubbing forest administration upto the 1857 rebellion a melancholy failure, the Governor-General had called in 1862 for the establishment of a department that could ensure the sustained availability of the enormous requirements of the different railway companies for

no. 2149, 23 December 1876, from acting secretary to government, revenue department, Madras, to secretary to GOI, legislative department.

sleepers, which 'has now made the subject of forest conservancy an important administrative question' (quoted in Trevor and Smythies 1923, p. 5). The magnificent forests of India and Burma, one official recalled, 'were being worked by private enterprise in a reckless and wasteful manner and were likely to become exhausted if supervision were not exercised' (Webber 1902, pp. xii–xiii).

The crisis had assumed major proportions as only three Indian timbers—teak, sal, and deodar—were strong enough in their natural state to be utilized as railway sleepers. Sal and teak, being available near railway lines in peninsular India, were very heavily worked in the early years, necessitating expeditions to the north-western Himalaya in search of deodar forests. The deodar of the Sutlej and Yamuna valleys was rapidly exhausted in the years following the inception of the forest department—over 6,500,000 deodar sleepers were supplied from the Yamuna forests alone between 1869 and 1885 (Paul 1871; Hearle, 1888).[4]

The imperial forest department was formed in 1864, with the help of experts from Germany, the country which was at that time the leading European nation in forest management. The first inspector-general of forests, Dietrich Brandis, had been a botanist at Bonn University before his assignment in India. The awesome task of checking the deforestation of past decades required, first and foremost, forging legal mechanisms to assert and safeguard state control over forests. It was in this dual sense that the railways constituted the crucial watershed with respect to forest management in India—the need was felt to start an appropriate department,[5] and for its effective functioning legis-

---

[4] Each mile of railway construction requires 860 sleepers, each sleeper lasting between 12 to 14 years. In the 1870s it was calculated that well over a million sleepers were required annually. While European sleepers were imported in some quantities, the emphasis was always on substituting them by Indian timbers. See D. Brandis, 'Memorandum on the Supply of Railway Sleepers of the Himalayan Pines Impregnated in India', *Indian Forester*, V, 1879.

[5] Although state control was not unknown in the early decades of colonial

lation was required to curtail the previously untouched access enjoyed by rural communities. This was an especially difficult task as, in many cases, the proprietary right of the state in forests had been 'deliberately alienated' in favour of peasant and tribal communities (Brandis 1897, p. 52; cf. also Ribbentrop 1900, and Dasgupta 1980). Before its late recognition of the strategic importance of forests, the policy of the colonial state had been to recognize forests and waste land as the property of the village communities within whose boundaries these fell (Stebbing II, pp. 464ff).

The first attempt at asserting state monopoly was through the Indian Forest Act of 1865. This was replaced thirteen years later by a far more comprehensive piece of legislation. Yet the latter act (to serve in time as a model for forest legislation in other British colonies) was passed only after a prolonged and bitter debate within the colonial bureaucracy. This controversy, enumerated in some detail below, has a particular resonance for us today: the protagonists of the earlier debate put forth arguments strikingly similar to those advanced by participants in the contemporary debate about the environment in India.

An Early Environment Debate

Hurriedly drafted, the 1865 act was passed to facilitate the acquisition of those forest areas that were earmarked for railway supplies. It merely sought to establish the claims of the state to the forests it immediately required, subject to the proviso that existing rights not be abridged. Almost immediately, the search commenced for a more stringent and inclusive piece of legislation. A preliminary draft, prepared by Brandis in 1869, was circulated among the various presidencies. A conference of forest officers, convened in 1874, then went into the defects

---

rule, the setting up of a separate department marked a qualitative shift in colonial perceptions of the strategic value of forests. For early attempts to enforce state monopoly over trees such as teak and sandalwood, see Cleghorn (1860).

of the 1865 act and the details of a new one. The conference provided the basis for a memorandum on forest legislation, prepared by Brandis in 1875. The latter memorandum, further worked on by Brandis and a senior civil servant, B.H. Baden-Powell, culminated in the Indian Forest Act of 1878.

In these successive iterations the state was concerned above all with removing the existing ambiguity about the 'absolute proprietary right of the state'. A vocal advocate of state monopoly deplored the 'unfortunate but irrevocable action of government authorities in days past' which had taken many forest areas wholly out of the category of state property. Even forests where the state had in theory retained its 'absolute' proprietorship were 'everywhere used by all classes to get what they wanted'. Villagers had got accustomed to graze cattle and cut wood wherever they wished, the writer complained, because 'nobody cared whether [they] did or not' (Baden-Powell 1875).

Here colonial officials were, perhaps wilfully, confusing 'open access' with 'common property'—for the peasantry's customary use of forests was not random but governed and regulated by community sanctions. Clearly, a firm settlement between the state and its subjects over their respective rights in the forest represented the chief hurdle to be overcome. As Brandis put it, 'Act VIII of 1865 is incomplete in many respects, the most important omission being the absence of all provisions regarding the definition, regulation, commutation and extinction of customary rights . . . [by the state]'.[6] In the heated debate about how best to accomplish this separation of rights, three distinct positions emerged. The first, which we call *annexationist*, held out for nothing less than *total* state control over *all* forest areas. The second, which one may call *pragmatic*, argued in favour of state management of ecologically sensitive and strategically valuable forests, allowing other areas to remain under communal systems of management. The third position (a mirror image of the first) we call *populist*. This completely

[6] NAI, Forests, B progs, nos 37-47, December 1875, 'Explanatory Memorandum on Draft Forest Bill', by D. Brandis, IGF, 3 August 1869.

rejected state intervention, holding that tribals and peasants must exercise sovereign rights over woodland. These three perspectives on state control dovetailed with three distinct views on the sociology, history, politics and ecology of forest resource use. They deserve to be reconstructed in full, for the issues they raised and debated with such intensity a hundred years ago are very much with us today.

The bedrock of the *annexationist* position was the claim that all land not actually under cultivation belonged to the state. Of course it was not easy to wish away the access to forests—subject naturally to the norms of the community—that peasants so patently exercised down the centuries, right until the formation of the forest department. Officials argued that such customary use, however widespread and enduring, was exercised only at the mercy of the monarch. Here they used precedents, selectively citing Tipu's edict banning the cutting of sandalwood as proof that India's rulers had ultimately reserved to themselves the right of ownership over forests and forest produce. Baden-Powell claimed 'the state had not, it is true, exercised that full right: the forests were left open to any one who chose to use them; *but the right was there*' (Baden-Powell, 1875, pp. 4-5, emphasis in original). In this strictly legalistic interpretation only those rights of use which were *explicitly granted by the state* (presumably only in writing) were to be entertained. Thus Baden-Powell made a clever distinction between 'rights' defined as 'strict legal rights which unquestionably exist, and in some instances have been expressly recorded in land settlement records'—and 'privileges'—defined as 'concessions of the use of grazing, firewood, small wood, etc., which though not claimable as of legal right, are always granted by the policy of the government for the convenience of the people'.[7]

This tortuous distinction (in effect, a legal sleight-of-hand) was buttressed by an early version of the theory of 'oriental despotism' in which eastern chiefs were believed to have

[7] NAI, Forests, B progs, nos 37-47, Dec. 1875, 'Draft Forest Bill prepared by Mr. Baden-Powell'.

powers far more extensive than those enjoyed by their contemporaries in medieval Europe. Adducing no evidence, Baden-Powell nevertheless claimed that 'the right of the state to dispose of or retain for public use the waste and forest area, is among the most ancient and undisputed of features in oriental Sovereignty'.[8] 'In India', an official primer on forest law likewise affirmed, 'the government is by ancient law ... the general owner of all unoccupied and waste lands' (Anon. 1906, p. 20). Whatever the historical evidence for this claim (scanty, at best), its purpose was clear: to pave the way for the formal assertion of ownership over forests and waste by the colonial state. The 'right' of oriental governments in the forest, insisted Baden-Powell, 'passed on to, and was accepted by, the British government' (Baden-Powell 1882, p. 9). Others were more blunt. 'The right of conquest', thundered one forest official, 'is the strongest of all rights—it is a right against which there is no appeal.' (Amery 1875, p. 27).

Counterposed to this claim of an age-old right was the total denial of the legitimacy of any state intervention in the forest. The Madras government, which emerged as the most articulate official spokesman for village interests, rejected Baden-Powell's tendentious distinction between legally proven 'rights' and 'privileges' exercised without written sanction. 'All instances of the use of the forest by the people', it argued, 'should be taken as presumptive evidence of property therein'.[9] Both 'private grantees and village and tribal communities', an early nationalist organization likewise pointed out, 'have cherished and maintained these rights [in the forest] with the same tenacity with which private property in land is maintained elsewhere'.[10]

[8] B.H. Baden-Powell, 'Concessions', *Indian Forester*, XXV, 1899, p. 358.

[9] NAI, legislative department, A progs, nos 43-142, March 1878, 'Remarks by the Board of Revenue, Madras', 5 August 1871. This file, containing the major documents pertaining to the 1878 act, is hereafter referred to as LD file of 1878.

[10] Memorial, 3 March 1878, from Puna Sarvajanik Sabha, and the inhabitants of the city and camp of Pune, in LD file of 1878.

If this view was to be allowed, then it seemed the claim of the state was virtually non-existent. For—

There is scarcely a forest in the whole of the Presidency of Madras which is not within the limits of some village and there is not one in which, so far as the Board can ascertain, the state asserted any rights of property unless royalties in teak, sandalwood, cardomoms and the like, can be considered as such, until very recently. All of them, without exception are subject to tribal or communal rights which have existed from time immemorial and which are as difficult to define as they are necessary to the rural population . . . . Nor can it be said that these rights are susceptible of compensation, for in innumerable cases, the right to fuel, manure and pasturage, will be as much a necessity of life to unborn generations as it is to the present . . . . (In Madras) the forests are, and always have been, common property, no restriction except that of taxes, like the Moturpha and Pulari, was ever imposed on the people till the Forest Department was created, and such taxes no more indicate that the forests belong to the state than the collection of assessment shows that the private holdings in Malabar, Canara and the Ryotwari districts belong to it.[11]

Intermediate between those two extreme positions was the moderate voice of the inspector-general of forests, Dietrich Brandis, the exemplar of what we have termed the 'pragmatic' approach. Brandis allowed that in certain cases the state had indisputable rights; however, he was with the Madras board of revenue in disputing Baden-Powell's contention that rights had to be 'proved' in writing before they could be said to exist. In most forest areas, he believed, villagers were accustomed to freely graze their cattle, cut wood, etc., subject only to some restrictions which rulers imposed from time to time. Drawing on a cross-cultural comparison, he pointed out that

the growth of forest rights in India has been analogous to the growth of similar rights of user in Europe. There are many

[11] Source cited in footnote 9.

well-known cases in which forest rights in Europe have arisen out of a specific growth and in such cases the extent of the right is construed by the terms of the grant and is not necessarily restricted by the limitations adverted to. In most instances however, they have grown up out of the use by the surrounding villages of the common waste and forest. Forest rights in India have had a similar origin and development as in Europe, with that important difference that the arbitrary dealings of the Native Rulers have interfered with the growth of these rights and have in many cases restricted or extinguished them.

Not that he was approving of such arbitrary action. Contesting Baden-Powell's invocation of the case of the Amirs of Sindh (chieftains who had enclosed forests for hunting), Brandis said:

the fact that the former Rulers in many cases have extinguished such customary usage of the forest in a summary manner and without compensation is hardly an argument in point, for these were cases of might versus right. As against other individuals and communities the customary rights to wood and pasture have as a rule been strenuously maintained (Brandis, 1875, pp. 13-14).[12]

Other officials used the European analogy to quite different ends. If for Brandis the forest history of Europe called for a similar treatment of village rights in India, for others it merely served as a warning *not* to grant these rights. Thus a committee set up by the government of Bombay in 1863 went so far as to claim that in *both* India and England the governing powers could assert a total state monopoly whenever they wished. Claiming the right of the sovereign in England, since ancient times, to 'make forests of any extent over the lands of his subjects', they urged the application of a similar principle in India.[13] For

[12] One does not know whether Brandis was unaware of this, but in Europe too there were many instances of the monarch abruptly extinguishing customary rights in the forest. See, for example, Thompson (1975) for England, Agulhon (1982) for France, and Linebaugh (1976) for Germany.

[13] See NAI, legislative department, A progs, nos 32-38, Feb. 1865.

Baden-Powell the lesson of European forest history was not to allow, in India, the building up of rights which could encumber timber production by the state (Baden-Powell 1892, p. 7). Moreover, even if the development of common rights was analogous, the rights permissible to free-born citizens in England were not feasible in a colonial territory. Thus—

> in England by the Common Law, all proprietors of land own everything up to the sky and down to the centre of the earth except gold and silver mines, which by prerogative, belong to the Crown. But in a ceded and conquered country like India, this English Common Law and Crown prerogative does not apply at any rate beyond the limits of the Presidency towns (Baden-Powell 1882, p. 50).

Brandis, a comparative newcomer to colonial administration—and from a country which was at the time very much a beginner in the colonial game—took a different stance. The settlement of rights, he insisted, must be done in a 'just and equitable manner' (Brandis 1875, p. 12). For him, identical acts could call upon the same legal justification, even if one was committed in colonial India, the other in 'free' England. 'There has been much thoughtless talk', he told a meeting in Brighton in 1872,

> as if the natives of India, in burning the forests and destroying them by their erratic clearings were committing some grave offence. If the matter is carefully analysed they will be found to have the same sort of prescription which justifies the commoner in the New Forest to exercise his right of pasture, mast and turbary (Brandis 1897, p. 53).

If Baden-Powell concluded from European history that the colonial state must be more emphatic in asserting its claims, and Brandis that it must grant to its subjects the rights prevalent in Europe, the Madras government sharply challenged the principle of state forestry in Europe itself. The board of revenue compared Brandis' first draft of a forest act to the French Code

Forestier, that 'most stringent of forest rules' and itself the consequence of 'a long feudal tyranny, followed by the storms of a revolution, and the despotism of an empire'; indeed 'no system could be more opposed either in its history or its provisions to the corresponding circumstances in India'. Faced with the Indian Forest Act of 1878, the governor of Madras had to go even further back to find an appropriate analogy from European history. Condemning the new legislation as a 'Bill for confiscation instead of protection', he said 'it was probably the same process which the Norman Kings adopted in England for their forest extension'.[14]

Very different proposals flowed from these different readings of Indian and European forest history. The 'annexationists' urged the constitution of all wooded areas as state forests, following a settlement of rights on the interpretation advanced by Baden-Powell. Thus the agricultural secretary, Allan Octavian Hume, sharply rebuked the vocal Madras official W. Robinson for his opposition to state encroachment on customary rights. Commenting on his decision to recognize rights of ownership in forests cultivated in rotation by swidden agriculturists in South Kanara, Hume cautioned 'the government of India to watch carefully and satisfy itself that [Robinson's] kindly and warm-hearted sympathy for the welfare of the semi-savage denizens of the Kanara forests does not lead him into a too lavish dissipation of the capital of the state'.[15] Sentiments such as Hume's informed the proposals for a generalized takeover of forest and waste by the state. As Brandis found to his dismay, the majority of the participants at the crucial Forest Conference of 1874 disagreed with his more modest claims for state control, holding out for the constitution of all forests as state reserves controlled by the forest department.[16]

[14] 'Remarks by the Board of Revenue, Madras', 5 August 1871, and minute by the governor of Madras, 9 February 1878, both in appendix SS, LD file of 1878.

[15] NAI, Forests, B progs, no 10, Sept. 1876, note by A.O. Hume, 24 June 1876.

[16] NAI, Forests, B progs, no 3-8, July 1874, 'Memorandum by D. Brandis,

In sharp contrast, the Madras government believed that state intervention should be minimal, fully respecting existing rights. The collector of the Nilgiris, for example, insisted that forest officials actively seek out evidence of communal rights, rather than wait for headmen to put forward their claims. Objecting to Brandis' draft bill of 1869, he remarked that the procedure it envisaged would pit two unequal antagonists. While its provisions were 'too arbitrary, setting the laws of property at defiance', the bill left 'the determination of the forest rights of the people to a Department which, in this Presidency at all events, has always shown itself eager to destroy all forest rights but those of Government'. Showing a prescient awareness of the territorial aspirations of the forest department, the board pleaded for the involvement of civil courts in the arbitration of forest rights. As it stood, the bill had stacked the dice heavily against the interests of villagers, for the forest department, 'which acquires new importance by every forest right which it strangles will be the arbitrator'.[17]

Typically straddling these two positions, Brandis advocated the *restricted* takeover of forests by the state. He justified this middle course both on the grounds of equity—respect for age-old rights—and efficiency—as the only feasible course. Brandis urged the administration to 'demarcate as state forests as large and compact areas of valuable forests as can be obtained free of forest rights of persons', while leaving the residual areas—smaller in extent but more conveniently located for their supply—under the control of village communities. He hoped for the creation of three great classes of forest property based on the European model: state forests, forests of villages and other communities, and private forests. State ownership had to be restricted on account of the 'small number of ex-

---

IGF, on several matters discussed at the Forest Conference, dated the 1st June 1874'.

[17] 'Remarks by the Board of Revenue', 5 August 1871, and appendix A to the above ('Abstract of Collectors' Reports on the Forest Bill'), both in the LD file of 1878.

perienced and really useful officers' in the colonial forestry service, *and* out of deference to the wishes of the local population. Thus:

> the trouble of effecting the settlement of forest rights and privileges on limited well-defined areas is temporary and will soon pass away, whereas the annoyance to the inhabitants by the maintenance of restrictions over the whole area of large forest tracts will be permanent, and will increase with the growth of population.[18]

Walking a tightrope between the imperatives of colonial administration and the claims of social justice, Brandis, quite remarkably for his time and milieu, placed considerable trust in the ability of village communities to manage their own affairs. He wrote appreciatively of the extensive network of sacred groves in the subcontinent, which he termed 'the traditional form of forest preservation' (Brandis 1897, pp. 14-15). Displaying an early 'ethnobotanical' interest in indigenous systems of tree and plant classification, he circulated a list of local names, urging 'younger officers, with more leisure and more extensive opportunities, to take up the study of the names of trees and shrubs used by the [tribes] of Central India' (Brandis 1876, appendix). He also praised Indian rulers for their forest sense, singling out the Rajasthan chiefs who, in strenuously preserving brushwood in a dry climate, 'have set a good example, which the forest officers of the British government will do well to emulate' (Brandis 1873, pp. 24-5). He was especially keen on reviving and strengthening village communal institutions. When his requests for official initiative in the formation of village forests were repeatedly turned down, he argued the fruits of well-managed communal forests, recognized by law, as existing in several European countries. On a visit to Mysore he expressed the hope that at some future date he would 'find

---

[18] This paragraph draws on three memoranda by Brandis, namely Brandis (1875), and the unpublished memoranda of 1869 and 1874, cited in footnotes 6 and 16 above.

the advantages of true communal forests recognized not in Mysore only but in all parts of India where a village organization exists', for it seemed to him 'particularly desirable to strengthen the old village organization by consolidating and ameliorating the grazing grounds, forest and waste land of the village community'.[19]

Brandis' task was an uphill one. His sentiments may have been noble but they were not shared by his peers and masters in the British colonial system. Rapping him on the knuckles, Brandis' boss, the agricultural secretary, said the inspector-general's 'views as to rights of aboriginal tribes, forest villages etc., are to my mind clearly in advance of my own, and *a fortiori* of those of the government of India'.[20] Meanwhile, the Madras government was chastised by the secretary of state for its 'laxity with respect to the forest rights of Government'.[21] Under pressure from both London and Fort William, it finally capitulated, and in 1882 agreed to an act closely modelled on the 1878 Indian Forest Act.[22]

And so the internal resistance to the 1878 act crumbled. As the next chapter documents, it prefigured the far more wide-spread *popular* resistance to colonial forest management. Within official circles, however, the question was firmly resolved in favour of the 'annexationists', and a policy of state annexation was embarked upon. The concrete proposals were embodied in Brandis' memorandum of 1875 which, with Baden-Powell's paper in the Forest Conference of the previous year, formed the basis of the 1878 act.

Based on Baden-Powell's distinction between 'rights' and

[19] See Brandis' memoranda of 1869, cited in footnote 6, and 'Memorandum by D. Brandis, IGF, on the district forest scheme of Mysore', 1 June 1874, in NAI, Forests, B progs, nos 12-15, June 1874.

[20] NAI, Forests, progs nos 43-55, March 1875, note by A.O. Hume, 19 August 1874.

[21] NAI, Forests, B progs nos 9-10,1879, no. 13 (revenue forests), London, 28 August 1879, from secretary of state to governor, Madras.

[22] See NAI, Forests, progs nos 18-27, July 1882, and progs nos 9-31, January 1883.

'privileges', the act was a comprehensive piece of legislation which, by one stroke of the executive pen, attempted to obliterate centuries of customary use by rural populations all over India. It provided for three classes of forest. 'Reserved forests' consisted of compact and valuable areas, well connected to towns, which would lend themselves to sustained exploitation. In reserved forests a legal separation of rights was aimed for, it being thought advisable to safeguard total state control by a permanent settlement that either extinguished private rights, transferred them elsewhere, or in exceptional cases allowed their limited exercise. In the second category, the so-called 'protected forests' (also controlled by the state), rights were recorded but not settled. However, control was firmly maintained by outlining detailed provisions for the reservation of particular tree species as and when they became commercially valuable, and for closing the forest whenever required to grazing and fuelwood collection. Given increased commercial demand and their relatively precarious position from the government's point of view, protected areas were gradually converted into reserved forests where the state could exercise fuller control. Thus the 14,000 square miles of state forest in 1878 (the year the act was passed) had increased to 56,000 square miles of reserved forests and 20,000 square miles of protected forests in 1890—the corresponding figures a decade later being 81,400 and 3300 square miles respectively (Stebbing, I, pp. 468ff). The act also provided for the constitution of a third class of forests—village forests—although the option was not exercised by the government over the most part of the subcontinent. Finally, the new legislation greatly enlarged the punitive sanctions available to the forest administration, closely regulating the extraction and transit of forest produce and prescribing a detailed set of penalties for transgressions of the act.

Forest Policy Upto 1947

As advocates of state monopoly well understood, the strict

regulation (and preferably extinction) of traditionally exercised rights was a *sine qua non* for the activity of commercial timber production. Under the provisions of the 1878 act, each family of 'rightholders' was allowed a specific quantum of timber and fuel, while the sale or barter of forest produce was strictly prohibited. This exclusion from forest management was, therefore, both *physical*—it denied or restricted access to forests and pasture—as well as *social*—it allowed 'rightholders' only a marginal and inflexible claim on the produce of the forests. The principle of state monopoly also formed the cornerstone of the important forest policy statement of 1894. Influenced by a devastating official indictment of the commercial orientation of forest management (Voelcker 1893), the policy was also a response to the 'serious discontent among the agricultural classes' caused by strict forest administration. While apparently more favourably disposed to village needs, the policy cautioned that these should be met only 'to the utmost point that is consistent with imperial interests'.[23]

Superbly equipped to maintain strict state control over forest utilization, the 1878 act provided the underpinnings for the 'scientific' management of forests, enabling the working of compact blocks of forest for commercial timber production. Consistent with this legal and institutional structure, the administration of the forests reserved by the state—some 99,000 square miles in 1947—was contingent on the imperial interests it served—first, during the era of railway expansion, and later, during the two world wars. At the same time, the forest department had to generate an adequate revenue, in keeping with a cardinal principal of imperial policy, namely that the administrative machinery had to be self-supporting. As such, a constant endeavour was to find markets for the multiple species of

[23] Regional Archives Dehradun, list no. 22, file no. 244, circular no. 22F, 19 October 1894, revenue & agricultural (forests). One must distinguish between policy statements and legislative enactments. Whereas it is always possible to make conciliatory gestures in the former, it is the latter which will actually be in operation.

India's tropical forests, of which only a few, often comprising less than 10 per cent of the canopy, were readily saleable. The inaccessibility of many forest areas and the stagnant nature of industrial development further inhibited the full commercial utilization of forest produce (Smythies 1925, pp. 57ff).

TABLE 4.1

REVENUE AND SURPLUS OF FOREST DEPARTMENT 1869–1925

Yearly average for the period	Revenue (Rs million)	Surplus (Rs million)	Per cent of column 3 to column 2
1869-70 to 1873-74	5.6	1.7	30
1874-75 to 1878-79	6.7	2.1	31
1879-80 to 1883-84	8.8	3.2	36
1884-85 to 1888-89	11.7	4.2	36
1889-90 to 1893-94	15.9	7.3	46
1894-95 to 1898-99	17.7	7.9	45
1899-1900 to 1903-4	19.7	8.4	43
1904-1905 to 1908-9	25.7	11.6	45
1909-1910 to 1913-14	29.6	13.2	45
1914-1915 to 1918-19	37.1	16.0	43
1919-1920 to 1923-4	55.2	18.5	34
1924 to 1925	56.7	21.3	38

SOURCE: Stebbing III, p. 620.

Nevertheless, as Table 4.1 indicates, the department consistently showed a handsome surplus on account. This was made possible by the requirements of urban centres for fuelwood, furniture, building timber, etc., while supply was facilitated by the improved communications which the railway network brought about (Tucker 1979). Thus the Himalayan forests provided bamboo, sal and several species of conifer for the urban markets of Punjab and the United Provinces, and for the military cantonments and hill stations that were a creation of colonial rule (Walton 1910; Hearle 1889). The railways, by now wholly government owned, continued to be an important customer of the forest. Urging closer co-operation, one committee pointed out that 'in many cases the interests of the two departments are identical' (GOI 1929, p. 30).

After years of research, the treatment of several woods for use as railway sleepers was made possible on a commercial scale in 1912. These timbers included the chir and blue pines. In the years that followed, the extensive pine forests of Garhwal and Kumaun were reserved—largely obviating any need to import wood or to search for metal and concrete substitutes (Guha, Ramachandra, 1989a). The teak export trade continued to pay, with well over one million sterling worth of teak wood being imported annually into Britain (Anon. 1920). The development of 'Minor Forest Produce' (hereafter MFP)—i.e. excluding timber—was also taken up in the twentieth century. This MFP was found to have a variety of industrial uses. And as India was the only source in the empire for several of the more valuable MFPs, e.g. resin and turpentine, tanning materials such as kath and myrabolans, and essential oils, foreign trade in these products showed a rapid rise. For example, the export trade in shellac was valued at more than two and a half million pounds in 1917-18 (Smythies 1925, pp. 82-91).

During this period the large areas of forest under India's princes were also drawn in, though indirectly, into the orbit of colonial capitalist expansion. The exploitation of these forests, either by the agency of the colonial state or directly by the princes, introduced qualitative changes in the relationship between ruler and subject. Over time, native rulers became 'generally very much alive to the value of their forest properties' (Smythies 1925, p. 27). The magnificent deodar forests of the Himalayan state of Tehri Garhwal had early attracted the attention of the colonial state, and in 1865 it successfully negotiated a lease on the important deodar and chir forests in Tehri Garhwal. These forests were divested of the existing rights of user of the surrounding population and commercially managed by the Imperial Forest Department from 1865 to 1925. Their enormous value being evidenced by the average annual profit of over Rs 1.6 lakhs (for 1910-25), the king did not renew the lease, henceforth working the forests—with professional help from the forest department and with legislation modelled on the 1878 act—himself (Guha, Ramachandra, 1989a). The deodar forests of the adjoining hill states of present-day Himachal Pradesh were also leased in by the colonial government, with deodar being 'valued daily more and more for sleepers'. The British similarly cast a covetous eye on the magnificent sal forests in the Himalayan principality of Sikkim.[24] Meanwhile, several states in Central India, such as Rewa, became important suppliers of MFP such as lac and myrobalans (Smythies 1925).

The strategic value of India's forests, first made evident in the building of the railway network, was forcefully highlighted during the world wars. In the war of 1914-18 timber and bamboos were supplied for the construction of bridges, piers, wharves, buildings, huts and ships. In little over a year (April 1917 to October 1918) 228,076 tonnes of timber (excluding railway sleepers) were supplied by the specially created 'timber branch' of the munitions board, and 50,000 tonnes of fodder grass exported to help military operations in Egypt and Iraq. Approximately 1.7 million cubic feet of timber (mostly teak) were exported annually between 1914 and 1919, and the indigenous resin industry proved to be a great boon at a time when American and French supplies were unavailable (Stebbing I, p. 36; III, ch. XIX; Smythies 1925, pp. 13, 82, 84, etc.).

The impact of the Second World War was more severely felt on the forests of the subcontinent. Early in 1940, a timber directorate was set up in Delhi to channel supplies of forest produce from the provinces. India was the sole supplier of timber to the Middle East theatre, and later to the Allied forces in Iraq and the Persian Gulf. The war became an 'over-riding

[24] NAI, Forests, progs nos 30-35 for October 1878, and B progs nos 83-5 for December 1876. See also *Indian Forester*, XLVII, 1921, pp. 80-2.

objective' as timbers had to be found to replace the few that hitherto ruled the market and had become unobtainable. The cessation of the import of structural steel too brought an urgent demand for wood substitutes (GOI 1948; Champion and Osmaston 1962, ch. 4).

To meet the exigencies of war, 'fellings and sawings were pushed to the remotest corners of the Himalayas and the densest forests of the Western Ghats'. In the United Provinces the demand for chir and sal timber was 'virtually unlimited', and the forest department's instructions were 'to produce the maximum outturn possible'. By the end of 1944 it had supplied, to the defence department alone, 909,000 tonnes of timber. Not surprisingly, working-plan prescriptions in reserved forests were 'considerably upset' during the war. In Bombay too the yield prescriptions were widely departed from, the margin in some cases being upto 400 per cent (Champion and Osmaston 1962).

Table 4.2 gives some indication of the war demand and efforts to meet it. The figures relate only to recorded fellings; the available evidence points to considerable over-fellings; in forests, both of private owners and native states, as well as unrecorded felling in government forests. The fellings recorded show an increase, over pre-war outturn, of 65 per cent. However, it was admitted that due to the varying circumstances in which felling took place, an accurate estimate of the damage done to forest capital was not possible. For the government forests, these excess fellings were estimated to be on average as much as six annual yields (GOI 1948, pp. 107-8). As can be seen from Table 4.2 the accelerated fellings in the last years of the war coincided with a sharp drop in the area covered by working plans, implying that much felling was carried out without the supervision required to ensure proper regeneration. In general, the damage done in areas not covered by working plans would have been greater, and at the same time undetectable.

TABLE 4.2

INDIA'S FORESTS AND THE SECOND WORLD WAR

Year	Outturn of timber and fuel (m. cuft)	Outturn of MFP (Rs m)	Revenue of FD (Rs. m.)	Surplus of FD (Rs. m.)	Area sanctioned under working plans (sq. miles)
			(at current prices)		
1937-38	270	11.9	—	—	62,532
1938-39	299	12.3	29.4*	7.2*	64,789
1939-40	294	12.1	32.0	7.5	64,976
1940-41	386	12.5	37.1	13.3	66,407
1941-42	310	12.7	46.2	19.4	66,583
1942-43	336	12.9	65.0	26.7	51,364
1943-44	374	15.5	101.5	44.4	50,474
1944-45	439	16.5	124.4	48.9	50,440

NOTE : * Average for the period 1934-5 to 1938-9.

SOURCE : Compiled from *Indian Forest Statistics, 1939-40 to 1944-45* (Delhi, 1949).

The Balance Sheet of Colonial Forestry

In so far as the main aim of the new department was the production of large commercial timber and the generation of revenue, it worked willingly or unwillingly to enforce a separation between agriculture and forests. This exclusion of the agrarian population from the benefits of forest management, anticipated by opponents of the 1878 act, continued to draw sharp criticism from within the ranks of the colonial intelligentsia. In the words of an agricultural chemist, the forest department's objects

> were in no sense agricultural, and its success was gauged mainly by fiscal considerations; the Department was to be a revenue paying one. Indeed, we may go so far as to say that its interests were opposed to agriculture, and its intent was rather

to exclude agriculture from than to admit it to participation in its benefits (Voelcker 1893, pp. 135-6).

While advocating the creation of fuel and fodder reserves to more directly serve the interests of the rural population, Dr Voelcker used the characteristic justification that the increased revenue from land tax—which such a reorientation would bring—would more than compensate any loss of revenue from a decline in commercial timber operations. Faced with such criticism, colonial foresters were unrepentant. 'It is the province of the forest department to grow *timber*', stated one, 'pasturage is the province of the agricultural department, and should be taken up by that department'.[25] Grazing and shifting cultivation, the life-blood of tens of millions of Indians, were singled out by foresters as activities to be totally banned in areas under their control. Such hostility bears the mark of its origins, for, in other countries dominated by German forestry techniques, agriculture and forestry were likewise considered separate and often opposed activities (cf. Raumolin, 1986; Peluso 1989).

The priorities of colonial forestry were essentially commercial in nature. This trend was reinforced by the financial crunch faced by the government following the revolt of 1857, which kept every department on its toes. At periodic intervals government committees asked the forest department to generate even more revenue, and from Brandis onwards senior officials had to justify the activities of the department on commercial grounds (Stebbing I, pp. 463-4). Testifying to the Royal Commission on Agriculture, the inspector-general of forests explained that as 'the Forest Department has always been considered a commercial department', and revenue only came from large timber forests, it was forced to neglect shrub forest and pasture under its control (Anon. 1927, p. 256). Indeed, a commercial orientation was built into the education of forest officials. Thus the analogy with business enterprise, one wholly

[25] GKB, 'Some notes on the connection existing between forestry and agriculture in India', *Indian Forester* XV, 1889, p. 331.

inappropriate for an activity with such a long gestation period (and from which societies derive inestimable and unquantifiable benefits in the form of environmental stability) was nonetheless widely used in training manuals for junior officials (cf. D'Arcy 1910).

To fulfil these twin demands of commercial timber and revenue, the forest department intensified its exploitation through two major devices. First, it made remote forests accessible by improving transportation networks. As one United Provinces forester proclaimed, 'communications are the veins and arteries along which forest revenue flows and from its earliest days the Department has been active in "opening up the jungles" with a proper system of cart roads and paths' (Ford Robertson 1936, pp. 15-16). Simultaneously, foresters made the accessible areas more profitable by increasing the proportion of commercially valued species in the growing stock. Silvicultural techniques of ringing, girdling and fire manipulation successfully transformed many mixed oak-conifer forests in the Himalaya into pure coniferous strands (Guha, Ramachandra, 1989a). From Brandis onwards, foresters have looked down upon oaks, the climax vegetation of the area, as having 'much too slow a rate of growth to justify their maintenance as component parts of the high forest' (Brandis 1882, p. 124). Likewise, working plans in South India prescribed the conversion of evergreen forests into single-species teak forests (Dhareshwar 1941).

We may briefly mention two related processes of ecological change under colonialism. First, there is the intimate connection between the Raj and shikar. From the middle of the last century, a large-scale slaughter of animals commenced in which white hunters at all levels—from the viceroy down to the lower echelons of the British Indian army—participated. Much of this shooting was motivated by the desire for large 'bags'. While one British planter in the Nilgiris killed 400 elephants in the eighteen sixties, successive viceroys were invited to shoots in which several thousand birds were shot in a single day in attempts to claim the 'world record'. Many Indian princes sought to emulate the shikar exploits of the British. The Maharaja of Gwalior, for example, shot over 700 tigers early in this century. Although it is difficult to estimate the impact of such unregulated hunting on faunal ecology, some of the consequences were clear by the time India gained independence, as reflected in the steadily declining populations of wild species such as the tiger and the elephant (Bennet 1984; Elliot 1973; Sukumar 1989).

An equally major transformation in forest ecology concerned the sale, at extremely low prices, of large expanses of woodlands to Europeans for the development of tea, coffee and rubber plantations. Although many areas had been taken over before 1864, in its early years the forest department was besieged with requests for land by coffee and tea planters who enjoyed considerable influence in the colonial administration.[26] In fact the state's desire to commercialize the forests went hand in hand with the allotment of vast areas to planters. The development of a road and railway network to facilitate the export of tea, coffee and rubber also served to hasten the pace of timber exploitation. The plantation economy itself had a high level of timber demand for fuel and packaging—the tea industry in eastern India alone requiring wood for over a million chests annually. In this manner the expansion of plantations bore a direct relation to the shrinking areas under forest cover (Pandian 1985; Sinha 1986; Tucker 1988).

However, perhaps the most serious consequence of colonial forestry was the decline in traditional conservation and management systems around the forest. Disregarding the proposals of Brandis and the Madras government, the state was quite lukewarm about the constitution of community forests. This was in line with overall colonial policy, for, as Voelcker pointed out, 'the tendency of our system of government has, to a considerable extent been to *break up* village communities, and

---

[26] See evidence of A. Rodger, offg IGF, in Anon (1927), p. 256.

now for the most part they are heterogeneous bodies rather than communities' (Voelcker 1893, p. 16, emphasis in original). In the one presidency where *panchayat* (village) forests were promoted to any significant extent—Madras—it was a case of too little too late. While waiting thirty years after the 1878 act before creating village forests, the government had imposed a set of rules that quickly bureaucratized the panchayats and impaired their functioning (Pressler 1987). Elsewhere the provision in the act for constituting village forests remained a 'dead letter', and the stipulation that these forests be first constituted as state reserves aroused the suspicion of peasants (Ribbentrop 1900). The consequence of the alienation of peasants from forests they had earlier protected was anticipated by the Poona Sarvajanik Sabha in 1878. Contesting the new act's excessive reliance on state control, it argued that the maintenance of forest cover could more easily be brought about by

> taking the Indian villagers into the confidence of the Indian Government. If the villagers be rewarded and commended for conserving their patches of forest lands, or for making plantations on the same, instead of ejecting them from the forest land which they possess, or in which they are interested, emulation might be evoked between neighbouring villages. Thus more effective conservation and development of forests in India might be secured and when the villagers have their own patches of forests to attend to, Government forests might not be molested. Thus the interests of the villagers as well as the Government can be secured without causing any unnecessary irritation in the minds of the masses of the Indian population.[27]

But it was not to be. The state's takeover of forests and the subsequent working of these on commercial lines had, as one corollary, the diminution of customary rights, as well as a second—a slow but significant process of ecological decline. Attracted to India by among other things 'the seemingly immeasurable extent of its natural resources' (Whitcombe 1971,

---

[27] See, for example, NAI, Forests, progs nos 7-11, July 1875.

p. ix), the British had by the turn of the nineteenth century acquired firm control over these resources. However, the loss of forests and pastures, earlier communally owned and managed, severely undermined the subsistence economy of the peasant. Simultaneously, British land policy worked towards the increasing differentiation of the peasantry and the decline of communal institutions. Losing his autonomy, the peasant was forced further out of production for use and into the vortex of the market economy (cf. Scott 1976, for a similar process in colonial Indochina).

Forest management was easily the most significant element in the state takeover of natural resources which had earlier acted as a buffer for the peasant household. Yet colonial policy had other, often unforeseen, ecological consequences. Large-scale irrigation works in UP and Bihar resulted in waterlogging and soil salinity in some areas. According to Whitcombe this created an unprecedented strain in the economy of the Doab. In Bihar the breakdown of traditional small-scale community irrigation systems was believed to be a factor in rural impoverishment and the rise of *kisan sabhas* in the 1930s (Whitcombe 1971; Sengupta 1980). While there is limited research yet on the specific changes in different geographical regions, clearly the century and a half of colonial rule had introduced manifold social and ecological changes whose interdependence has rarely been appreciated.

CHAPTER FIVE

The Fight for the Forest

> In the olden days small landholders who could not
> subsist on cultivation alone used to eat wild fruits like
> figs and jamun and sell the leaves and flowers of the
> flame of the forest and the mahua tree. They could also
> depend on the village grazing ground to maintain one
> or two cows and two or four goats, thereby living
> happily in their own ancestral villages. However, the
> cunning European employees of our motherly govern-
> ment have used their foreign brains to erect a great
> superstructure called the forest department. With all
> the hills and undulating lands as also the fallow lands
> and grazing grounds brought under the control of the
> forest department, the livestock of the poor farmers
> does not even have place to breathe anywhere on the
> surface of the earth.
> —Jotirau Phule, 1881, in Keer and Malshe 1969

From the perspective of the Indian villager, the ecological and
social changes that came in the wake of commercial forestry
were not simply an intensification of earlier processes of change
and conflict. Clearly, many of the forest communities (especial-

ly hunter-gatherers and shifting cultivators) had for several centuries been subject to the pressures of the agrarian civilizations of the plains. However, while these pressures themselves ebbed and flowed with the rise and fall of the grain-based kingdoms of peninsular India, they scarcely matched in their range or scope the magnitude of the changes that were a consequence of the state takeover of the forests in the late nineteenth century. Before this the commercial exploitation of forest produce was largely restricted to commodities such as pepper, cardamom and ivory, whose extraction did not seriously affect either the ecology of the forest or customary use. It was the emergence of timber as an important commodity that led to a qualitative change in the patterns of harvesting and the utilization of forests. Thus when the colonial state asserted control over woodland earlier controlled by local communities, and proceeded to work these forests for commercial timber production, it represented an intervention in the day-to-day life of the Indian villager which was unprecedented in its scope. Second, the colonial state radically redefined property rights, imposing on the forest a system of management and control whose priorities sharply conflicted with earlier systems of local use and control. Finally, one must not underestimate the changes in forest ecology that resulted from this shift in management systems. Significantly, the species promoted by colonial foresters—teak, pine and deodar in different ecological zones—were invariably of very little use to rural populations, while the species they replaced (e.g. oak, terminalia) were intensively used for fuel, fodder, leaf manure and small timber.

In these varied ways, colonial forestry marked an ecological, economic and political watershed in Indian forest history. The intensification of conflict over forest produce was a major consequence of changes in the patterns of resource use it initiated. This chapter analyses some of the evidences on conflicts over forest and pasture in colonial India. Based on both primary and secondary sources, it outlines the major dimensions of such conflicts by focussing on the genesis, the geographical spread, and the different forms in which protest manifested itself.

Hunter-Gatherers: The Decline Towards Extinction

Until the early decades of this century, almost a dozen communities in the Indian subcontinent depended on the original mode of sustenance of human populations, namely hunting and gathering. Their distribution encompassed nearly the entire length of India, with the Rajis of Kumaun in the north to the Kadars of Cochin in the south. The abundant rainfall and rich vegetation of their tropical habitats facilitated the reproduction of subsistence almost exclusively through the collection of roots, fruit, and the hunting of small game. While cultivation was largely foreign to these communities, they did engage in some trade with the surrounding agricultural population, exchanging forest produce such as herbs and honey for metal implements, salt, clothes, and very occasionally grain. With minimal social differentiation, and restraints on the over-exploitation of resources through the partitioning of territories between endogamous bands, these hunter-gatherers, if not quite the 'original affluent society' (cf. Sahlins 1971) were, as long as there existed sufficient areas under their control, able to subsist quite easily on the bounties of nature.

Predictably, state reservation of forests sharply affected the subsistence activities of these communities, each numbering a few hundred—and with population densities calculated at square miles per person rather than persons per square mile. The forest and game laws affected the Chenchus of Hyderabad, for example, by making their hunting activities illegal and by questioning or even denying their existing monopoly over forest produce other than timber. The cumulative impact of commercial forestry, and the more frequent contacts with outsiders that the opening out of such areas brought about, virtually crippled the Chenchus. As suspicious of mobile populations as most modern states, in some parts the colonial government forcibly gathered the tribals into large settlements. Rapidly losing their autonomy, most Chenchus were forced into a relationship of agrestic serfdom with the more powerful cultivating castes. Further south, the Chenchus of Kurnool, almost in desperation, turned to banditry, frequently holding up pilgrims to the major Hindu temple of Srisailam (von Fürer Haimendorf 1943a; Aiyappan 1948).

As with the Chenchus, other hunter-gatherer communities were not numerous enough to actively resist the social and economic changes that followed state forest management. Forced sedentarization and the loss of their habitat induced a feeling of helplessness, as outsiders made greater and greater inroads into what was once their undisputed domain. Thus the Kadars succumbed to what one writer called a 'proletarian dependence' on the forest administration, whose commercial transactions and territorial control now determined their daily routine and mode of existence. In this manner the intimate knowledge of his surroundings that the Kadar possessed was now utilized for the collection of forest produce marketed by the state. In the thickly wooded plateau of Chotanagpur, meanwhile, the commercialization of the forest and restrictions on local use led to a precipitous fall in the population of the Birhor tribe—from 2340 in 1911 to 1610 in 1921 (Ehrenfeld 1952 ; Roy 1925).

While the new laws restricted small-scale hunting by tribals, they facilitated more organized shikar expeditions by the British. The disjunction between the favours shown to the white shikari and the clampdown on subsistence hunting had serious consequences. While there were few formal restrictions on the British hunter until well into the twentieth century, hunter-gatherers as well as cultivators for whom wild game was a valuable source of protein found their hunting activities threatened by the new forest laws.

The Baigas of Central India, for example, were famed for their hunting skills. They were 'expert in all appliances of the chase', and early British shikaris relied heavily on the 'marvellous skill and knowledge of the wild creatures' that they possessed. Yet the stricter forest administration, dating from the turn of the century, induced a dramatic decline. Writing in the

1930s, Verrier Elwin noted that while their love for hunting and meat persisted, the old skills had largely perished. There remained, however, a defiant streak, and as one Baiga said, 'even if Government passes a hundred laws we will do it. One of us will keep the official talking; the rest will go out and shoot the deer' (Ward 1870; Best 1935; Elwin 1939). In the Himalayan foothills, too, where there was an abundance of game, villagers continued to hunt despite government restrictions, taking care to be one step ahead of the forest staff—a task not difficult to accomplish, given their familiarity with the terrain.[1]

Among shifting cultivators, there was often a ritual association of hunting with the agricultural cycle. Despite game laws, the Hill Reddis of Hyderabad clung to their ritual hunt—called Bhumi Devata Panduga or the hunt of the earth god—which involved the entire male population and preceded the monsoon sowing. The reservation of forests also interfered with the movement of hunting parties across state boundaries. In 1929 a police contingent had to be called in to stop a party of Bison Marias from Bastar state, armed with bows and spears, from crossing into the British-administered Central Provinces. This, of course, constituted an unnatural intervention, as the ritual hunt was no respector of political boundaries. Nevertheless, in later years the authorities were successful in confining the Maria ritual hunt to Bastar, the game caught steadily declining in consequence (von Fürer Haimendorf 1943b; Grigson 1938).

The 'Problem' of Shifting Cultivation

Shifting or jhum cultivation was the characteristic form of agriculture over large parts of India, especially in the hilly and forested tracts where plough agriculture was not always feasible. Jhum typically involves the clearing and cultivation of patches of forest in rotation. The individual plots are burnt and cultivated for a few years and then left fallow for an extended

[1] See 'Gamekeeper', 'Destruction of Game in Government Reserves During the Rains', *Indian Forester*, XIII (1887), pp. 188-90. Cf. also Corbett (1952).

period (ideally, a dozen years or longer), allowing the vegetation and soil to recoup and recover lost nutrients. Cultivators then move on to the next plot, abandoning it in turn when its productivity starts declining. Although in parts of the Western Ghats Hindu castes did depend on this mode of resource use, it was usually practised by 'tribal' groups for whom jhum was a way of life encompassing, beyond the narrowly economic, the social and cultural spheres as well. The corporeal character of these communities was evident in the pattern of cultivation, where communal labour predominated, with different families adhering to boundaries established and respected by tradition. The overwhelming importance of jhum in structuring social life was strikingly manifest, too, in the many myths and legends constructed around it in tribal cosmology.

As in many areas of social life, major changes awaited the advent of British rule. For, almost without exception, colonial administrators viewed jhum with disfavour as a primitive and unremunerative form of agriculture in comparison with plough cultivation. Occasionally the British, out of political compulsions, were constrained to allow the continuance of jhum, as in the hill tracts of the Western Ghats formerly controlled by the Maratha kingdom. The Marathas were among the last to fall to the East India Company, and shifting cultivators in their territories continued to rise periodically against the British, right until the insurrection led by Vasudev Balwant Phadke in the 1880s. Elsewhere, however, the British strove strenuously to curb or destroy shifting agriculture. Influenced both by the agricultural revolution in Europe and the revenue-generating possibilities of intensive (as opposed to extensive) forms of cultivation, official hostility to jhum gained an added impetus with the commercialization of the forest. Like their counterparts in other parts of the globe, British foresters held jhum to be 'the most destructive of all practices for the forest'.[2] There was a very good reason for this animosity—if 'axe cultivation

[2] Cf. Muhafiz-i-Jangal (pseud), 'Jhooming in Russia', *Indian Forester*, II (1876), pp. 418-19.

was the despair of every forest officer' (Elwin 1943, p. 8), it was largely because timber operations competed with jhum for territorial control of the forest. This negative attitude was nevertheless tempered by the realization that any abrupt attempt to curtail its practice would provoke a sharp response from jhum cultivations. Yet the areas cultivated under jhum often contained the most valued timber species.[3] In the circumstances, the curbing of jhum was an intractable problem for which the colonial state had no easy solution.

A vivid account of the various attempts to combat jhum can be found in Elwin's classic monograph on the Baiga (Elwin, 1939, esp. chapter 2), a small tribe that inhabited the Mandla, Balaghat and Bilaspur districts of present-day Madhya Pradesh. The first serious attempt to stop shifting cultivation in the 1860s had as its impetus the civilizational zeal of the chief commissioner of the province, Richard Temple. In later years, though, it was the fact that the marketable value of forest produce 'rose in something like geometrical proportion' which accounted for the 'shifting of emphasis from Sir Richard Temple's policy of benevolent improvement for their own sake to a frank and simple desire to better the Provincial budget'. A vigorous campaign to induce the Baiga to take to the plough culminated in the destruction of standing jhum crops by an over-enthusiastic deputy commissioner. When many tribals fled to neighbouring princely states, the government advised a policy of slow weaning from axe cultivation.

In fact, such difficulties had been anticipated by the settlement officer in 1870; he observed that 'it has been found quite impracticable, as well as hard and impolitic, to force the Baigas to give up their dhya (jhum) cultivation and take to the plough'. He advised limits on jhum rather than a total ban. A more cautious policy was dictated, too, by the dependence of the

---

[3] As the chief commissioner of the Central Provinces put it, 'the best ground for this peculiar cultivation is precisely that where the finest timber trees like to grow'. Sir Richard Temple, quoted in J.F. Dyer, 'Forestry in the Central Provinces and Berar', *Indian Forester*, LI (1925), p. 349.

forest department on the labour of the Baigas, for they were most proficient at wood-cutting and the collection of forest produce. As a consequence, the government established the Baiga *chak* (reserve) in 1890, covering 23,920 acres of forest, where they planned to confine all jhum cultivators. The area chosen was described as 'perfectly inaccessible [and] therefore useless as a timber producing area'. While permitting jhum within the reserve, the administration stressed an overall policy of discouraging it elsewhere. In this they were partially successful, as Baiga villages outside the chak, faced with the prospect of leaving home, accepted the terms of plough cultivation. While many Baigas continued to migrate into neighbouring princely states, within the chak itself the population of jhum cultivators steadily dwindled.

Baiga opposition took the form of 'voting with their feet', and other forms of resistance that stopped short of open confrontation—such as the non-payment of taxes and the continuance of jhum in forbidden areas. The new restrictions inculcated an acute sense of cultural loss, captured in a petition submitted to the British government in 1892. After jhum has been stopped, it said—

> We daily starve, having had no foodgrain in our possession. The only wealth we possess is our axe. We have no clothes to cover our body with, but we pass cold nights by the fireside. We are now dying for want of food. We cannot go elsewhere. What fault have we done that the government does not take care of us? Prisoners are supplied with ample food in jail. A cultivator of the grass is not deprived of his holding, but the government does not give us our right who have lived here for generations past (Elwin 1939; Ward 1870).

In some areas tribal resistance to the state's attempt to curb jhum often took a violent and confrontationist form. This was especially so where commercialization of the forest was accompanied by the penetration of non-tribal landlords and moneylenders who came to exercise a dominant influence on the indigenous population. Elwin himself, talking of the periodic disturbances among the Saora tribals of the Ganjam Agency, identified them as emanating from two sources: the exactions of plainsmen and the state's attempts to check axe cultivation. Thus, Saoras were prone to invade reserved forests and clear land for cultivation. In the late 1930s, several villages endeavoured to fell large areas of reserved forests in preparation for sowing. The Saoras were ready for any penalty—when the men were arrested and put in jail, the women continued the cultivation. After returning from jail the men cleared the jungle again for the next year's crop. As repeated arrests were unsuccessful in stopping Saoras from trying to establish their right, the forest department forcibly uprooted crops on land formally vested in the state (Elwin 1945).

Perhaps the most sustained resistance, extending over nearly a century, occurred in the Gudem and Rampa hill tracts of present-day Andhra Pradesh. Inhabited by Koya and Konda Dora tribesmen (predominantly jhum cultivators), under British rule the hills were subject to a steady penetration of the market economy and the influx of plainsmen eager to exploit its natural wealth. Road construction led to rapid development in the marketable trade of tamarind, fruit, honey and other forest products that were exported to urban centres and even to Europe. Traders, from the powerful Telugu caste of Komatis, also took on lease (from local chiefs) tracts of forest as well as the trade in palm liquor. As in other parts of India, they were actively helped by the colonial government, which had banned the domestic brewing of liquor (an important source of nutrition in the lean season) and farmed out liquor contracts in a bid to raise revenue. Simultaneously, commercial forest operations were begun on a fairly large scale, and, as elsewhere, the creation of forest reserves conflicted with the practice of jhum. Slowly losing control over their lands and their means of subsistence, many tribals were forced into relations of dependence with the more powerful plainsmen, either working as tenants and sharecroppers in the new system of market agriculture or as forest labour in the felling and hauling of timber.

Among the many small risings or *fituris* documented by David Arnold, several were directly or indirectly related to forest grievances. The Rampa rebellion of 1879-80 arose in response to the new restrictions concerning liquor and forest regulations. Complaining bitterly against various exactions, the tribals said that 'as they could not live they might as well kill the constables and die'. The rebellion broke out in March 1879 and spread rapidly to neighbouring areas. The rebels, led by a minor tribal chieftain, Tammam Dora, attacked and burnt several police stations, executing a constable as an act of ritual sacrifice. While Tammam Dora was shot by the police in June 1880, the revolt spread to the Golconda Hills of Vishakhapatnam and the Rekepalle country in Bhadrachalam. The latter territory had earlier been part of the Central Provinces, and its transfer to Madras led to greater restrictions on the practice of jhum. Here, protest emanated directly from forest grievances and, as in other fituris, police stations—a highly visible symbol of state authority—were frequent targets. It took several hundred policemen and ten army companies to suppress the revolt, a task not finally accomplished till November 1880.

The last recorded fituri was, like its predecessors, closely linked to restrictions on tribal access to the forest. This occurred in 1922-3 and was led by a high-caste Hindu from the plains called Alluri Sita Rama Raju, who was able to transform a local rising into a minor guerilla war. Including dispossessed landholders and men convicted for forest offences, Rama Raju's men were actively helped by villagers who gave them food and shelter. After raids on police outposts had netted a haul of arms and ammunitions, Raju's band was able to evade the police by its superior knowledge of the hilly and wooded terrain. Unsuccessful in his attempts to spread the rebellion into the plains, Rama Raju was finally captured and shot in May 1924 (Arnold 1982; von Fürer Haimendorf 1945a).

Interestingly, as the Indian princes sought to emulate their

British counterparts in realizing the commercial value of their forests, they too came in conflict with shifting cultivators. Regarding the state takeover as a forfeiture of their hereditary rights, in several chiefdoms tribals rose in revolt against attempts to curb jhum. A major rebellion took place in Bastar state in 1910, directed against the new prohibitions concerning jhum, restrictions on access to forests and their produce, and the *begar* (unpaid labour) exacted by state officials. The formation of reserved forests had resulted in the destruction of many villages and the eviction of their inhabitants. In order to draw attention to their grievances, some tribals went on hunger strike outside the king's palace at Jagdalpur. Mostly Marias and Murias, the rebels, affirming that it was an internal affair between them and their ruler, cut telegraph wires and blocked roads. Simultaneously, police stations and forest outposts were burnt, stacked wood looted, and a campaign mounted against *pardeshis* (outsiders), mostly low-caste Hindu cultivators settled in Bastar. Led by their headmen, the rebels looted several markets and attacked and killed both state officials and merchants. In a matter of days, the rebellion engulfed nearly half the state, or an area exceeding 6000 square miles. Unnerved, the king called in a battalion of the 22nd Punjabis (led by a British officer) and detachments of the Madras and Central Province police. Armed with bows, arrows and spears, the rebels unsuccessfully engaged the troops in battle. In a decisive encounter near Jagdalpur, over 900 tribals, of all ages from 16 upwards, were captured.[4]

In 1940 a similar revolt broke out in Adilabad district of Hyderabad state. Here, Gonds and Kolams, the principal cultivating tribes, were subjected to an invasion of Telugu and Maratha cultivators who flooded the district following the improvement of communications. Whole Gond villages fell to immigrant castes. In the uplands, meanwhile, forest conservan-

[4] Based on National Archives of India, New Delhi, foreign department, Secret—I progs, nos. 34-40, for August 1911, and nos. 16-17 for September 1910; Grigson (1939); Clement Smith (1945).

cy restricted jhum, with cultivated land lying fallow under rotation being taken into forest reserves. Following the forcible disbandment of Gond and Kolam settlements in the Dhanora forest, the tribals, led by Kumra Bhimu, made repeated but unsuccessful attempts to contact state officials. After petitions for resettlements were ignored, the tribals established a settlement on their own and began to clear forests for cultivation. An armed party which came to burn the new village was resisted by Bhimu's Gonds, who then took refuge within a mountain fastness. When the police asked them to surrender, they were met with the counter demand that Gonds and Kolams should be given possession of the land they had begun to cultivate. The police thereupon opened fire, killing Bhimu and several of his associates (von Fürer Haimendorf 1945b).

Elsewhere in Hyderabad state, the Hill Reddis of the Godavari valley were at the receiving end of the new forest laws. The restriction of jhum to small and demarcated areas forced the Reddis to shorten fallow cycles, or to prolong cultivation on a designated patch until deterioration set in. Interestingly enough, as forest laws were not quite as stringent across the Godavari in British territory, tribals moved across in response to a ban on jhum—returning to Hyderabad when the ban was lifted. While not resorting to open protest, the Reddis thus made evident their dislike of the ban (von Fürer Haimendorf 1943b; 1945b). Likewise the population of shifting cultivators in one taluk of Nasik declined by 24 per cent in a single year (1874): fed up with restrictions on jhum, they fled to neighbouring princely states.[5]

These repeated protests had a significant impact on government policy. In some parts of Madras Presidency, certain patches were set aside for tribals to continue jhum. For although 'the forest department would welcome the complete stoppage of podu [jhum] it is not done for fear of *fituris* [tribal uprisings]'

[5] National Archives of India (NAI), rev. agl. (forests) progs nos. 1-3, January 1877.

(Aiyappan 1948, pp. 16-17). Elsewhere the state found a novel way of pursuing commercial forestry without further alienating tribal cultivators. This was the 'taungya' method of agro-silviculture—developed in Burma in the nineteenth century—where jhum cultivators were allowed to grow food crops in the forest provided they grew timber trees alongside. Thus, after a few years, when the cultivator moved on to clear the next patch, a forest crop had been established on the vacated ground. Taungya, which rendered possible at a 'comparatively low cost' the establishment of the labour force necessary for forest works, is still widely in operation. It helped forestall the very real possibility of revolt among tribals who were to be displaced by a prohibition upon their characteristic forms of cultivation. (Sometimes, though, even taungya cultivators thwarted the state, for example by planting only upon those areas likely to be inspected by touring officials). Ironically enough, its success has even led to the reintroduction of jhum in tracts where it had died out or been put down at an earlier stage (Blanford 1925; Baden-Powell 1874; Champion and Seth 1968).

More commonly, the cumulative impact of market forces and state intervention forced the abandonment of jhum in favour of the plough or wage labour. Even where the practice continued, the disruption of the delicate balance between humans and forests—initially through the usurpation of forests by the state, and later through rises in population—has led to a sharp fall in the jhum cycle. A form of agriculture practised for several millenia has become unsustainable in the face of external forces over which it had very little control.

Settled Cultivators and the State

Notwithstanding the spatial separation between field and forest, over the most part of India plough agriculturists (mostly caste Hindus) were scarcely less affected by forest reservation than cultivators. For they too depended on their natural habitat in a variety of ways. An adequate forest cover was ecologically necessary to sustain cultivation, especially in mountainous tracts where terrace farming predominated. And with animal husbandry a valuable appendage to cultivation, the forest was a prime source of fodder in the form of grass and leaves. Forests also provided such essential inputs as fuel, leaf manure, and timber for construction and agricultural implements.

Here too state reservation enforced changes in the traditional pattern of resource utilization, even if these changes were not quite as radical as in the case of shifting cultivators. Under the provisions of the 1878 act, the takeover of a tract of forest involved settling the claims of surrounding villages. Under the new 'legal' (i.e. codified) arrangements, the previously unlimited rights of user were severely circumscribed. These restrictions affected two distinct classes of agriculturists, and in somewhat different ways. In areas dominated by cultivating proprietors, and where differentiation was not too marked, those affected by state forestry primarily consisted of middle to rich peasants, many of whom were graziers rather than agriculturists. On the other hand, in tracts which exhibited more advanced forms of class differentiation, it was a different social stratum that was at the receiving end. These were adivasi (tribal) and low-caste communities which supplemented their meagre earnings as tenants and sharecroppers with the extraction and sale of fuel, grass and other minor forest produce.

An example of the first form of deprivation comes from the Madras Presidency. There, several decades after forest reservation, villagers had vivid memories of their traditional rights over the forest, continuing to adhere to informal boundaries demarcating tracts of woodland claimed and controlled by neighbouring villagers. The tenacity with which they clung to their rights was visibly manifest, too, in the escalation of forest offences (averaging 30,000 per annum)—with the killing of forest personnel a not infrequent occurrence. A committee formed to investigate forest grievances was puzzled to find that villagers interpreted the term 'free grazing' quite differently from the committee itself. While quite prepared to pay a small fee, peasants understood 'free grazing' to mean 'the right to graze all over the forests', i.e. a continuation of the territorial control over the forest that they formerly enjoyed. Thus the demand for grazing was accompanied by the demand for free fuel and small timber—in effect 'for the abolition of all control and for the right to use or destroy the forest property of the state without any restriction whatever'. Commenting on the widespread hostility towards state forest management, the committee observed that 'the one department which appears at one time to have rivalled the forest department in unpopularity is the salt department, which, like the forest department, is concerned with a commodity of comparatively small value in itself but an article for daily use and consumption' (Anon 1913; Baker, C.J. 1984).

Not surprisingly, the opposition to state forestry was far more intense among the lower castes and tribals. In the Thane district of coastal Maharashtra, an important source of income for tribal households was the sale of firewood to Koli fishermen. This trade was severely affected by the stricter control exercised over the forest since the later decades of the nineteenth century. Typically, the early manifestations of discontent were peaceful, e.g. petitioning the local administration. When this had no impact, collective protest turned violent. Surrounding the camp of a deputy collector, a group of villagers demanded that 'the forests be thrown open, palm tax be abolished, country liquor [be sold] at one anna a seer, salt at one anna a paili, rice at Re 1/1/4 per maund and that the Government should re-deem their mortgaged land and restore it to them'. In another incident, a large number of tribals carrying firewood to the market were intercepted by the police. In protest, the adivasis stacked wood on a nearby railway line and refused to allow a train to pass. Sensing the prevailing mood of defiance, the officer in charge of the force allowed them to proceed to the market (Singh 1983).

A similar turn of events is reported from the Midnapur district of Bengal Presidency. In one area called the Jungle

Mahals, land owned by the Midnapur Zamindari Company (MZC)—an associate of the important British managing agency firm of Andrew Yuile—and other large landlords was cultivated by Santhal tribal tenants. While early lease deeds clearly specified that all land was to be handed over to the lessee, the coming of the railway and consequently of a thriving timber trade influenced the zamindars to impose sharp restrictions on the Santhals. Again, the tribals first tried the courts and other means of legal redress. However, the conditions of economic distress prevailing in the aftermath of World War I provoked a more militant response. Thus in 1918 the forest-dwelling Santhals proceeded on a campaign of *haat* (market) looting, their principal targets being upcountry cloth traders who were moneylenders as well.

Some years later, and after the intervention of Congress nationalists, the Jungle Mahals witnessed a movement more sharply focussed on the question of forest rights. In early 1922 Santhals working as forest labour went on strike. Following a scuffle between employees of the MZC and the strikers, the Congress directed the Santhals to plunder the forests. Further incidents of haat looting (including the burning of foreign cloth) and attempts to restrict the export of paddy were also reported. In one subdivision, Silda, Santhals began to plunder jungles leased to timber merchants. When a police party tried to confiscate the newly-cut wood, they were beaten up (Dasgupta 1980).

Another form of the assertion of traditional rights was manifest when Santhals began to loot fish from ponds controlled by individual zamindars. In April 1923 there was a wave of fish pond looting and breaches of the forest law over an area of 200 square miles, from Jhargram in Midnapur to Ghatshila in the Singhbhum district of Bihar. While recognizing this to be an 'illegal' act, the tribals argued that tank-raiding would force the zamindars to concede their customary rights over forests. The Santhals, the district magistrate commented, 'will let you know how in his father's time all jungles were free, and *bandhs* (ponds)

open to the public. Sometimes he is right . . . '. When the protests were supported by a dispossessed local chieftain, even the
belief that their acts were illegal was abandoned. Indeed, as
alarmed officials reported, 90 per cent of the crowd believed
that through their acts they were merely bringing back a golden
age when all jungles were free (Sarkar 1984).

The defiance of forest regulations also formed part of the
countrywide campaigns led by the Indian National Congress
in 1920-2 and 1930-2. Gandhi's visit to Cudappah in south-east-
ern India in September 1921 was widely hailed as an oppoi -
tunity to get the forest laws abolished. In nearby Guntur, peasants actually invaded the forests in the belief that 'Gandhi Raj'
had been established and the forests were now open. Ten years
later, during the Civil Disobedience movement, the violation of
forest laws was far more widespread. In Maharashtra, where
women played a significant part, nearly 60,000 villagers in
Akola district marched into government forests with their cattle. In Satara district peasants, arguing that grazing restrictions
deprived the sacred cow of its daily food, resolved not to pay
the grazing fee. Encroachment on reserved forests was followed
by the felling of teak trees and the hoisting of the national
tricolour on a teak pole, in front of a temple dedicated to Shiva.
Women also played a key role in a similar campaign in the
coastal district of North Kanara (in present-day Karnataka),
garlanding and smearing ritual paste on men who went off to
the forest to cut the valued sandal tree. There too the timber was
loaded onto carts and stacked in front of a local temple. The
arrests of men inspired the women, who invoked Sri Krishna
(the deity who had gone to the forest), when symbolically
breaching the rules themselves. In the Central Provinces, meanwhile, tribals came forth in great numbers to participate in the
organized violation of forest laws. While formally conducted
under the rubric of the Congress, these movements actually
enjoyed a considerable degree of autonomy from that organization; moreover, the many violent incidents were clearly in
defiance of nationalist leaders, wedded as the latter were to an

ideology of non-violence (Sarkar 1980; Halappa 1964; Baker, D.E.U. 1984; Brahme and Upadhya 1979).

Perhaps the most sustained opposition to state forest management was to be found in the Himalayan districts of present-day Uttar Pradesh. Dominated by magnificent stands of coniferous species, these hill forests have been—as the only source of softwoods—one of the most valuable forest properties in the subcontinent. At the same time, the forests here have also played a crucial role in sustaining agriculture in the mountainous terrain, this role being strikingly reflected in the traditional systems of resource conservation evolved to inhibit the over-exploitation of village forests.

In the period of colonial rule this region was divided into two distinct socio-political structures—the princely state of Tehri Garhwal and the British administered Kumaun division. However, as the forests of Tehri Garhwal came under commercial management even earlier (*c.* 1865), in both areas peasant resistance to this encroachment on customary rights was remarkably sustained and uniform. In Tehri, important if localized movements occurred in 1904, 1906, 1930 and 1944-8, in all of which forest grievances played an important and sometimes determining role. Through the collective violation of the new laws and attacks on forest officials, the peasantry underscored its claim to a full and exclusive control over forests and pasture. As in other pre-capitalist societies where the ruler relied on a traditional idiom of legitimacy, protest was aimed at forest management and its back-up officials, not at the monarch himself. In Kumaun division, on the other hand, social protest was aimed directly at the colonial state itself, and at the most visible signs of its rule, namely pine forests under intensive commercial management, and government buildings and offices. It reached its zenith in the summer of 1921, when a wide-ranging campaign to burn forests controlled by the forest department virtually paralyzed the administration, forcing it to abolish the much disliked system of forced labour and to abandon effective control over areas of woodland. Largely autonomous of organized nationalist activity (as represented by the Congress), the movements of 1916, 1921, 1930 and 1942 in Kumaun division brought to the fore the central importance of forests in peasant economy and society. Notwithstanding differences in the social idiom of protest—not unexpected in view of the somewhat different socio-political structures and styles of rule —in both Tehri Garhwal and Kumaun division forest restrictions were the source of bitter conflicts, unprecedented in their intensity and spread, between the peasantry and the state (Guha, Ramachandra 1989a).

Everyday Forms of Resistance: The Case of Jaunsar Bawar

In a penetrating study of rural Malaysia, the political scientist James Scott (1986) has observed that while most students of rural politics have focused on agrarian revolt and revolution, these are by no means the characteristic forms of peasant resistance. Far more frequently, peasants resort to methods of resisting the demands of non-cultivating elites that minimize the element of open confrontation—for example non-co-operation with imposed rules and regulations, the giving of false and misleading information to tax collectors and other officials, and migration. In colonial India, too, the peasantry often resorted to violent protest only after quasi-legal channels—such as petitions and peaceful strikes—had been tried and found wanting. Whereas the historical record is heavily biased towards episodes of violent revolt—the times when the peasant imposes himself rather more emphatically on the processes of state—it is important not to neglect other forms of protest which were not overtly confrontationist in form.

Often, these other forms of resistance preceded or ran concurrently with open conflict. Thus, in many areas the breach of forest laws was the most tangible evidence of the unpopularity of state management: the available evidence showing that typically the incidence of forest 'crime' followed a steadily escalating trend. While this would be true of regions where sustained protest did occur (such as those described above), the absence of an organized movement quite evidently did not signify an approval of state forestry.

That the conflict between villagers and colonial forest management did not always manifest itself in open revolt is clearly shown by the experience of Jaunsar Bawar, the hilly segment of Dehra Dun district that bordered Tehri Garhwal on the west. From the early 1860s the forests of Jaunsar Bawar had attracted the attention of the state. These forests were important for three reasons—as a source of wood for the railway, as 'inspection' forests for training students at the Forest School in nearby Dehra Dun, and for supplying fuel and timber to the military cantonment of Chakrata. In the ensuing settlement of 1868 the state divided the forests into three classes. While forests of the first class were wholly closed for protection, villagers had certain rights of pasturage and timber collection in the second class. The third class was to be kept for the exclusive use of peasants, with the caveat that they were not allowed to barter or sell any of the produce.

Early protests were directed at this government monopoly. The confused legal status of Class III forests, village leaders argued (it was not clear who held actual proprietary right, the state or the village), was compounded by the refusal to allow rightholders to dispose of their timber as they pleased. If peasants believed that they could not dispose of the produce of Class III forests as they liked, their control was only a formal one, the government on its part was loath to give up its monopoly over the timber trade. Extending over three decades, and conducted through a series of petitions and representations, this was in essence a dispute over the proprietary claims of the two parties. As the superintendent of the district observed, villagers were concerned more with the legal status of Class III forests than its extent—indeed 'they would be contented to take much less than they have now, if they felt it was their own'.[6] Nor were

<hr/>

[6] Uttar Pradesh Regional Archives, Dehra Dun (hereafter UPRA); Post-Mutiny Records (hereafter PMR); file no. 71, department XI, list no 2

they tempted by money for forests they claimed as theirs, with one frustrated official complaining: 'the Jaunsaris are a peculiar set and no reasonable amount of compensation will satisfy them'.

The unsettled state of forest boundaries had made the peasantry suspicious that the government would slowly take over Class III forests and put them under commercial management. On a tour of the district, the lieutenant-governor of the province encountered repeated complaints on the 'severity of the forest rules, dwelling chiefly on the fact that no forest or wasteland was made over to them in absolute proprietary right, and so they were afraid that at some future period government might resume the whole of it and leave them destitute'. As one hillman succinctly put it, 'the forests have belonged to us from time immemorial, our ancestors planted them and have protected them; now that they have become of value, government steps in and robs us of them'.[7] The official urged a revision of forest boundaries and the confirming of village proprietorship in Class III forests, as 'nothing would tend to allay the irritation and discontent in the breasts of the people so much as giving them a full proprietary title to all lands not required by government'.[8]

(hereafter, L2); Memorandum by H.G. Ross, superintendent of Dehra Dun, on verbal complaints made to the lieutenant-governor by Syanas (headmen) of Jaunsar and Bawar, n.d. (prob. 1871 or 1872); NAI, department of rev. agl. (forests), progs. nos. 9-10, July 1876, no. 24, 21 April 1876, from CF, NWP, to government NWP, PWD.

[7] A comparatively wealthy *inamdar* in Thana district of the Bombay Presidency, fighting to protect his forest rights, made a similar complaint about the avarice of the forest department: 'In the earlier days when the plantation was comparatively young, the forest department left it to your memorialist to foster and nurture the growth of the trees; as soon as they are come to be of any value, the department steps in with its prohibitory and threatening orders'. See memorial of Naro Ramachandra Parchurey, inamdar of Asnouli, Tanna collectorate, to Marquis of Salisbury, secretary of state, 6 July 1874, in NAI, rev. and agl. (forests), progs no. 34, April 1875.

[8] UPRA, PMR, file no. 2 department I, L2, superintendent, Dehra Dun, to

At the level of everyday existence, the restrictions on customary use under the Forest Act were regarded as unnecessarily irksome. Thus the government tried, not always with success, to restrict the use of deodar (cedar, the chief commercial species) by villagers, arguing that while the peasants were 'clearly entitled to wood according to their wants, nothing is said about its being *deodar*'. This legal sleight of hand did not always succeed, as villagers insisted on claiming deodar as part of their allotted grant—the wood being extensively used in the construction of houses. Again, the takeover of village grazing lands and oak forests to supply the fuel and grass requirements of Chakrata cantonment were grievances district officials acknowledged as legitimate, even if they could do little about it within the overall structure of colonial administration. Particularly contentious were proposals to regulate and ban the traditional practice of burning the forest floor before the monsoons for a fresh crop of grass. While this closure was regarded by the forest department as essential for the reproduction of timber trees, it led to the drying up of grass, and consequently a shortage of green fodder, as well as a proliferation of ticks.[9] Pointing to deodar forests where numerous young seedlings had sprung up despite constant grazing and even occasional fires, villagers were openly sceptical of the department's claim that closure was 'scientific'.[10] An additional reason for the persistent hostility towards grazing restrictions was the liberal allowance extended to nomadic cattle herders from the plains. These herdsmen were important as suppliers of milk to the cantonment and to lumbermen working in the forest. They were of the Muslim community of Gujars and, it was pointed out, they were allowed access to forest pasture even in areas

---

commissioner, Meerut div., no. 340, 15 September 1873.

[9] UPRA, PMR, L2, file no. 244, note by C. Streadfield, superintendent, Dehra Dun, 1 November 1898.

[10] See E.C. McMoir, 'Cattle Grazing in Deodar Forests', *Indian Forester*, VIII (1882), pp. 276-7.

where sheep and cattle belonging to the local peasantry were banned.[11]

The forest department also banned the use of the axe by peasants claiming their allotment of timber. Villagers demurred, arguing that the saw was too expensive, that they were not familiar with its use, that split wood lasted longer than sawn, and finally that since their forefathers had always used the axe, so would they. As a consequence, attempts to insert a clause in the land settlement of 1873 prohibiting the use of the axe came to naught. Although the settlement had considerably enhanced the land revenue, the main grievance expressed continued to be the infringement of village rights over forest. Village headmen first asked for a postponement of the settlement, and then drove a hard bargain, agreeing to the new revenue rates and the continuance of forest restrictions only on condition they were allowed the use of the axe in obtaining their grants of timber from forest land.[12]

If such petitions represented an appeal to the 'traditional' obligations of the state, the peasants of Jaunsar Bawar also resorted to extra-legal forms of protest that defied the government's control over forest extraction and utilization. Before an era of motorized transport, commercial forestry depended on fast-flowing hill rivers to carry felled logs to the plains, where they were collected by timber merchants and sold as railway sleepers. The floating logs were considered the property of the forest department; nearly 2 million sleepers were floated annually down the Yamuna and its chief tributary, the

---

[11] B.B. Osmaston, deputy conservator of forests, Jaunsar div., to assistant superintendent, Jaunsar Bawar, no. 483, 19 March 1899, source cited in fn. 6.

[12] UPRA, PMR, L2, file no. 244. Report on Forest Administration in Jaunsar Bawar, submitted by superintendent, Dehra Dun, to comm., Meerut Div., no. 520/244, 10 December 1900; L2, UPRA, PMR, L2, dept. XXI, file no., 244, E.C. Buck, offg secretary to board of revenue, NWP, to C.A. Elliot, secretary to government of NWP; UPRA, PMR, L2, file no. 2, no. 47, 17 February 1872, from settlement officer, Jaunsar Bawar, to comm., Meerut div.

Tons. Although villagers dwelling on the river banks had been 'repeatedly warned that government property is sacred', thefts were endemic. As 'every Jaunsari knows well all about the working of the Government forests and the floating of timber', officials tried to stop pilfering by levying heavier sentences than those sanctioned by the Forest Act. Thus, while each sleeper was worth only Rs 6, it was not unknown for villagers caught in possession of a sleeper to be sentenced to two months' rigorous imprisonment or a fine of Rs 30. Stiff sentences needed to be enforced, magistrates argued, as 'river thieves are pests and a deterrent fine is necessary'. Such measures failed to have the anticipated effect, and as late as 1930, a full sixty years after the state takeover of woodland, the superintendent of the district was constrained to admit that 'pilfering, misappropriating and stealing government and State timber' was 'a chronic form of crime in Jaunsar Bawar'.[13]

As in eighteenth-century England (Thompson 1975), while the infringement of forest laws was viewed as 'crime' by the state, it represented here too, as an assertion of customary rights, an incipient form of social protest. In Jaunsar Bawar the theft of floating timber and the defacement of government marks were accompanied by other forms of forest 'crime' wherein the peasantry risked a direct confrontation with the authorities—notably the infringement of laws preventing forest fires. In a fascinating incident, the head priest of the major temple of the area, which was dedicated to the god Mahashu Devta at Hanol, organized a firing of the pine forest to get rid of both the dry grass and the insects it harboured. The tall grass also attracted deer, who were a hazard to the adjoining crop-lands. Under the direction of the priest, Ram Singh, several villagers set fire to the forest on the night of 13 July 1915. Under section 78 of the Forest Act, villagers were liable to inform the forest staff of any fire in their vicinity. This they proceeded to

[13] See Trials, nos. 98 of 1925, 36 of 1927, 53 of 1930, and unnumbered trials dated May 1922, 15 June 1922, 7 April 1923, all in basta (box) for 1927-30 for Chakrata tehsil, in the Criminal Record Room, Dehra Dun collectorate.

do, but only several hours after the fire had been started. Ram Singh then advised a low-caste labourer, Dumon Kolta, to call the forest guard, but to go slowly.

While early enquiries clearly revealed that the fire was not accidental, its occurrence near the Mahashu Devta temple and the involvement of its priest made it difficult for the state to convict those accused.[14] Indeed, several prosecution witnesses, after a meeting with village headmen at the Hanol temple, suddenly retracted their confessions in court. Though the headmen were looked upon by the state to act as a bulwark of the administration, they underlined their partisan stance by appearing en masse for the defence. One elder, Ranjit Singh (whose fields were closest to the forest that was fired), expressed his disavowal of the *wajib-ul-arz* (record of rights) whereby headmen were personally required to put out fires and collect other villagers for the same purpose. As he defiantly told the divisional forest officer, 'such a wajib-ul-arz should be burnt and that his ancestors were ill-advised to have agreed to such a wajib-ul-arz with the Government'.[15]

Such organized and collective violations were hardly as frequent, of course, as the numerous acts of individual 'crime'. What differentiates Jaunsar from other forest areas where protest took a more open and militant form is the reliance on individual and largely 'hidden' forms of resistance. What is worthy of note is that this was an equally effective strategy in thwarting the aims of colonial forest administration. As an official reflecting on the history of state forestry in Jaunsar Bawar remarked, 'prosecutions for forest offences, meant as deterrents, only led to incendiarism, which was followed by more prosecutions and the vicious circle was complete'.[16]

[14] The oath in the court of Jaunsar Bawar was taken in the name of Mahashu Devta.

[15] See criminal case 98 of 1915, in source cited in fn. 13. Ram Singh and five others were sentenced to terms of imprisonment ranging from three months to a year.

[16] M.D. Chaturvedi, 'The Progress of Forestry in the United Provinces', *Indian Forester*, LI (1925), p. 365.

Clearly, these ostensibly individual acts of violation relied on a network, however informal, of consensus and support within the wider community. With all strata of village society uniformly affected by commercial forestry, every violation of the forest act could draw sustenance from a more general distrust of state control. And as individuals could quite easily be subject to the due processes of colonial justice, this resistance could hardly 'hope to achieve its purpose except through a generalized, often unspoken complicity' (Scott 1987). This complicity is strikingly evident in the refusal to testify, or alternatively the giving of false and misleading information to officials—as in the case of Ram Singh and the Hanol temple.

The Decline of the Artisanal Industry

Apart from its all too visible impact on the cultivating classes, state forest management, by restricting access to traditional sources of raw material, also contributed to the decline of various forms of artisanal industry. Chief among these was bamboo, a resource vital to many aspects of rural life. Extensively used in house construction, basketweaving, for the manufacture of furniture and musical instruments, and even as food and fodder, this plant of enormous local utility was initially treated as a weed by colonial foresters—and early management plans advocated its eradication from timber producing areas. With the discovery in the early decades of this century that bamboo was a highly suitable raw material for papermaking, there was a radical shift: foresters now encouraged industrial exploitation while maintaining restrictions on village use. Many weavers were now forced to buy bamboo from government-run depots or the open market. Limited availability also led to new forms of social conflict within the agrarian population. Thus the Baigas, who had earlier supplemented slash-and-burn agriculture with bamboo weaving, lost this subsidiary source of income when the Basors, an artisanal caste specializing in basket work, asserted their 'trade union' rights to a monopoly of bamboo supplied by the forest department (Prasad and Gadgil 1981; Elwin 1939).

While bamboo, whether obtained surreptitiously from the forest or bought in the market, continues to play an important role in present-day village society, one form of indigenous industry that collapsed under colonial rule was the manufacture of charcoal-based iron. Again, we are indebted to Verrier Elwin for a sensitive study of the industry in its declining years. In his book on the Agaria, an iron-smelting tribe of the Central Provinces, Elwin describes in chilling detail how high taxes on furnaces and diminished supplies of charcoal led to a sharp fall in the number of operating furnaces—from 510 to 136 between 1909 and 1938. Although peasants preferred the soft, malleable metal of village smelters, the changing circumstances had virtually forced the Agaria out of business, especially as improved communications had made local iron uncompetitive when compared to imported British metal. Deeply attached to their craft, the Agarias resisted as best they could, by defying forest laws concerning charcoal burning or, alternatively, migrating to nearby chiefdoms where they were accorded more liberal treatment. In an extensive survey of Madras Presidency, the first inspector general of forests, Dietrich Brandis, provided confirmatory evidence of this decay, on account of limited fuel supplies and foreign competition, of an industry that was formerly very widespread (Elwin 1942; Bhattacharya 1972; Brandis 1882).

Significantly, proposals to set up iron works controlled by European capital did briefly evoke an interest in the conservation of trees for charcoal. Pointing out that the metallic content of Indian ores was nearly twice that of European ores, several administrators urged the reservation of large tracts of forest for the benefit of European-owned and managed works using the latest technological processes. Here, the expansion of charcoal-based iron production was based on the assumption that 'iron-making by hand in India will soon be counted among the things of the past'.[17] Brandis, while acknowledging that the abundance of wood in presently inaccessible areas made the promotion of charcoal iron a potential source of forest income, advocated a different form of utilization. Articulating an early version of 'intermediate' or 'appropriate' technology, he believed that any such attempt must build upon, rather than supplant, traditional forms of manufacture. In the event both proposals came to naught, and the industry died an inevitable if slow death.[18]

Other forms of artisanal industry, too, declined under these twin pressures—the withdrawal of existing sources of raw material and the competition from machine-made, largely foreign, goods. Thus the tassar silk industry, which depended on the collection of wild cocoons from the forest, experienced a uniform decline through most of India from the 1870s onwards. Here too decay could be attributed to the new forest laws: specifically to the enhanced duties levied on weavers collecting cocoons from the forest. Although, much later, the tassar industry experienced a revival under official patronage (chiefly in response to a growing export market), the household industry was in no position to compete with the newly-formed centres of production operating from towns. A parallel case concerns the decline of village tanners and dyers, likewise denied access to essential raw materials found in the forest.[19]

[17] Anon, 'Iron-making in India', *Indian Forester*, VI (1880), pp. 203, 208.

[18] See Dietrich Brandis, 'The Utilization of the Less Valuable Woods in the Fire Protected Forests of the Central Provinces, by Iron-Making', *Indian Forester* V (1879).

[19] This paragraph is based on information kindly supplied to the authors by Dr Tirthankar Roy of the Centre for Development Studies, Trivandrum, who is doing research on handicraft production during the colonial period. Fishing communities were also affected by forest laws, being forced to use inferior wood for canoes owing to the heavy duties levied on teak by the forest department. See Grigson (1938), pp. 163-4. Among other artisanal castes, evidence from Khandesh in Western India suggests that banglemakers were almost ruined by the fee imposed on fuelwood. See Maha-

One group on whom we have comparatively little information, but who would definitely have been affected adversely by forest laws, are pastoral nomads. The Gaddis of the northwestern Himalaya (present-day Himachal Pradesh) were denied grazing for their sheep by the constitution of reserved forests. Turning to the uncultivated waste and protected forests, they found that the communities of settled cultivators who controlled these areas were reluctant to allow their sheep to graze. Forest reservation thus fostered conflict between nomads and peasants, with officials worried that the Gaddis would 'eventually go to the wall in the struggle with the village communities'. In fact the abrupt changes in the pastoral cycle pitted the Gaddis not merely against the peasants but against the forest administration as well. Ironically, even as restrictions on grazing increased, the simultaneous expansion of the lowland market for meat and wool propelled Gaddis to increase their flocks.[20]

Conclusion

The Social Idiom of Protest

In this chapter, through a synthesis of the available evidence from both primary and secondary sources, we have tried to indicate the quite astonishing range of conflicts over access to nature in British India. These conflicts were entirely consistent with the wide variety of ecological regimes, and correspondingly of social forms of resource use, which prevailed in the Indian subcontinent. Our survey reveals some interesting regularities in the forms within which protest characteristically expressed itself, notably against the state's attempts to abrogate

---

rashtra state archives, revenue department, file 73 of 1884 (personal communication from Dr Sumit Guha, St Stephen's College, Delhi).

[20] See NAI, rev. and agl. (forests), B progs no. 76, May 1875, and Tucker (1986).

traditional rights over the forest. In essence, state monopoly and its commercial exploitation of the forest ran contrary to the subsistence ethic of the peasant. To adapt a contrast first developed by E.P. Thompson in his study of the eighteenth-century food riot, if the customary use of the forest rested on a moral economy of provision, scientific forestry rested squarely on a political economy of profit (Thompson 1971).

If state monopoly severely undermined village autonomy, then what is striking about social protest is that it was aimed precisely at this monopoly. In many areas, peasants first tried petitioning the government to rescind the new regulations. When this had no visible impact they issued a direct challenge to state control, in the form of attacks on areas controlled by the forest department and worked for profit. Whether expressed covertly, through the medium of arson, or openly, through the collective violation of forest laws, protest focussed on commercially valuable species—pine, sal, teak, and deodar in different geographical regions. Quite often these species were being promoted at the expense of tree varieties less valuable commercially but of greater use to the village economy. While challenging the proprietary right of the state, peasant actions were remarkably discerning. Thus in the Kumaun movement cited above, the 'incendiary' fires of the summer of 1921 covered 320 square miles of exclusively pine forests. In other words, by design rather than accident, the equally vast areas of broad-leaved forests *also controlled by the state* were spared as being of greater use to hill agriculture (cf. Guha, Ramachandra 1989a). As in peasant movements in other parts of the world, arson as a technique of social protest had both a symbolic and an utilitarian significance—the latter by contesting the claim of the state over key resources, the former by selectively choosing targets where the state was most vulnerable.

Historical parallels with other peasant movements far removed in time and space are evident, too, in the close association of protest with popular religion. A religious idiom also reflected the sense of cultural deprivation consequent on the loss of control over resources crucial to subsistence. In many areas the customary use of nature was governed by traditional systems of resource use and conservation that involved a mix of religion, folklore, and tradition in regulating both the quantum and form of exploitation (cf. Chapters 1, 2 and 3). The suppression and occasionally even obliteration of these indigenous systems of resource management under colonial auspices was acutely felt by different communities, albeit in somewhat different ways. The Baigas, for example, resisted attempts to convert them into plough agriculturists by invoking their myth of origin, in which they had been told specifically not to lacerate the breasts of Mother Earth with the plough. As Elwin observes, 'every Baiga who has yielded to the plough knows himself to be standing on *papidharti*, or sinful earth'. Even if not entirely a willing one, this conversion was not without divine retribution. And as one Baiga put it, 'when the *bewar* [slash and burn] was stopped, and we first touched the plough . . . a man died in every village' (Elwin 1939, pp. 106-7).

The Gonds, aboriginal plough cultivators, were similarly afflicted by a melancholia, or what Elwin has elsewhere called a 'loss of nerve' (Elwin 1943). Gonds were convinced that the loss of their forests signalled the coming of Kaliyug, an Age of Darkness, in which their extensive medical tradition was rendered completely ineffective. So insidious and seductive was the power of modern civilization that even their deities had gone over to the camp of the powerful. Unable to resist the changes wrought by that ubiquitous feature of industrial society, the railway, 'all the gods took the train, and left the forest for the big cities', where with their help the urban dweller prospered (Elwin 1958, p. 58, Elwin 1960, p. 80; Hivale and Elwin 1935, pp. 16, 17).

The belief that traditional occupations were sanctioned by religion was evident, too, in the obvious reluctance of the Agaria to abandon iron smelting. According to *their* myth of origin, both slash-and-burn and plough cultivation were sinful. In the old days, when they were faithful to iron, the Agaria believed they had enjoyed better health; now that government taxes and scarcity of charcoal had forced many iron workers to take to cultivation, their gods no longer provided immunity from diseases. The real point of conflict with authority concerned charcoal burning—vividly reflected in the numerous dreams that hinged on surreptitious visits to the jungle, and which often culminated in the Agaria being intercepted and beaten up by forest officials (Elwin 1942, pp. 264-8).

The Mechanisms of Protest

Researches over the past two decades have quite convincingly demonstrated that while the peasant operates in a world largely composed of 'illiterates', and consequently many peasant movements lack a written manifesto, his actions are imbued with a certain rationality and internally consistent system of values. It is the task of the scholar, therefore, to reconstruct this ideology, an ideology that informs the peasant's everyday life as much as episodes of revolt, even where it has not been formally articulated. In this chapter too, we can discern, from a reconstruction of different episodes of social protest, a definite ideological content to peasant actions. Protest against enforced social and ecological changes clearly articulated a sophisticated theory of resource use that had both political and cultural overtones.

Of special significance is the wide variety of strategies used by different categories of resource users to oppose state intervention. Hunter-gatherers and artisans—small and dispersed communities lacking an institutional network of organization —were unable to directly challenge state forest policies. They did, however, try and continue their activities by breaking the new regulations, resorting chiefly to what one writer has called 'avoidance protest', i.e. protest that minimized the element of confrontation with the state (for example, migration and petty crime: cf. Adas 1981). In the long term, though, these groups were forced to abandon their traditional occupation and eke out a precarious living by accepting a subordinate role in the dominant system of agricultural production. Both slash-and-burn and plough agriculturists were able to mount a more sustained opposition. Their forms of resistance ranged from individual to collective defiance, from passive or 'hidden' protest to open and often violent confrontation with instituted authority. Tightly knit in cohesive 'tribal' communities, the characteristic response of jhum cultivators to forest laws was militant resistance, one that was almost wholly outside the stream of organized nationalism. The fate of this protracted resistance varied greatly across different regions. Occasionally, the colonial state capitulated, allowing the continuance of traditional forms of cultivation. More frequently the state reached an accommodation with these communities, restricting but not eliminating jhum cultivation. The resultant shrinkage of forest area available for swidden plots, when coupled with rising population, led gradually to a reduction in fallow cycles and declining yields. A large proportion of jhum cultivators, therefore, have also had no alternative to becoming landless labourers.

Settled cultivators have perhaps been more successful in retaining some degree of control over forest resources. The new laws, while sharply limiting access, did not, unlike in the cases given above, seriously threaten the livelihood of agriculturists and graziers. With subordinate forest officials often hailing from the same castes, the peasantry was often able to obtain forest produce through bribing rangers and guards. In such cases, while the *cost of access* may have increased significantly, the deprivation of forest resources was very rarely total. Moreover, Hindu peasants protesting forest restrictions were more successful in using the resources and strategies of modern nationalism (petitions, litigation) in advancing their own interests.

Whatever the specific modalities of protest in different time periods, and across different regions and forms of resource use, it was in its essence 'social'—reflecting a general dissatisfaction with state forest management, and resting heavily on traditional networks of communication and co-operation. It is note-worthy that, almost uniformly, traditional leaders of agrarian society—for example clan and village headmen—played a key role in social mobilization and action. Since the colonial state looked upon them as local bulwarks of power and authority, such leaders were subjected to conflicting pressures; however, they usually decided to throw in their lot with their kinsmen. Second, one may indicate the tenuous hold exercised by the premier nationalist organization, the Congress, over most of the movements described in this chapter. Although individuals like Gandhi may have recognized the importance of natural resources such as salt and forest produce in the agrarian econ-omy, even protest formally conducted under the rubric of Congress often enjoyed considerable autonomy from its leader-ship. Social protest over forests and pasture pre-dated the involvement of Congress: even when the two streams ran con-current, they were not always in tune with each other. Finally, these conflicts strikingly presaged similar conflicts in the post-colonial period. Thus contemporary movements asserting local claims over forest resources have, if unconsciously, replicated earlier movements in terms of their geographical spread, in the nature of their participation, and in the strategies and ideology of protest (chapter 7).

The bitter and endemic opposition to colonial forestry, spanning as it did the entire spectrum of agrarian society, testifies to the foresight of those on the losing side in the debate over the 1878 act. Hostile to village control and sceptical of the peasant's ability to manage his own resources, forest officials claimed that the 'ryot is a short-sighted individual and probab-ly will not see that his cherished popular privileges must dis-appear in any case before railroads and increased cultivation and that his best chance, and in fact, only chance, is in a well conducted forest establishment'.[21] Such rationalizations were

---

[21] NAI legislature department, progs 43-152, February 1878, appendix KK, no. 1931, 24 February 1870, from offg. CF, Madras, to acting secretary to govt. of Madras.

rejected by early nationalists and sympathetic officials, both being aware that forests were much more than an economic resource for the majority of the Indian population. The act would leave 'a deep feeling of injustice and resentment amongst our agricultural communities', the Madras board of revenue pointed out with uncanny prescience; indeed the act would 'place in antagonism to Government every class whose support is desired and essential to the object in view, from the Zamindar to the Hill Toda or Korambar'.[22] While deploring the severance of the intimate connections between plough cultivation and the forest, peasants also pointed to the adverse effects the act would have on the forest tribes which earned their livelihood through hunting, gathering and the sale of forest produce. The new restrictions, they pointed out, would force these tribes to seek other modes of subsistence—perhaps even into plundering from the peasants themselves. For no fault of their own, therefore, these forest tribes would be converted by the colonial state into criminals, with thousands being 'thrown into the jails at the cost of the general public'.[23] While such opposition may have been in vain, we can retrospectively see its justification in the fulfilment of its direct predictions. And, as the following chapters document, the colonial forestry debate has more than a fleeting relevance to contemporary developments.

The movements described in this chapter were both short-lived and unsuccessful, yet their legacy is very much with us today.

[22] See Appendix SSS in ibid.

[23] NAI, dept. of rev. & agl. (forests), B progs, no. 54, March 1878, memorial to Baron Lytton, viceroy of India, from inhabitants of Kolaba collectorate, 21 December 1877 ('signed by about 5000 people'). In fact many of the tribes later designated by the colonial administration 'criminal'—for example the Chenchus of Hyderabad and the Lodhas of Bengal—were hunter-gatherers deprived of their livelihood by the new forest laws.

CHAPTER SIX

Biomass for Business

Two Versions of Progress: Gandhi and the Modernizers

A detailed treatment of the transition from colonial rule to independence would take us too far afield (see Sarkar 1983). To properly appreciate the evolution of forest policy since 1947, however, we must set it in the context of the overall development strategy adopted by the government of independent India. The national movement had thrown up two alternative scenarios for the reconstruction of Indian economy and society. One vision was associated with Mahatma Gandhi, under whose tutelage the Indian National Congress emerged as the chief vehicle of mass nationalism. The kernel of Gandhi's social philosophy is contained in a slim tract, *Hind Swaraj*, written in 1909, which contains a massive indictment of modern western civilization. Rejecting modern industry in its totality, the pioneer organizer of indentured labour in South Africa pleaded for a revival of the organic village communities of the pre-colonial and pre-industrial past. Gandhi's idealization of the village community and the integration within it of craft production was central to the transformation from elite to mass nationalism. For it was his peculiar genius that enabled the Congress to reach out into the countryside and take into its orbit the broad masses of the people. In this political 'appropriation' of the peasantry, Gandhi's ideology, and more particularly the moral idiom in which it was couched, was to strike a sympathetic chord among social groups peripheral to the urban and Westernized sections of Indian society. Weighed down by the pressures of the state and intermediary classes, the peasantry saw in Gandhi's challenge an opportunity to recover its lost autonomy. Gandhi's appeal was strengthened by his distinctive personal style—ascetic, charismatic and all-inclusive in nature, it enabled him to fit easily into the saintly tradition of Hinduism. Another contributory factor was his reliance on a religious idiom and his invocation of symbols like the prayer meeting and hunger fast, though it has been suggested that his affinities lay more with the folk, as opposed to the classical tradition of Hinduism (cf. Chatterjee 1984; Nandy 1980).

In an apparent paradox, the Gandhian era of Indian politics saw the juxtaposition of a peasant-based politics with the increasing influence of Indian capitalists over the Congress organization. It is a central, largely unresolved question of Indian historiography that while Gandhi always gave 'theoretical primacy' to the peasant (Sarkar 1983, pp. 208-9), it was the Indian industrial class that was able to use nationalism as a vehicle to wrest concessions from the British. The isolation of the economy during World War I and the protective measures reluctantly offered to Indian industry in the years immediately following it had given a considerable filip to indigenous manufacture, notably in new areas like sugar, cement, and paper (the pioneering steel plant having already been set up by Jamsetji Tata in 1907). Simultaneously, the development of the Congress as a mass organization afforded entrepreneurs like G.D. Birla, growing in strength and confidence, an opportunity to serve as its major source of funds. While initially reluctant to support the Congress, they quickly perceived that their aims were in congruence with Gandhi's doctrinal insistence on non-violence and his desire to avoid a chaotic upheaval by mobilizing all social groups, including landlords and capitalists, against the British. Gandhi's theory of the capitalist as 'trustee' of the workers was sufficiently ambiguous, too, for the camouflaging of the shrewdly tactical support extended by industrialists to the Congress by protestations of good faith.

Whatever the anomalies in Gandhi's own thought and practice, it is clear that in the path of economic development eventually charted by the Indian nation the Mahatma's ideals were made redundant with a quite alarming rapidity. Most Indian nationalists drew a wholly different conclusion from the colonial experience, arguing that India's subjugation was a consequence of its intellectual and economic backwardness. In this perspective, as contrasted with the dynamic and progressive West, India was a once-great civilization that had stagnated and atrophied under the dead weight of tradition. Its revitalization could only come about through an emulation of the West, intellectually through the infusion of modern science, and materially through the adoption of large-scale industrialization. The person most closely associated with this view is of course Jawaharlal Nehru, Prime Minister for nearly two decades after independence.

As a nationalist leader who had spent many years in British prisons, Nehru's attitude towards the West was an ambivalent one—admiration for its industrial progress coupled with a bitterness resulting from the colonial experience. Other leaders more openly praised the West for awakening India out of its slumber. An early and influential statement may be found in the work of the Mysore engineer and statesman, Sir M. Visveswaraya. As Visveswaraya saw it, the choice before the Indian people was stark:

> They have to choose whether they will be educated or remain ignorant; whether they will come into closer contact with the outer world and become responsive to its influences, or remain secluded and indifferent; whether they will be organized or disunited, bold or timid, enterprising or passive; an industrial or an agricultural nation, rich or poor; strong and respected or

weak and dominated by forward nations. The future is in their own hands. Action, not sentiment, will be the determining factor (Visveswaraya 1920, pp. 273-4).

Operative here are the standard assumptions of modernization theory, even if Visveswaraya was writing several decades before that body of literature made its first appearance. Through rapid industrialization and urbanization, and the creation of a strong nation state, India could 'catch up' with the West. As exemplars of a radically compressed process of state-induced industrialization, Meiji Japan, Stalinist Russia, and Bismarckian Germany were variously held aloft as the beacon. Not surprisingly, this vision coincided with that of the rising Indian capitalist class. In the Bombay Plan of 1944, leading industrialists had agreed upon the importance of a strong and centralized state. This plan also stressed the need for government investment and control in heavy industry and public utilities, areas in which private investment would not easily be forthcoming (Thakurdas, *et al.* 1944; Chattopadhyay 1985).

What Visveswaraya termed the 'industrialize or perish' model of economic development was formally institutionalized in the Second Five Year Plan, for which underdevelopment was 'essentially a consequence of insufficient technological progress' (GOI 1956, p. 6; cf. also Mahalanobis 1963). Underlying a strategy of imitative industrialization was the adoption of the most 'modern' technologies, with little regard for their social or ecological consequences. In theory there were, of course, many options available to the Indian state. The technologies adopted could be capital or labour intensive; they could be oriented towards satisfying the demand for luxury goods or fulfilling the basic needs of the masses; they could degrade the environment or be non-polluting; they could use energy intensively or sparingly; and they could use the country's endowment of natural resources in a sustainable fashion or liquidate them; and so on.

In a sharply stratified society like India, these choices were critically affected by three interest groups: capitalist merchants and industrialists, the technical and administrative bureaucracy, and rich farmers. The influence of the capitalists was reflected in the massive state investments in industrial infrastructure—e.g. power, minerals and metals, and communications, all provided at highly subsidized rates—and in the virtually free access to crucial raw materials such as forests and water. Large landowners, for their part, ensured that they had an adequate and cheap supply of water, power, and fertilizer for commercial agriculture. Finally, the bureaucrat–politician nexus constructed an elaborate web of rules and regulations in order to maintain control over resource extraction and utilization. In this manner, the coalescence of economic interests and the seductive ideology of modernization worked to consolidate dominant social classes. This strategy willingly or unwillingly sacrificed the interests of the bulk of the rural population— landless labour, small and marginal farmers, artisans, nomads and various aboriginal communities—whose dependence on nature was a far more direct one.

Forests and Industrialization: Four Stages

The continuity between the forest policies of colonial and independent India is exemplified by the national forest policy of 1952. Upholding the 'fundamental concepts' of its predecessor—the forest policy of 1894—it reinforces the right of the state to exclusive control over forest protection, production, and management. With the integration of the princely states into the Indian union, the forest department in fact considerably enlarged its domain in the early years of independence. While inheriting the institutional framework of colonial forestry, however, the new government put it to slightly different uses. The one major difference in the post-1947 situation has been the rapid expansion of forest-based industry. As we argue below, the demands of the commercial–industrial sector have replaced strategic imperial needs as the cornerstone of forest policy and management. Here, one can distinguish four stages in the industrial orientation of Indian forestry.

In the first stage, foresters relied exclusively on traditional 'sustained yield' selection methods to meet the growing commercial demand. Under this regime a proportion of the more mature trees is selectively extracted at some fixed time interval, such as thirty years, with the expectation that the stock will replenish on its own between two episodes of extraction. A powerful incentive to industrial expansion was provided in the shape of handsome state subsidies in the supply of forest raw materials. These subsidies cut across conventional political alignments. In Kerala, one of the first acts of the first elected communist government in the world was to commit the administration to supply bamboo and other raw materials at Re 1 per tonne for a rayon factory set up by the Birlas, the largest industrial house in the country. Meanwhile, existing forest operations were also intensified. In the Himalayan coniferous forests, for example, rotation periods were progressively reduced (from 160 to 100 years for the chir pine) as consumers were willing to settle for trees of smaller and smaller girth. Simultaneously, research helped find new uses for hitherto unmarketable trees. Thus the large areas of twisted chir pine in Kumaun—unsuitable both for resin tapping and railway sleepers—were sold to paper mills once their suitability for pulping had been established (Guha, Ramachandra 1989a, chapter 6).

While these concessions were consistent with the strategy of state subsidies to private industry, conventional management practices were unable to keep step with the escalating commercial demand. Due to a variety of reasons—including an inadequate data base, the failure to take account of rural demand, excessive grazing and fire, and the violation of standing prescriptions—the selection system did not generate the expected 'sustained' yields. A new strategy of intensive forestry was called for. One of its early and most influential proponents was a visiting expert of the Food and Agricultural Organization, who called upon the forest department to adopt a more dynamic approach. An 'expanding economy on the eve of modern industrialization', he observed, 'requires the *highest* tonnage of production of organic raw material within the *shortest* possible period, and at the *lowest* possible cost' (Von Monroy 1960, p. 8, emphasis added). Forest officials took up the challenge, arguing that the extremely low productivity was due to the 'uneconomic' and 'conservation oriented' approach that had hitherto characterized Indian forestry. The emphasis of the new strategy would be on the production of 'economically attractive resources', i.e. plantations of quick-growing, high-yielding tree species, to replace 'inferior' slow growing ones. Through their emphasis on rapid industrialization, foresters hoped the five year plans would 'compel' the government to 'revise' its policy from one of satisfying the demands of the rural population towards more directly serving the developing forest-industries sector (Sagreya 1979, pp. 15ff, 169; Nair 1967; Chandra and Srivastava 1968). Then in the early seventies the National Commission on Agriculture retrospectively set the official seal on industrial forestry by recommending a strategy whose first element 'would have to be production forestry for industrial wood production' (NCA 1976, p. 39).

From the early sixties the central government provided financial incentives, in the form of central plan funds, to encourage state governments to take up industrial plantations. 'Production' forestry has had as its mainspring the clear-felling of existing forest stands and their replacement by fast-growing commercial species. As dwindling forest stocks and traditional methods of 'sustained yield' harvesting were found inadequate to meet the growing commercial and industrial demand, foresters set aside working plans for programmes of clear-felling and the plantation of quick-growing, chiefly exotic, species. These plantations, the official manual of silviculture admits, were necessitated by the shortage of timber caused by the 'too rapid exploitation' of the mature stock of natural forests (Champion and Seth 1968, p. 444).

The attempts to increase the economic productivity of forests relied on two distinct kinds of monoculture. The first and more widespread strategy involved the raising of eucalyptus and tropical pine plantations for industrial raw material. Additionally, foresters were encouraged to grow species like teak and rosewood which could be converted into high-quality furniture and generate valuable foreign exchange. Indeed, on account of its revenue-generating potential, foresters were advised to plant teak, *wherever possible*, in and outside of its forest habitat (Champion and Seth 1968). Encouraging such trends, foreign aid agencies believed 'it would be highly advantageous for the Indian economy to replace a significant percentage of the mixed tropical hardwood species with man-made forests of desirable [sic] species such as eucalyptus, tropical pine and teak' (USAID 1970, p. viii).

The salient question, which the votaries of industrial forestry never stopped to ask, was 'desirable' for whom? By hastening the conversion of mixed forests into single species stands, monoculture was putting the final touches to the separation of forestry from subsistence agriculture. Indeed, the local populations adversely affected by the new plantations have reacted sharply to its imposition (see chapter 7). However, more proximate ecological causes underlie the failure of plantation forestry to realize projected yields. The expected yields from eucalyptus plantations varied from 10 tonnes/ha/year on poor sites, to 30 tonnes/ha/year on favourable sites. However, available data from 25 forest ranges in Karnataka show actual yield varying from 10 to 43 per cent of projected yield. In Haliyal division, a region with abundant rainfall, yields were as low as 0.86 to 2.22 tonnes/ha/year, with an average of 1.4 tonnes/ha/year, i.e. 10 per cent of the lower limit of the projected yields. In Bangalore, a dry zone, yields were 20 per cent of those projected (Gadgil, Prasad and Ali 1983). Similar results have been obtained from Kerala, where a study of 70 eucalyptus plantations revealed that annual increments were between 15 per cent and 30 per cent of those estimated by the forest department (Krishnakutty and Chundamannil 1986).

In some areas, in fact, productivity was close to zero. In many high-rainfall tracts of the Western Ghats, eucalyptus plantations were taken up on a large scale by clear-felling excellent rain forests. These were everywhere attacked by a fungus known as pink disease. In effect, tropical rain forests were converted into man-made deserts.

Even when judged on its own narrow terms, therefore, plantation forestry has been a miserable failure. Faced with a continuing crisis of raw-material supply, the wood-based industry has, since the middle of the last decade, adopted yet a third strategy to supplement harvesting from natural forests and the creation of man-made plantations. It has turned increasingly to farmers for the supply of fibrous raw material. Although the market price of wood is far higher than the subsidized rates at which it was being supplied produce from government forests, companies have preferred to deal directly with private farmers.

This third stage in the industrial orientation of forest policy has witnessed a veritable revolution in cash-crop agriculture. In the last decade, millions of farmers have taken to planting tree crops, which are hypothecated and sold on maturity to rayon and paper manufacturers. Ironically, the propagation of eucalyptus has been closely tied to a programme of 'social forestry' whose stated aims are quite different, namely supplying fuel, fodder, and small timber to agriculturists. In theory, social forestry programmes have three components: plantation on individual holdings ('farm forestry'), fuel woodlots on government land and along roads and canals, and community forests planted and managed by villages on common land. In principle, the programme emphasizes the last component—community forestry. However, its original aims were quickly subverted. A mid-term review by the World Bank, one of the programme's chief sponsors, conclusively showed that of its three components only farm forestry was at all successful.

In Uttar Pradesh, for example, community self-help woodlots achieved only 11 per cent of their targets, whereas farm forestry overshot its target by 3430 per cent, an unprecedented rate of success for a government-sponsored programme. Observable trends in other states were very similar. Within the farm-forestry programme, the percentage of seedlings reaching big farmers (i.e. those whose holdings exceed two hectares) was over 60 per cent (CSE 1985; Blair 1986).

And what do these farmers plant? Overwhelmingly, commercial species such as eucalyptus. Indeed, nearly 80 per cent of all seedlings distributed by the forest department to farmers were of eucalyptus. There has been a veritable eucalyptus revolution in states such as Karnataka, Gujarat and Haryana, with perhaps a million hectares of farmland being brought under different varieties of the tree. Eucalyptus has been praised by foresters as the panacea for all ills and bitterly attacked by environmentalists as being totally unsuited to Indian conditions. Its critics invoke social as well as environmental arguments. Although the programme of clear-felling rain forests to raise plantations of exotic species was quite ill-advised, the ecological impact of eucalyptus on farmland (as compared to other cash crops such as sugarcane) is less clear. Perhaps the social implications are more serious. In some areas, it is replacing food crops (ragi), in other areas cash crops (cotton). With an assured market and handsome advances offered by industry, many farmers now find it profitable to switch from traditional agricultural crops to eucalyptus even on irrigated holdings. However, as it is much less labour intensive than the crops it replaces, this substitution is in effect displacing agricultural labour from existing sources of employment in conditions of high rural unemployment. Where eucalyptus displaces food crops, it may increase the cost of grains for the poor, in so far as they earlier obtained a portion of their wages as grain and are now forced to turn at a greater real cost to the market. Finally, it has been observed that eucalyptus, as it involves little supervision and is not browsed by animals, is an attractive option for absentee landlords, especially the urban gentry. In these several ways, farm forestry is very likely intensifying the already grave inequalities within the agrarian sector (Shiva *et al.* 1982; Chandrashekar *et al.* 1987).

The explanation for the eucalyptus epidemic is a relatively straightforward one. As the state, upon whom the private sector had traditionally relied, exhausted the forests under its command, industrialists have turned to private farmers.

According to one study (Prasad, personal communication), whereas the average yield and cost of production for government plantations were 2 tonnes/ha/year and Rs 2000 respectively, the corresponding figures for farmers were greater than 10 tonnes/ha/year and between Rs 500–1000 respectively (one must note here that the price at which government supplied wood to industry from its plantations was vastly lower than the actual cost of production). So farmers are more productive than the industry-oriented plantations of the forest department. While indirectly availing of state subsidies in the form of free seedlings and technical help, private farmers have emerged as a far more reliable ally for an industry plagued with chronic raw-material shortages.

Indeed the hiatus between precept and practice is striking even for a government programme. Social forestry, claims a leading forester, 'involves the people at all levels with raising forests as their own assets for their own use'. It aims 'to provide forest goods and services in rural areas where these are needed the most' (Tewari 1981). The programme, a high-level committee likewise affirms, 'is the practice of forestry for meeting the felt needs of rural areas, as against that for meeting the (needs) of the commercial and industrial interests' (GOI 1980, p. 5).

In official rhetoric, therefore, 'social forestry' revives a plea made by Voelcker nearly a century earlier (Voelcker 1893) for the creation of 'fuel and fodder reserves' to overcome the separation between forestry and agriculture. Yet within a decade it stands exposed as oriented almost exclusively towards commercial farmers and industrial units. In so far as it has bypassed more pressing questions of social equity and environmental stability while pursuing commercial ends, farm forestry is akin to the earlier policy of clear-felling natural forests to raise industry-oriented plantations. In this sense, as a leading environmentalist has observed, the recent afforestation of parts of India has been as negligent of the needs of the vast bulk of the rural population as the continuing deforestation in other parts of the country (Agarwal 1986).

While abandoning the forest department for the commercial farmer, the paper and rayon industries have also been lobbying intensely for the allotment of government land as captive plantations. Along with a massive import of wood and paper pulp, the move for captive plantations can be said to constitute an emerging fourth stage in the industrial orientation of forest policy. In one very important case, a company of the giant Birla group, Harihar Polyfibres Ltd (KPC), has formed a joint-sector company, Karnataka Pulpwoods Ltd, with the government of the state of Karnataka. KPL has been allotted 75,000 acres of land, spread over six districts, for growing eucalyptus as raw material for the exclusive use of Harihar Polyfibres.

The formation of KPL has been challenged in the supreme court as being harmful to the interests of peasants, who were fulfilling their own biomass requirements from the land handed over to the new company. The court judgment (awaited at the time of writing) will be of considerable significance, for it may determine the principles on which public land can or cannot be used by private industry. The controversy raises with particular cogency the question of 'biomass for whom and for what?' If the judgment is in favour of KPL, it could inaugurate a fourth stage in the industrial orientation of forest policy, in which large industry is allowed to lease land at highly favourable terms. While the ministry of environment and forests in New Delhi has indicated its opposition to captive plantations (whether undertaken directly by the concerned industry or in the joint sector), many state governments are eager to go ahead with KPL-style schemes. Industries are eagerly queuing up in half a dozen states, including Orissa, Madhya Pradesh, and Maharashtra.

TABLE 6.1

FOUR STAGES OF INDUSTRIAL FORESTRY

Period	Method	Species	Agency	Prime beneficiary
1947	Selection felling	Indigenous commercial species	Forest department	Industry
1960-85	Clearfelling and mono-cultural plantations	Chiefly exotics	Forest department	Industry
1975	Farm forestry	Chiefly exotics	Commercial farmers	Commercial farmers and industry
1985	Import and captive plantations	Exotics	Joint sector	Industry, importers

The Balance Sheet of Industrial Forestry

Whereas between 1860 and 1947 forests were a strategic raw material crucial for imperial interests—such as railway expansion and the world wars—since independence the commercial–industrial sector has been the prime beneficiary of state forest management. The growth in wood-based industries, and the expansion in demand for processed wood products, have been the determining influence on forest policy in this period. While the ends may be different, the means to achieve these ends have been very similar in the two periods. Both the 'hardware' and 'software' of forest administration in independent India have been closely modelled on colonial forestry.

The continuity between colonial and post-colonial forestry

regimes is most clearly manifest in the system of ownership. The state has contrived to uphold its monopoly over forest ownership. In some ways it has even strengthened its hold, as for example through the Forest Conservation Act, 1980, which actively discourages the participation of individuals and communities in forest plantation and protection. Until very recently it has also inhibited tree plantations by individuals and communities, reserving to itself the right of disposal of commercially valuable species *wherever planted*. State monopoly is reinforced by the preference for macroplanning, wherein national priorities take precedence over local priorities. As enshrined in the National Forest Policy of 1952, the exclusion of local communities from the benefits of forest management is legitimized as being in the 'national interest', namely that the 'country as a whole' is not deprived of a 'national asset' by the mere 'accident [*sic*] of a village being situated close to a forest' (GOI 1952, p. 29).

The rationale for government ownership is the belief that private individuals and groups will not invest in tree crops whose gestation period often exceeds a lifetime. However, as Part I of this book shows, many castes and communities have had informal systems of natural resource management. Moreover, these decentralized and small-scale systems were far better adapted to the rhythms and demands of subsistence agriculture, husbandry, and crafts production. State management has substituted a set of *external* constraints for a set of *internal* constraints which operated in a local, communal context. Meanwhile as the 'national interest' has virtually been equated with the industrial sector, local populations have been further alienated from the activity and practice of forest management.

Another element of continuity is in the monopoly of technically trained experts on decisions concerning forest management. Foresters draw a very clear line between 'professionals' and 'non-professionals', recognizing neither the local user's knowledge about forest conditions nor his/her definition of a resource and priorities in its management. Resource use is thus separated from resource management. Again, the ideology of scientific forestry is clearly at variance with the facts. For peasants have, in using the forests for centuries, drawn upon an intimate knowledge of local ecological conditions accumulated and passed on through the generations (see Fortmann and Fairfax 1989).

TABLE 6.2

Forest Revenue and Surplus, Selected Years
(at current prices)

Average for period	Revenue (Rs million)	Surplus (Rs million)
1951-52 to 1954-54	240-1	133.9
1956-57 to 1958-59	418.4	247.2
1961-62 to 1963-64	693.8	371.5
1966-67 to 1968-69	1075.0	508.7
1969-70 to 1970-71	1358.7	623.8
1975-76	2927.0	1275.0
1976-77	3355.0	1466.0
1980-81	4725.5	1547.2

Source : NCA (1976); PUDR (1982).

Thirdly, the forest department, assigned the role of a revenue generating organ by the colonial state, continued to be a money-spinner for the government of independent India (Table 6.2). The emphasis on revenue generation, encouraged by many state governments, has contributed to the overexploitation of growing stock. A narrow commercial orientation is also reflected in research priorities. A recent attempt at consolidating forest research produced individual bibliographies for commercially valuable species such as teak, sal and chir pine, whereas the many varieties of oak, so crucial for sustaining Himalayan agriculture, only merited a single bibliography. Actually, the broad-leaved forests of the upper Himalaya, condemned by the British as valueless, have in recent years attracted the attention of the commercial sector, after work at the

Forest Research Institute established their suitability for use as badminton rackets (Guha, Ramachandra 1989a). Again, the continuing raw-material crisis of the paper industry has encouraged research on agricultural residues as possible substitutes for scarce forest raw material. In both cases, scientists have unwittingly deprived local populations of a resource earlier earmarked exclusively for their use.

Fourth, in the system of forest management which has now prevailed for over a century, no social group has any stake in the long-term husbanding of forest resources. This is especially true of the three segments of our society most closely connected with forest utilization: the rural poor, forest-based industry, and the forest department itself. Unfortunately, the self-interest of none of these sectors is served by a proper maintenance of the tree cover. The rural poor can at best derive very low wages by working as forest labourers or by selling firewood, and since they do not share in the profits made from the forest produce these wages always remain low, at the subsistence level. While the rural poor gain little by protecting the tree crop, so far they have always succeeded in establishing their ownership over a patch of land by cutting down the trees and putting it to the plough. This is one reason why 2.5 million hectares of forest land has been lost to cultivation between 1951 and 1976 (see Table 6.3).

TABLE 6.3

The Loss of Forest Area for Various Purposes Between 1951 and 1976

Purpose	Area (thousand ha)
River valley projects	479.1
Agricultural purposes	2506.9
Construction of roads	57.1
Establishment of industries	127.2
Miscellaneous purposes	965.4

Forest-based industry and timber merchants both gain least in the short run by preserving forest stock. Instead, they can maximize immediate profit by concentrating on minimizing the present cost of resources. This is what they have done, in the process frequently resorting to violations of forestry regulations. Further, they have been given little incentive for investing in the preservation of resources. The very low prices, well below replacement cost, at which they had access to resources meant that they had no motivation to invest substantially in resource regeneration. Of course in recent years, when the forest department has failed them, industry has turned to helping private farmers grow wood, by providing them a remunerative price and loan facilities. But by and large the industrial sector has so far concentrated only on exploiting newer and newer species in more remote areas, as the currently used resources have been exhausted one by one (see below).

Meanwhile, the bureaucratic apparatus, with its diffusion of responsibility and lack of any accountability, provides no motivation to a good officer for the proper management of resources under his charge, nor disincentives for those who mismanage. Forest officers are frequently transferred, never spending more than three or four years in one assignment. As a consequence, there is little commitment within the forest bureaucracy towards good husbanding of the resources over which they are temporarily in charge.

Sequential Exploitation: A Process Whereby a Whole Flock of Geese Laying Golden Eggs is Massacred One by One

During the British regime timber remained the main commodity in demand—teak, initially for the construction of ships and gun carriages, later for building-construction and furniture; deodar, pine, sal and some of the evergreen tree species for railway sleepers. There were of course other demands, such as wood for charcoal-making in the early days of the railways. But by and large the thrust of forest management was on the gradual conversion of India's forests into single species stands of teak, sal and conifers. The working plans ultimately aimed at bringing about this change, and if the natural mixed forests were overexploited, this was a matter of little concern. The pace of such overexploitation was especially great during the two world wars, and the forest working plans written immediately after World War II uniformly speak of the need to give the ravaged forests a long period of rest.

But no such rest was forthcoming, because India achieved independence soon after the end of World War II and launched on a course of industrial development. Forest-based industry in India had its hesitant beginnings with the use of bamboo for paper manufacture only in the 1920s. In 1924-5 just 5800 tonnes of bamboo were so used; by the beginning of the World War II this had risen to 58,000 tonnes. By 1987, however, paper and board production had risen to 2.66 million tonnes, corresponding to a raw-material consumption of over 5 million tonnes, a thousandfold increase over a period of sixty years. There has been an even more rapid expansion in the capacity of a number of other forest-based industries: plywood, polyfibre, rayon, and matchsticks to mention only the most important ones.

The stated policy in independent India was to enhance the forest stocks by 50 per cent, raising the overall area under forest from 22 per cent to 33.3 per cent. The existing forest stocks were then meant to be used sustainably, while additional areas were to be brought under tree cover. There was, however, no apparent attempt to match the growing capacity of forest-based industry with sustainable yields from existing forest stocks. Firstly, there was a wholly inadequate data base to assess sustainable yields from any forest area. Even for *Bambusa arundinacea*, which had been established as an excellent raw material for paper in 1912, the nature of the growth curve of an individual bamboo and the effect on growth of extraction and grazing remained to be understood (Prasad and Gadgil 1981). And there was no understanding at all of the complex rain-forest ecosystems of the Western Ghats, the north-eastern hill states, and the Andaman and Nicobar islands, which provided raw material for the exploding plywood industry (FAO 1984; Saldanha 1989). At the same time, the growth in industrial capacity followed the economic rationale of a continuing increase, so long as investment was perceived to be profitable enough in the short run by the entrepreneur. Indeed such growth in industrial capacity parallels the logic of growth in the fishing fleet explored by Dasgupta (1982). Dasgupta shows that fishing boats will continue to be added so long as the net gain, i.e. the balance of gross profit minus the harvesting cost, remains above the threshold of the minimal acceptable level of profitability. This is likely to lead to overexploitation, if the market price of the produce is high relative to the harvesting and processing costs. Economists therefore recommend a tax to hike costs to a level that would avoid the excessive growth of harvesting effort. In the case of forest-based industry in independent India, exactly the opposite situation prevailed. The industries were subsidized so heavily, and could hike up the prices of their produce so freely in a seller's market, that their profitability has remained high, even as forest stocks have plummetted. Thus in the 1950s the paper industry was provided bamboo at the throwaway price of Rs 1 per tonne, when the prevailing market price was over Rs 2000 per tonne. Indeed, as early as 1860 Cleghorn records that local basket weavers were being charged at the rate of Rs 5 per tonne. Even in the 1980s, bamboo prices were raised only to Rs 200 to 500 per tonne, when market prices were well over Rs 5000 per tonne. The result of this state-subsidized profitability of forest-based industry has been an explosive growth in industrial capacity, and a non-sustainable use of forest stocks that may be summed up in the words of a forester speaking of the evergreen forests of Karnataka's Western Ghats: 'Most of the areas which were worked during the past have deteriorated considerably and it is doubtful if ever they would regenerate to their original structure' (Rai 1981).

It is worthwhile to follow the pattern of the over-use of

forest resources over the last thirty years. This pattern provides a chilling illustration of *sequential overexploitation*, i.e. the exhaustion of resources in a sequence of continuing decline in quality as well as in quantity. Such overexploitation can be discerned along six dimensions: (i) the mode of acquiring the resource, whether by gathering or production; (ii) control over the land from which the resource is acquired; (iii) the locality from which the resource is acquired, whether close to or far from where the industry is situated; (iv) the kind of terrain from which the resource is acquired, i.e. easy or difficult of access; (v) the plant species used, more or less suitable for the purpose; and (vi) the size of the tree used.

Thus the West Coast Paper Mill in northern Karnataka was set up in 1958 in the belief that the neighbouring state-owned reserved forest would supply *in perpetuity* all the requirements of the mill from the natural growth of bamboo, essentially at bare harvesting cost. By 1978 the mill had expanded to 200 tonnes per day, although less and less bamboo was available from the forests originally allotted to the mill. The mill gradually replaced bamboo with hardwood, also from the natural forests, and a large proportion of plantation-grown eucalyptus. Today only 10 per cent of the mill's raw material is bamboo, obtained at about Rs 650 per tonne (after the government has revised royalty rates) from nearby forests, while the rest is mainly eucalyptus (65 per cent)—a significant proportion from farm land—casuarina (13 per cent) and mixed hardwood (10 per cent) costing about Rs 1000 per tonne at mill site. There has thus been a continuous shift in raw material, from that merely extracted from natural forests at little cost, to that produced on plantations or fields with substantial inputs and at a far higher cost (Guha, S.R.D. 1989).

The ownership of land from which the resources are being supplied has also shifted in sequence. Initially all resources for a mill like Harihar Polyfibres in Karnataka came from state-controlled reserved forest land, which was used to supply raw materials at highly subsidized prices. As these supplies were no longer adequate, the mill shifted to purchasing eucalyptus grown on private farmlands. Here the element of state subsidy was restricted to the supply of free seedlings to farmers; thus the mill had to spend substantially larger amounts for the raw material. More recently, as we have seen, the mill has begun shifting the focus of resource production to erstwhile village common lands to be planted up by a joint-sector company, Karnataka Pulpwoods Limited.

Third, forest-based industries were started off with catchments close to the factory site from which the raw materials would come, supposedly in perpetuity. Thus the West Coast Paper Mill at Dandeli was expected to derive its resources from the districts of Uttara Kannada and Belgaum, while the Mysore Paper Mill at Bhadravathi was expected to do so from Shimoga district. As Figures 6.1 and 6.2 show, however, the resources of these areas have long been exhausted. While the joint sector Mysore Paper Mill then had to tap the entire state, the private sector West Coast Paper Mill is scrounging for bamboo and other woods from all over the country (Gadgil and Prasad 1978).

Fourth, the industrial demand has initially been met from the flat, more easily accessible, terrain. As the resources of such a terrain are exhausted through the process of selection felling, these areas are clear-felled and brought under the so-called conversion circle to develop teak or eucalyptus plantations. At the same time, the much steeper terrain earlier constituted as protection circle (from the point of view of watershed conservation) is brought first under selection and then conversion circle. Figure 6.3 schematically shows how this process has gone on in the Quilon forest division of Kerala (FAO 1984).

A fifth dimension of sequential overexploitation is the acceptance of less and less suitable species, as the more desirable ones are exhausted. As Table 6.4 shows, the Indian Plywood Manufacturing Company at Dandeli has increased the species utilized from 36 in 1946 to 61 in 1975, continually adding new localities for exploitation as well.

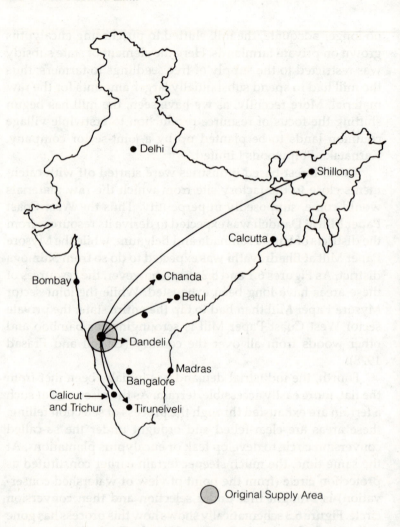

Figure 6.1
Areas from which the West Coast Paper Mills, Dandelli, began to draw
bamboo in the late 1970's (after Gadgil and Prasad, 1978).

○ Original Supply Area

Figure 6.2
Areas from which Mysore Paper Mills, Bhadravati, began to draw bamboo in
the late 1970's (after Gadgil and Prasad, 1978).

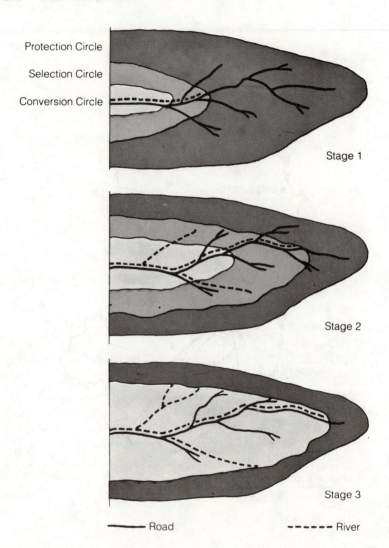

Protection Circle

Selection Circle

Conversion Circle

Stage 1

Stage 2

Stage 3

———— Road   - - - - - River

Figure 6.3

Successive changes in designation of areas under protection, selection and
conversion circles in the Quilon Forest Division of Kerala over the period
1950–1980 (after FAO, 1984).

TABLE 6.4

SPECIES AND AREAS ALLOTTED TO THE INDIAN PLYWOOD
MANUFACTURING CO. LTD, DANDELI AND ITS ALLIES

Year	Number of species allotted	Concession areas added
1946	36	Gund, Virnoli, Kulgi, Sambrani & Dandeli Ranges
1948	45	Nil
1959	48	Anshe - Ulve, Supa plateau series 2 & 3, Dandeli R. series 6 and 7. More areas of Yellapur, Sonda, unorganized forests of Mundgod, Nirsol slopes, Sonda high forests, Yekkambi
1961	52	Nil
1974	53	
1975	61	Nil

SOURCE : Gadgil and Subash Chandran (1989).

Finally, there is a general though not overwhelming tendency to decrease the minimum girth for exploitation through selection felling. Table 6.5 shows the fluctuations in the exploitable girths under a succession of working plans for Ankola in coastal Karnataka. Rather than go to very low-girth sizes under selection felling, however, the tendency is to clear-fell forests being exhausted under selection felling regimes to raise plantations.

In the case of Indian forestry, one can thus discern a whole complex of processes leading to resource exhaustion. These processes vary greatly, depending on the part of the country and the industry concerned. However, four broad phases are discernible. In the first phase, lasting till the 1960s, selection fellings from natural forests were the mainstay of wood-based industry. When this was found inadequate, large-scale programmes of clear-felling and the raising of plantations of fast-growing species such as eucalyptus were launched with the

TABLE 6.5
EXPLOITABLE SIZE OF TIMBER UNDER WORKING PLANS OF ANKOLA HIGH FORESTS

Name of the tree	Coppleston 1901	Pearson 1918	Miller 1918	Millet 1927	War felling 1940-45	Mundkur 1955	
						WC I	WC II
Tectona grandis	6½-7'	6'	6'	6'	4'	6'	6'
Terminalia tomentosa	–	7-6'	6'	5'	5'	3'	6'
Terminalia paniculata	–	–	7'	7'	5'	5'	6'
Lagerstroemia microcarpa	–	7-6'	7'	7'	5'	5'	6'
Dalbergia latifolia	–	6'	6'	7'	5'	5'	6'
Adina cordifolia	–	8-7'	7'	7'	5'	5'	6'
Other species	–	6'	7'	7'	5'	variable	variable

WC I — Working Circle I — Plains Working Circle
WC I I — Working Circle I I — Teak bearing areas

SOURCE : Gadgil and Subash Chandran (1989)

backing of special plan schemes by the central government. While clear-felling provided large amounts of wood, the productivity of plantations so raised was well below what was expected. Notably enough, this large-scale plantation effort had been launched without any careful trials of eucalyptus, or indeed any other species such as tropical pines. Consequently, by the mid 1970s came the next phase—of 'social' forestry, whose single remarkable success has been the raising of industrial softwoods on agricultural lands, and whose major failure relates to biomass for rural needs. The latest phase is a three-pronged attack, beginning in the 1980s, to fully open up the resources of untapped areas such as Arunachal Pradesh and the Andaman and Nicobar islands, liberalize the import of pulp and timber, and take over village common lands for industrial wood production.

The Profligacy of Scientific Forestry

The strategies of resource use introduced by the British and continued by the government of independent India make a sharp contrast with earlier traditions of ecological prudence. As Parts I and II of this book document, the traditional patterns organized sustainable resource use by the implementation of a number of thumb rules such as the provision of refugia like sacred groves and sacred ponds, protection to keystone resources like *Ficus* trees, protection to specially vulnerable or critical life-history stages such as nesting birds, certain (probably conservative) quotas on how much fuelwood or leaf manure may be extracted from a village forest, and the diversification of the use of biological resources by endogamous groups. These thumb rules were bound to be arbitrary, and were implemented on the basis of magico-religious sanctions and social conventions.

A very different belief system was crafted on the European continent and brought to India by the British. The central tenet of this European belief system was the primacy of the objective of making maximum profit on the market. The currency in which this profit was measured was money; so that the whole diversity of resources that was earlier of significance to humans could now be transformed into money. This happened of course because there were now technologies available to change resources from one form into another, and into products that would fetch money; and new technologies were being continually invented to transform them in newer ways. All this meant that the goal of immediate profit from the most valuable resource of the moment was far more attractive than the goal of long-term conservation of a diversity of resources. The world dominance of European culture was a result of the European discovery of how to acquire mastery over nature, as well as how to translate this knowledge into technologies which manipulate nature. Along with the market, therefore, it was science and technology that became the most respected elements within the belief system of Europe. This science and technology had explicitly stated assumptions about the working of nature: it recognized only those natural forces whose working could be observed empirically. At the physical and chemical levels, where one is dealing with relatively simple phenomena, this methodology worked very well—Newton's laws of motion, the steam engine, and cannons that could be fired accurately from ships were among its many triumphs. The same methodology was then sought to be applied to more complex phenomena, including the working of ecosystems and human societies.

There were serious difficulties in applying the 'scientific' method at the level of these more complex phenomena. Consider, for instance, the functioning of a tropical humid forest, which is an interacting system of hundreds of plant species, along with thousands of species of micro-organisms as well as animals of varying sizes. To this day we do not even have a complete inventory of all the living organisms from a single hectare of any one tropical humid forest. We are also quite ignorant of how the populations of these thousands of species interact with each other. Only within the last few years have we realized, for instance, that insect predation on seeds or fungal infections on seedlings may profoundly influence these systems. Even if we were to leave aside ecosystem dynamics and concentrate on the population of a single species, we are able to say little about its population dynamics. For instance, we know very little about the 'regeneration niches' of most tropical-forest tree species. Forgetting even the population and focusing on individual plants, we know little about the growth patterns of tropical forest trees, or of the timing and periodicity of their seed production.

How can one then apply this supposedly 'scientific' method in decisions on how to manipulate a resource base such as a tropical humid forest? Obviously, all that is possible are a few crude prescriptions based on rules of thumb. If the object was the conservation of resources, these rules would differ scarcely at all from pre-scientific prescriptions of earlier times, precisely because our empirical knowledge of the workings of such a system has progressed only marginally beyond the empirical knowledge possessed by people who observed these systems, albeit informally, for generations. In our 'scientific' system sacred groves may be replaced by preservation plots, but the notion is the same, and the establishment of preservation plots has exactly the same arbitrariness.

However, if the object is not the conservation of a diverse resource base but the maximization of profits in the short run, rule-of-thumb prescriptions are obviously likely to be quite different. Their orientation, as we know too well, is quick harvests, and the replacement of a diversity of commercially less-valuable species by commercially valuable species—as perceived at that point in time. Add to this the fact that the maximization of profits has to accrue to a state apparatus and not to local people, and you get an additional rule of thumb, namely that as much land as possible should be brought under as complete a control as is possible by the apparatus of state. This is precisely what British forestry management attempted to do in India. While the British had radically different objectives from the traditional forestry management of village populations, they were hardly better informed about the working of forests as a result of 'scientific' investigations: such knowledge simply did not exist. It was therefore quite correct to term it 'forestry in the commercial interests of the state'; it was quite erroneous to call it 'scientific forestry in the interest of resource conservation'—as it was in fact incorrectly called.

Why was this misnomer applied? It was clearly a double misrepresentation of both the objectives and of the methodology employed to achieve those objectives. The objectives were represented as 'sustained yield' in the 'national interest', although in practice the yield was rarely sustained and the interests served were much narrower than society as a whole. The methodology too was misrepresented as 'scientific', an ideological device related to the high regard which science enjoyed in European society because of its success in dealing with simpler phenomena.

Let us take the objectives first. Did the consequences match the professed objective of sustained yield? Indeed not. The forest resource base was not used sustainably; rather, the pattern of its utilization is best described as successive overexploitation. For example, forests taken over by the state were classified into two categories: protected forests, taken over by the state but available to villagers for their requirements of gathered material; and reserved forests, fully at the disposal of the state and supposedly managed on a sustained-yield basis. (This classification itself acknowledges that there was no intention to manage the protected forests on a sustained-yield basis). Reserved forests were further categorized into protection forests and production forests. Protection forests were on sites such as steep hillsides or banks of streams, where an undisturbed vegetation cover was considered necessary for maintaining soil cover and the hydrological cycle. If resource conservation was the genuine objective of forest management, the delineation of such protection forests would have been independent of the commercial feasibility of their exploitation. In fact, protection forests were originally declared in areas difficult of access; as these areas become accessible, they have been reclassified as production forests. This, for instance, has been the case with hill-slope forests near the Kudremukh iron ore project in Karnataka. The terrain near the crestline of the Western Ghats where this project is located was earlier without any roads, and was declared 'protection forest' on the grounds that it covered steep hill-slopes. It was reclassified as 'production forest' as soon as the project led to the construction of roads into the area. Similarly, the high-level oak, fir and spruce forests of the Himalaya have been converted into production forests with the expansion of the road network into those areas.

The second issue relates to the methodology of scientific forestry: can it be appropriately termed scientific? The basis of modern science is its careful grounding in empirical fact. It proposes a model of how nature works, based on systematic observation; it then suggests that certain predictions follow if this model is adequate; it verifies these predictions, and if falsified, makes appropriate changes in its model. This model suggests further predictions, which are then sought to be verified in an ongoing process. Now, the 'scientific' working of forests ought to start with a model based on empirical observation, and make predictions about the yields being of such-and-such quantitative level, and that they would change in such-and-such fashion with time, given a certain system of management. These predictions would then be verified, to check if they have worked in practice; and if not, the model would be altered accordingly. This cycle would then become an ongoing one.

None of the elements of these processes occur in the exercise of 'scientific' forestry. There is a wholly inadequate data base which underpins the initial model of how the forest works; there is no proper verification to see if the prescriptions have worked, nor why they have or have not worked; and there is no appropriate adjustment of the model in the light of any attempted verification. Tropical forests are exceedingly diverse species-rich systems, quite unlike the species-poor temperate forests. The nutrient cycle in tropical forests is quite distinctive, too, with the bulk of nutrients being held in the standing biomass, rather than in the soil. These facts imply that ecosystem and community-level interactions—for instance soil–plant relationships and inter-species interactions—are of far greater significance in tropical-forest dynamics. These are essentially ignored in the models of the working of temperate forests, such as single-species stands of pines that temperate-region foresters deal with; they have been equally ignored in the 'scientific' forestry introduced into India. Temperate foresters also ignore population dynamics, since they work with single-species stands maintained at a certain density, and Indian forestry thus also ignored population dynamics. Temperate foresters treated the dynamics of growth of an individual plant as almost the only necessary empirical data base, and this was also the approach adopted by 'scientific' forestry in India. The model then was that every tree species has a characteristic growth curve, such that the increment to biomass increases till the tree reaches a certain size and then begins to come down. The main prescription asked for was the right size for cutting the tree, so that some function of the timber yield is maximized. But the elementary data required for this, namely the growth pattern, is hardly known for any Indian species or for any exotic species in Indian conditions.

The bewildering variety of species also made the tropical forest very different from the temperate forests with which the German foresters were familiar. Dietrich Brandis drew attention to this signal difference when he called the low proportion of marketable species in any forest 'a peculiarity of forestry in India' (Brandis 1884, p. 12). But far from applying themselves to an understanding of the complexities of the forest ecosystem, colonial foresters were under considerable pressure to immediately change the species composition of the forest in favour of commercially valued trees. Yet increasing the proportion of commercially valued species was itself a 'most difficult problem . . . ' (Ribbentrop 1900, p. 163). It was therefore hardly surprising that existing attempts at inducing reproduction were often unsuccessful—and in many areas the department was 'living as yet to a certain extent on capital' (Ribbentrop 1900, p. 183). Quite apart from the ignorance of community-level interactions, the estimates of growing stock on which 'sustained yield' prescriptions were based were themselves flawed. But if Indian forest management deviated from the European model in the extreme paucity of data, the government did little to remedy the gap—indeed, foresters were told explicitly by the inspector-general of forests that constraints of time and money made it 'utterly impracticable and futile to try and elaborate working plans on advanced European models' (Smythies and Dansey 1887, p. 9). In other words, the proper enumeration of growing stock—an essential prerequisite for sustained-yield prescriptions—was out of the question. But even a century later, when in fact the scale of intervention in forest ecosystems has increased dramatically, there is the same attitude towards empirical data. Thus, while special experimental plots have been set up to collect information on species growth rates, the data on these have hardly ever been maintained or analysed properly.

This disregard for empirical data was revealed most strikingly by the Bastar pine plantation project. In the 1970s a project was proposed to grow the tropical pine *Pinus carribbeana* over some 40,000 hectares in the tribal district of Bastar in Madhya Pradesh. It was proposed that a 500 hectare plantation be grown initially for a five-year period to assess the performance of the species at this site—the decision on whether to pursue the project further was to be based on this experience. At the end of five years, when the larger project was being pushed, there was opposition to it from a number of quarters, including tribals, for whom the replacement of 40,000 hectares of natural forest (from which they gathered a number of resources) would have meant serious deprivation (see chapter 7). In view of this opposition, the central government appointed an expert group under the chairmanship of the inspector-general of forests to examine the project. One of the present authors served on that committee. When the committee requested data on the experimental plantation, none materialized. In fact no data had been properly maintained at all. This attitude to empirical rigour explains the widespread failures of 'plantation' forestry, narrated earlier in this chapter, to realize more than a small percentage of expected yields.

The forestry practices introduced by the British and continued thereafter are thus neither scientific nor conservation oriented. Their objectives have been threefold, namely (i) the demarcation and consolidation of forest land taken over by the state and alienated from access to the local people; (ii) the imposition of certain restrictions on the rate at which harvests are made from the forests. These restrictions do not ensure sustainable harvests; rather they have served to regulate the quantity of the material harvested to match commercial demands; (iii) the conversion of natural forests with a wide variety of resources valued by the local population into plantations of a relatively small number of species of maximal commercial value. While the environmental consequences of these objectives have been little short of disastrous, the unpopularity of 'scientific' forest management with the mass of the Indian population is a powerful indicator of its social inappropriateness. We have already dealt with the opposition to colonial forest management; the next chapter narrates the continuing resistance to state forest management in independent India.

CHAPTER SEVEN

Competing Claims on
the Commons

The continuing march of commercial forestry has greatly intensified conflicts between those whose interests it seems to serve
(chiefly the state and the commercial–industrial sector), and
those whose interests it seems to deny (chiefly the poorer
sections of the rural population). These conflicts apparently
came to a head with the debate around the 1980 Draft Forest
Act. The Act, which aimed at greatly strengthening the already
considerable powers enjoyed by the forest bureaucracy, was
opposed by grassroots organizations who argued that its punitive sanctions would be used against powerless groups such as
tribals and poor peasants. The controversy around the Act and
around the pine plantation in Bastar in Central India helped
fuel a larger debate on forest policy as a whole (Gadgil, Prasad
and Ali 1983; Guha, Ramachandra 1983).

This debate has brought in its wake a series of administrative changes which reflect the contending pulls on forest management. One set of changes works to strengthen the existing
system of state control, with exceptions made only for the
industrial sector. Thus, many states are entertaining proposals

to allot land to large industry as 'captive plantations'—though, significantly, the forest department is unwilling to hand over degraded reserved forests for the purpose, urging instead that industry be allotted other land owned by the state, including areas presently used as village commons. At the same time, another set of changes seems better disposed to ecological and social needs. These changes include the encouragement of voluntary organizations to take up afforestation in the countryside, and the ban on clear-felling imposed in several states. The government has also made important administrative changes. A new ministry of forests and environment was set up in 1985. In the same year, the National Wastelands Development Board was created as a nodal agency for afforestation. Severely hampered by the lack of access to land, in 1989 the Board was wound up and converted into a Technology Mission for Wastelands Development.

Only a decisive shift towards a more ecologically conscious and socially aware forest policy, however, is likely to diminish the severity of conflicts around the management and utilization of forest resources. This chapter (modelled on chapter 5, on the colonial period) provides a preliminary mapping of the conflicts over living resources in independent India. We distinguish between three generic types of forest-based conflict. To begin with, we follow the framework of chapter 5, successively analysing conflicts between the state on the one hand, and hunter-gatherers, shifting cultivators, settled cultivators, and artisans on the other (here we also deal with conflicts *within* the agrarian population). Well known from the colonial period, these conflicts all reflect a more basic clash between the commercial orientation of state forestry and the requirements of forest produce for subsistence on behalf of different sections of agrarian society. At the same time, while inheriting the framework of colonial administration and legislation, forest policy in independent India has been significantly influenced by the rapid expansion of the forest industries sector. This intensification of forest operations has brought in its wake new forms of conflict that were absent or at least not very visible in the earlier period. We then describe the characteristics of such conflicts *within* the forest, conflicts concerned with the distribution of gains from commercial forestry. Finally, the chapter examines a conflict which is the consequence not of intensive forest use but its obverse, i.e. the sharp curbs in certain areas on commercial *and* subsistence uses of the forest. We refer here to the massive network of wildlife sanctuaries, almost all of which have been established after 1947. Widely hailed as examples of successful conservation, these sanctuaries have often had a negative impact on the lives of the surrounding population. Our analysis of the conflicts around their management suggests that they rest, at least in part, on a narrow definition of biological conservation; enlarging this definition may perhaps be necessary to minimize future conflicts.

Hunter-gatherers

Even during the colonial period, hunter-gatherers in the Indian subcontinent had begun to lose control over their means of subsistence. The takeover of large areas of forest by the state and the expansion of the agricultural frontier have continued to threaten both hunter-gatherers and their natural environment.

Medical advances have also taken their toll, for example the reclaiming of the Terai, the malarial tract at the foot of the Himalaya. Till 1947 inhabited only by the hunter-gatherer communities of Bhoksa and Tharu, the Terai is now the centre of a prosperous agrarian economy, created mainly by refugees from Pakistani Punjab.

Many hunting and gathering communities have had only one survival strategy open to them—to put their enormous knowledge of flora and fauna at the service of the new owners of their habitat, the forest department. Thus the Jenu Kurubas of Mysore, with a tradition of helping the state in the capture of elephants, now collect honey and other forest produce on behalf of the forest department and merchants. In one taluk, Heggada Devan Kote, the department in the nineteen seventies was earning a revenue of Rs 2.5 million per annum from minor forest produce, collected mostly by Jenu Kurubas working for a small daily wage. These tribals have very little freedom of choice with respect to work; living in the forest, they either work for the department or face the threat of eviction. This near total dependence led one anthropologist to characterize the forest department–Jenu Kuruba relationship as 'feudalistic' (Misra 1977). The Hill Pandaram in Kerala, who also depend heavily on the collection of minor forest produce, are equally fearful of the forest department. Residing in what are now 'reserved forests', they live in mortal fear of government officials who often extract favours from them (Morris 1982). Even where hunter-gatherers are comparatively autonomous of the forest department, ecological changes have forced new adaptive strategies, for example the sale of small animals, honey and plants to nearby markets (cf. Sinha 1972 on the Birhors).

The Continuing 'Problem' of Shifting Cultivation

While hunter-gatherers have been powerless to effectively resist the forces of 'modernization', this has not always been the case with shifting cultivators who are, on the whole, a stronger and better organized group. However, in addition to economic and demographic pressures, shifting cultivators have had to contend with deep-seated official prejudice against this form of agriculture. Government reports have repeatedly affirmed the state's desire to do away *completely* with shifting cultivation. Such a policy rests on the unshakeable belief, expressed here by two economists, that shifting agriculture is invariably harmful for forest regeneration: '[Jhum] destroys the ecological balance and results in substantial soil erosion which subsequently leads to flooding of rivers [and] drying of hill springs' (Gupta and Sambrani 1978).

Recent anthropological work sharply contests this interpretation, providing abundant documentation that under conditions of stable population growth shifting agriculture is in fact a highly efficient and ecologically sustainable use of resources (cf. Geertz 1963; Conklin 1969). A major study of the Hill Marias of Abujmarh, one of the few surviving tribal communities in peninsular India who still depend exclusively on jhum, demonstrates that under the long fallow (twelve years) system practised by the Marias, both soil fertility and forest vegetation have sufficient time to recuperate (Savyasachi 1986). And as von Fürer-Haimendorf and his colleagues observe, 'some of the largest natural forests exist in areas inhabited by slash-and-burn cultivators for centuries, whereas intensive plough-cultivation has destroyed forests wherever it is practised' (Pingle, Rajareddy and von Fürer-Haimendorf 1982).

It is beyond our scope to adjudicate between these two conflicting interpretations. We would, however, like to highlight two points. First, one must remember that jhum is not merely an economic system with certain ecological effects; to its practitioners it is a way of life, the core of their material as well as mental culture. Secondly, many of the vocal opponents of jhum have not been at all critical of commercial forestry. In fact, most areas earlier used for shifting cultivation and taken over by the state have been subject to *greater*, not diminishing, forest exploitation, mostly for the market.

It is against this backdrop that we may view the continuing resistance of jhum cultivators to government forest policies. In Madhya Pradesh, jhum was banned in all areas covered by the Indian Forest Act, including large tracts earlier under princely states. Undeterred, tribals continued to follow the traditional rotations, although these areas had now been designated 're- served'. forests. When prosecutions and monetary fines failed to stop the cultivators, the forest department turned to the police, who made several arrests. The release of the arrested was then made conditional on a promise that they would take to plough cultivation. The transparent unwillingness to give up jhum was further illustrated by the Baigas, still confined to the *chak* in which Verrier Elwin had found them a quarter century earlier. While the forest authorities were 'hopeful of persuading [the] younger generation of Baigas to give up *bewar* altogether', the older generation was unyielding. They believed 'the Baigas were born to be kings of the jungle and the soil' and did not at all want to give up bewar, which provided 'the link with the past and with their ancestors' (NCAER, 1963, pp. 77-8).

Over many areas, the specific issue of jhum has been submerged in the larger question of tribal rights in the forest. Elwin and other anthropologists were hopeful that the new nation would redress the injustices the adivasis had suffered at the hands of the British. While their concerns found their way into important policy documents (including the Indian Constitution), there continued to be a wide gulf between policy and implementation. A special commission set up in 1960 to enquire into tribal problems was everywhere 'flooded with complaints from the tribals and their representatives against the forest administration'. Despite nearly a century of government control, the tribals were unshakeable in their belief that 'the forest belonged to them' (GOI 1961).

Viewing the forest department as a comparatively recent interloper, and undeterred by the provisions of the forest act, many tribal groups mounted a sustained challenge to the continuing denial of their rights. In 1957, a movement broke out among the Kharwar tribals of Madhya Pradesh, which called upon the people 'to stop payment of rent to revenue-collecting agents, utilise timber and forest produce without making any payment, defy magistrates and forest guards, and flout the forest laws which violated tribals' customary rights'. The movement slogan, *jangal zamin azad hai* (forests and land are free) succinctly expressed the opposition to external control and commercial use. For a time the movement brought forest operations to a standstill, dissipating only after the arrest of its leaders (Singh 1983).

More recently, attempts by the state to convert the mixed forests of Central India into monocultural plantations have met stiff resistance. The Bihar Forest Corporation's policy of replacing sal and mahua forests with teak has been sharply opposed by Ho, Munda and Santal tribals in the Chotanagpur area. In August 1979 the tribals, armed with bows and arrows, began cutting down the teak forests, asking simultaneously for their replacement with trees of species more useful to the local economy. The opposition to teak dovetailed with a wider movement of self-assertion which has demanded a separate tribal state of Jharkhand. A slogan of the movement, 'Sal means Jharkhand, Sagwan [teak] means Bihar', captures these links between the economic and ecological exploitation of the area. Outside Bihar, a World Bank aided project for raising Caribbean pine, as raw material for a new paper mill in the Bastar district of Madhya Pradesh, was stopped following opposition by tribal groups. And in the Midnapur district of Bengal, adivasis had opposed both the auction of forests and attempts to clear-fell sal in order to raise eucalyptus (PUDR 1982; Sengupta 1982; Anderson and Hubner 1988; Rana 1983).

This widespread and continuing resistance has, however, been no more than a holding operation. With the odds stacked against them, in most areas tribals have been forced to accept the new systems of forest working. Indeed the loss of their land has made thousands of tribals dependent on commercial forestry for a living. This integration of tribals into a capitalist system of wage labour has generated its own set of conflicts, dealt with later in the chapter.

The Changing Ecology of Settled Agriculture

However unsuccessful, the resistance of jhumiyas to state forest control seems to have been continuous, spilling over into the post-colonial period without any perceptible break. The situation has been somewhat different with respect to caste society, settled in villages whose core activity is plough agriculture, with the allied (and in a sense dependent) occupations of animal husbandry, craft production and services. Of course, in the three decades immediately preceding independence the peasants, who were the backbone of the Congress, had availed of the nationalist movement to advance their claims in the forest. The available evidence suggests that in the decades *following* independence, however, access to forests ranked rather low on the list of peasant grievances—i.e. there appears to have been a diminution of forest-based conflict between the peasantry and the state.

How can we explain this attenuation of conflict? To begin with, peasants were hopeful that the victory of the Congress would inaugurate a new era. As peasants, ever since the advent of Gandhi had been the mainstay of the Congress Party, it was reasonable to hope that, with their government in power, their interests would be looked after. Second, peasants were to a large extent preoccupied with consolidating the gains that were readily forthcoming after 1947. Zamindars (large landlords) had been among the most loyal supporters of the Raj; the confiscation of land under their control became one of the most urgent items on the national agenda. Thus, access to *land* became an overriding concern, and in the coming years substantial tenants (mostly from the middle castes) benefited greatly from the abolition of landlordism, now having clear titles to land on which they had previously enjoyed only a rather tenuous right of usufruct. Lastly, with the early sixties, and with the onset of the so-called Green Revolution, farmers in many parts of India switched to a new mix of agricultural technologies which in fact *reduces* their dependence on forest resources. With the state providing water, electricity, fertilizers and machinery at highly subsidized rates, the country's landscape has been dotted with pockets of fossil fuel agriculture, and the production of food and other cash crops for the urban market. Ironically, while chemical agriculture has (for its practitioners) reduced dependence on living resources, it has at the same time provided a powerful impetus for the destruction of forests through the construction of large dams for irrigation and power generation.

Chemical agriculture is feasible only in certain parts of the country; in other areas, a healthy forest cover continues to be crucial to the practice of subsistence agriculture. One such region, the Central Himalaya, gave rise to perhaps the best known of all forest conflicts, the Chipko movement. In this hilly terrain, the possibilities for both intensive and extensive agriculture are strictly limited; at the same time, the Himalaya contain the best conifer forests in the country. Control over forest (and over its changing species composition, with peasants preferring broad-leaved species and the forest department conifers) thus became a paradigm case of the conflict between subsistence and profit-oriented uses of the forest. In the past, it had given rise to some of the most bitter and intense conflicts, chronicled in chapter 5.

With the improvements in communications after 1947, especially after the 1962 India–China war, commercial exploitation of the Himalayan conifers for both timber and resin has greatly accelerated. Simultaneously, Gandhian workers tried to organize forest labourers into co-operatives which then bid, with mixed success, for timber and resin contracts. These co-operatives also began small-scale processing of forest produce — for example, resin distillation and the manufacture of agricultural implements and bee boxes—hoping to generate local employment. Here the intention was not so much to oppose commercial forestry as to enable villagers to gain a substantial share from its operations. These activities enjoyed only a limited success, with the government preferring to give contracts to large merchants from outside the hills and greater subsidies to large-scale industry in the plains.

Chipko was sparked off by the government's decision to allot a plot of hornbeam forest in the Alakananda valley to Symonds, a sports-goods company from faraway Allahabad. A few months before this, the Gandhian organization in the forefront of the co-operative movement, the Dashauli Gram Swarajya Sangh (DGSS) had been refused permission by the forest department to fell trees from the very same forest (which they wanted for making agricultural implements). This transparent favouritism provoked the villagers, led by the DGSS, to threaten to hug the trees (Chipko means to hug in Hindi) and prevent them being felled by Symonds' agents.

This was in 1973. In the next decade, Chipko spread rapidly to other parts of the Uttar Pradesh Himalaya. In over a dozen separate incidents, villagers successfully stopped felling operations. The auction of forest coupés was also disrupted. The movement has received wide publicity, and its two main leaders, Chandi Prasad Bhatt and Sunderlal Bahuguna, have emerged as among the best-known environmentalists in India. Notwithstanding its public image as an 'environmental' movement, however, Chipko is best viewed as a *peasant* movement. It resembles movements in the colonial period which defended customary rights in the forest—so crucial for subsistence—from encroachment by the state and the commercial sector. Chipko participants are very conscious of this long history of protest. Their basic demands are captured in this pithy statement by a peasant of Badyargarh: 'We got only a little food from our fields; when we could not get wood to cook even this paltry amount, we had to resort to a movement' (Guha, Ramachandra 1989a).

A decade after it began, Chipko's echoes were picked up in northern Karnataka, where a similar conflict between villagers and the forest department gave rise to the Appiko movement (Appiko means 'to hug' in Kannada). In this district, Uttara Kannada, the forest department had for several decades been promoting teak plantations after clear-felling the existing mixed semi-evergreen forests. Inspired by Chipko, in August 1983 the villagers of Sirsi taluk requested the forest department not to go ahead with selection felling operations in the Bilegal forest of Hulekal range. When their requests were unheeded, villagers marched into the forest and physically prevented the felling from continuing. They also extracted an oath from the loggers (on the local forest deity) to the effect that they would not destroy trees in that forest (Mani 1984).

The Chipko and, indeed, Appiko cases are somewhat atypical. The peculiar ecological characteristics of the regions in which they arose explain the intensity of social conflict (and popular concern) over forest resources. Deforestation in the Himalaya, while undermining the basis of the agrarian economy, has unleashed a series of landslides and floods that have taken a heavy toll of human life. At the other end of the country, the spice-garden farmers who dominate the economy of Uttara Kannada are critically dependent on leaf manure from the forest. These farmers, mostly from the influential caste of Havik Brahmins and far richer than the average Himalayan peasant, have also taken the lead in initiating programmes of eco-restoration in collaboration with scientists (Gadgil *et al.* 1986).

Elsewhere, as we have suggested, the lack of concern among the traditional social base of agrarian movements—the middle and rich peasantry—has contributed significantly to the absence of forest-based *movements*. This is not to say that other sections of agrarian society are not seriously affected by biomass shortages, especially women and the rural poor (with women from poor families being doubly affected). The crisis in the availability of woodfuel, and the impact of such shortages on the health of women and children, has been richly documented. It is less well known that shortages of fodder are equally pervasive, and in some areas even more serious. According to one estimate, while the annual demand for fuelwood in Karnataka is 12.4 million tonnes, the annual production is 10.4 million tonnes, a shortfall of 16 per cent. In the case of fodder, however, the corresponding figures are 41.5 and 13.5 million tonnes respectively—a shortfall of nearly 70 per cent (Gadgil and Sinha 1985).

The earlier chapters have argued that state control over large areas of forest has significantly restricted, though not completely eliminated, one source of biomass for rural populations. Another source that has been seriously affected in recent decades consists of grazing land and forests held in common by villagers, land which does not come under the purview of reserved forests. Seventy-five years ago, one scholar noted that in parts of Bengal common pastureland was being wrested by the landlord from the villagers (Mukerjee 1916). However, such threats to common land have greatly intensified since independence. A major study of common property resources (CPRs) in seven states shows the rapid decline in their area and physical productivity. Population pressure and the privatization of CPRs (partly by rich farmers but also due to their distribution to landless families by the state) are chiefly responsible for this decline. As it happens, poor families are the hardest hit, for large landholders have access to both fuel and fodder (for example, from agricultural wastes). Attempting to quantify this dependence, the study estimates that the income generated for each households of the poor from CPRs ranges between Rs 530 and 830 per annum. These figures are substantially higher than the income generated by several anti-poverty programmes. The restoration of the status and productivity of CPRs may therefore be a most effect ve anti-poverty strategy (Jodha 1986).

A case study of Rajasthan suggests that official policies have considerably hastened this process of privatization and degradation. Thus the supersession of customary law by codified law—in other words, the shifting of the locus of decision-making away from actual users—has created great uncertainty concerning the management of common lands. As traditional institutions which earlier regulated the use of CPRs are not recognized in law, there is a powerful incentive for individual farmers to claim possession of parcels of land previously held in common, and get such encroachments 'regularized'. As richer farmers have more influence with both politicians and administrators, the apparently inexorable decline of CPRs is intimately connected with the declining fortunes of the rural poor (Brara 1987).

While the commons dilemma testifies to the growing fissures within agrarian society, as it happens these lands are under threat from outside forces as well. A particularly important case in Karnataka involves the transfer of land previously under the control of the revenue department to a joint-sector company, formed to grow industrial wood for the exclusive use of one factory, Harihar Polyfibres (owned by the powerful industrial house of the Birlas). Contending that these areas have been traditionally used by villagers for fuel and fodder collection, a voluntary group has challenged the formation of the new company in the highest court of the land. While the case is being heard in the supreme court, villagers have organized several 'pluck and plant' satyagrahas, symbolically uprooting eucalyptus (a species of very little use to the local economy) and planting saplings of more 'useful' local species instead.

At the time of writing, the final judgement on the KPL case is awaited from the supreme court. Whichever way it goes, it is likely to be a landmark judgement, determining the principles whereby private industry can or cannot be granted public land for exclusive use. However, peasant opposition to the takeover of common lands by KPL draws on long-standing traditions in defence of customary rights. For example, in the village of Baad in Dharwad district, uncultivated land belonging to the family of a former *jagirdar* (land grantee) was leased to KPL for growing eucalyptus. Peasants challenged this decision in court, arguing that the land leased to KPL had traditionally been used by them for grazing cattle. They contended that by enclosing the plot, harrowing the land in strips, and planting eucalyptus saplings, the operations of KPL would adversely affect the supply of grass for their cattle. The villagers of Baad invoked earlier court cases (dating back to 1943) wherein they had successfully defended their collective right to graze cattle on the contested area without paying any fee to the jagirdar. In those cases, judges had upheld the villagers' claim that this land was *mufat gayaran* (free pasture): consequently the jagirdars were barred from levying a fee. Citing these precedents, villagers asked that these lands be retained as pastures and that KPL operations be stopped (see plaintiff's appeal in suit no. 133 of 1988, court of the civil judge, Dharwad; suit no. 128 of 1943, court of the extra joint sub-judge, Dharwad).

Biomass shortages have also intensified conflicts between settled cultivators and pastoral nomads. Traditionally, a significant proportion of India's population (perhaps as much as 5 per cent) depended on nomadic grazing. With large tracts of land earlier left uncultivated, nomads had available abundant grazing for their flocks in the monsoon season. As natural grass growth declined after the rains, they turned to stubble left after the harvest, and to fallow fields. The farmers themselves typically kept only a few livestock, primarily for draught power. They thus enjoyed a mutualistic relationship with the graziers, exchanging stubble for manure and dairy products, meat and wool for grain. In recent decades this relationship has come under great stress. On the one hand, the acreage of non-cultivated lands open for grazing has shrunk dramatically, not least due to the state takeover of forests. On the other hand, a growing market for dairy products and meat has encouraged many cultivators to increase their own livestock holdings, thereby limiting access to crop residues for pastoralists. These pressures have forced many nomadic communities to shift from grazing to cultivation, mostly on marginal and unproductive lands. Elsewhere, growing competition for shrinking fodder resources has led to bitter conflicts between graziers and cultivators. These sometimes violent conflicts between groups that earlier enjoyed a co-operative relationship have been reported from the states of Madhya Pradesh, Uttar Pradesh, Rajasthan and Maharashtra (Gadgil and Malhotra 1982; CSE 1985; Wade 1988).

A brief mention, finally of one other set of castes deprived of biomass, namely artisans. Undeniably, the major reason for their decline has been competition from organized industry—i.e. from the mass production of utensils, containers, furniture, etc., which were earlier manufactured within the village. Simultaneously, shortages of raw material have also been a contributory factor. Basket weavers dependent on reed in Kerala and on bamboo in Karnataka, and hemp workers in Uttar Pradesh, are among many artisanal communities which have faced deprivation in recent years, as the resource traditionally used by them has either been depleted or diverted to industrial uses.

Claiming a Share of the Profits

Changes in the proprietary status of the forests, as well as changes in its ecology, have clearly undermined the capacity of forest-dependent modes of subsistence—for example hunting, gathering, shifting cultivation, and some forms of plough agriculture and pastoralism—to reproduce themselves. As commercial forestry has continued its apparently unstoppable march, many forest-dependent communities have had to take recourse to alternative survival strategies. The most ready option, namely wage employment in commercial forest operations, ironically, concedes the inevitability of the new systems of forest working. One can see a classic process of proletarianization at work: divorced from the means of production (forest and land), forest dwellers are forced to accept a subordinate place in the new 'capitalist' system of production. This process has generated a set of conflicts characteristic of capitalism, in which labourers seek to improve their wages while capitalists seek to maintain high profit margins.

The basis of such conflict lies in the very mode of forest working in India, the so-called 'contractor' system. Although the state owns the forests, until very recently it has played little part in the actual extraction of timber and other forest produce. The procedure most widely followed is to mark, according to working-plan prescriptions, the trees to be felled in any given year. These trees are then collectively sold and auctioned to the highest bidder, who is now given a contract by the state. This 'contractor' is responsible for organizing labour, conducting felling operations, and transporting and supplying the converted logs directly to the actual users. A similar procedure is followed with respect to minor forest produce, wherein yearly contracts are offered to the highest bidder for the collection of any particular item—for example sal seeds—from a designated area of forest.

Corruption and waste are inherent in the contractor system. It is well known that at departmental auctions the contractor often bids a price far higher than the actual value of the marked trees, and then goes on to disregard silvicultural prescriptions by felling both unmarked and marked trees. The methods of extraction—for instance hurling logs down the hillside to a floatable stream—also cause great damage. By depressing collection wages, contractors realize staggering profits, often exceeding several hundred percent. Similar profit margins are realized by the processing industry, especially in the case of low bulk, high value items (such as perfumes) processed from minor forest produce (for illustrations, see Guha, Ramachandra 1983).

Recognizing these tendencies, policy documents have talked repeatedly of eliminating contractors, who, it is admitted, exploit both forests and labour. The need to replace contractors by forest labour co-operatives (FLCs) has been stressed in all the five year plan documents, in the 1952 forest policy, and by several commissions. A committee set up in 1967 to look into the tribal–contractor–forest nexus cynically observed that in this case they did not 'envisage the need for any changes in the wording of the existing [forest] policy' (GOI 1967, p. 13). The need to abolish intermediaries in forest working has been reiterated by the high-level committee for environmental protection, and in several meetings of the Central Board of Forestry (GOI 1980).

What has been the actual experience of the FLCs? Maharashtra is one state where the administration has taken some initiative in their formation. The districts of Thane and Dhulia in the state had been the centre of a major tribal upsurge in the 1940s, whose targets were the moneylender–forest contractor nexus (Parulekar 1976). Conceding the justice of these demands, the new Congress government tried to promote FLCs. However, their progress has been slow and halting.

Despite the presence of 444 FLCs in 1969-70 in the tribal parts of the state, co-operatives were in charge of only 40 per cent of the felling operations, with an equal share for contractors, and the remaining (20 per cent) in the hands of the forest department itself. Only one co-operative had taken the next step and started a sawmill to process timber. Lately, even these gains have been offset by the formation of the state's forest development corporation, whose brief is to augment the 'productivity' of forest lands by growing species such as teak. The new corporation has not recognized the earlier terms evolved between the government and the FLCs, and the number of forest blocks allotted to the latter has slowly dwindled (Muranjan 1974 and 1980).

In other states the experience has been even less encouraging. In Uttar Pradesh, the forest department was itself keen to encourage co-operatives, only to be told by the governor that since 'the forest department is a sort of a commercial department, it cannot be expected to extend concession in the transaction of its business, even to co-operative societies'. The government of Maharashtra (then Bombay) was actually invoked as an example not to be followed, for their schemes had 'cost the Bombay government quite dearly and considerable amounts were lost to the exchequer' (Guha, Ramachandra 1983). The favours shown to outside contractors and the processing industry were a major factor behind the rise of the Chipko movement. However, the most militant forest labour movements have been in tribal areas of Central India, concerned mainly with the terms of collection of minor forest produce. Protesting at their low wages, tribals have repeatedly struck work, refusing to deposit bundles at collection centres. In heavily forested districts, such as Srikakulam in Andhra Pradesh and Gadchiroli in Maharashtra, the affected tribals are being organized by Marxist revolutionaries, the so-called Naxalites (PUDR 1982; Calman 1985).

More recently, the controversy over the contractor system has resurfaced in Madhya Pradesh (MP). Responding to criticisms of exploitation of tribals by middlemen, in 1988 the MP government decided to bring the lucrative trade in tendu leaves (used for making *bidis*) under the co-operative fold. The collection rate for tendu leaves was fixed at Rs 15 per hundred bundles of a hundred leaves each, which compares favourably with the prevailing rates of Rs 12.90 in Maharashtra and Rs 9 in Orissa. At the same time, the MP government announced the formation of 2000 co-operative societies. It was claimed that these measures would benefit more than one million forest labourers, mostly tribals. The state takeover of the tendu leaf trade has been bitterly opposed by merchants and by politicians aligned to them. Scepticism has also been expressed about the feasibility of fostering co-operatives from above in the absence of local-level organizations (*The Economic Times*, 20 November 1988; *Economic and Political Weekly*, 18 March 1989). And with the change in government in MP in early 1990, moves have been afoot to abolish the co-operatives and give concessions to the merchants who earlier controlled the tendu leaf trade.

Despite successful struggles for wage increases, in most areas tribals continue to get only an infinitesimal share of the gains from commercial forestry. Nor have they benefited substantially from the abolition of the contractor system and the takeover of forest operations by newly-created government corporations. The state is not a model employer either, and since the contractor continues to dominate the trade in forest produce even where he does not anymore supervise extraction, resistance continues (Gupta *et al.* 1981).

Wild Life Conservation: Animals Versus Humans?

Amid the continuing ecological decline of the Indian subcontinent, the massive network of parks and sanctuaries constructed after 1947 apparently stands out as a magnificent exception. As chapter 4 suggests, the British, as proponents of shikar on a large scale, had very little interest in wild-life conservation. The consequences of record-breaking shikar sprees and habitat

destruction were apparent by the time India gained independence. The tiger population, estimated at 40,000 at the turn
of the century, had slumped to 3000. The cheetah was extinct in
1952. Other large mammals, such as the elephant and rhino, had
disappeared from areas in which they were formerly quite
numerous, while the Asiatic lion survived only in the Gir forest.

The initiative for wild-life preservation came from the erstwhile princes, who had a rather better record than the British
in maintaining their hunting preserves. The Indian Board for
Wildlife was set up in 1952; since then, a steady stream of parks
and sanctuaries has been constituted. A major conservation
effort, Project Tiger, was launched with the help of international
agencies in 1973, concerned exclusively with the protection and
enhancement of tiger populations (more than fifteen sanctuaries covering 25,000 sq. km. come under this project).

Judged on their own terms, these programmes have been
quite successful in stabilizing the population of some endangered species and in enhancing the population of others. Yet
this success has not been without its costs. Immediately after
independence, a well-known botanist had in fact warned the
proponents of wild-life sanctuaries of possible adverse effects
on the surrounding population, saying the interests of nature
lovers and the interests of cultivators were not easy to har-
monize (Randhawa 1949). His warnings were prescient, for
villagers living on the periphery of sanctuaries face serious
hazards against which they are insufficiently protected, especially crop damage and manslaughter. Destruction is particularly severe in areas adjoining forests inhabited by large
animals such as the rhino and elephant. A study conducted in
ten villages along the Karnataka–Tamil Nadu border estimates
that the damage done to food crops by elephants was about Rs
1.5 lakhs per year. While on the average 10-15 per cent of the
crop was destroyed, in some months fields were attacked by
elephants almost every day. Over a period of two years, eighteen human kills were also reported (Sukumar 1989). One area
in India where manslaughter by tigers has reached serious

proportions is the Sunderbans delta. While the tiger population has increased from around 130 to 205 in the last decade, it is believed that Sunderban tigers have taken a toll of perhaps a thousand human lives in the past twenty years. National parks already cover 3 per cent of India's land surface, and there are proposals to double this area by the end of the century. In displacing villagers without proper rehabilitation, prohibiting traditional hunting and gathering, and exposing villages on the periphery to the threat of crop damage, cattle lifting and man-slaughter, the parks are, as they stand, inimical to the interests of the poorer sections of agrarian society. In some cases, villagers have responded by setting fire to large areas in the national parks. In the Kanha National Park of MP—a Project Tiger area also famous for swamp deer—the dry season of 1990 saw a wave of fires sweep through nearly half the park. Denied access to the park for their requirements of forest produce, the villagers, aided by political extremists, have in this manner taken 'revenge' on the forest department (see *Sunday Observer*, 13 May 1990).

These conflicts come out sharply in a recent status report on national parks and sanctuaries in India. The report cited frequent clashes between villagers and park authorities over access to natural resources. Between 1979 and 1984, fifty-one such clashes were reported as having occurred in national parks, and sixty-six clashes as having taken place in sanctuaries. Commenting on incidents of death or injury to humans on account of attacks by wild animals, the report observed that the states of Andhra Pradesh, Arunachal Pradesh, Himachal Pradesh, Manipur and Rajasthan do not pay any compensation in such cases. Among the states that did report payment, compensation for fatalities was quite meagre, varying from Rs 200 to Rs 10,000. The day-to-day management of the parks and sanctuaries is also biased against local users, there being sharp curbs on customary use. Indeed, a greater proportion of parks allows the manipulation of habitat by plantations than allows grazing by the cattle of surrounding villages (Kothari *et al.* 1989).

This is not to say that the preservation of biological diversity is not important, only that it should follow different principles. For in India, as in other parts of the Third World, national park management is heavily imprinted by the American experience. In particular, it has taken over two axioms of the Western wilderness movement: that wilderness areas should be as large as possible, and the belief that *all* human intervention is bad for the retention of diversity. These axioms have led to the constitution of massive sanctuaries, each covering thousands of square miles, and a total ban on human ingress in the 'core' areas of national parks (See Guha, Ramachandra 1989b).

These axioms of 'giganticism' and 'hands off nature', though cloaked in the jargon of science, are simply prejudices. When it is realized that the preservation of *plant* diversity is in many respects more important than the preservation of large mammals, a decentralized network of many small parks makes far more sense. The widespread network of sacred groves in India traditionally fulfilled precisely those functions. Yet modern wilderness lovers and managers are in general averse to reviving that system: apart from rationalist objections, they are in principle opposed to local control, preferring a centralized system of park management. The belief in a total ban on human intervention is equally misguided. Studies show that in fact the highest levels of biological diversity are found in areas with some (though not excessive) intervention. In opening up new niches to be occupied by insects, plants and birds, partially disturbed ecosystems often have a greater diversity than untouched areas. The dogma of total protection can have tragic consequences, as illustrated by the case of the famous bird sanctuary in Bharatpur. Here, villages were abruptly told that they must stop grazing cattle in the sanctuary, a right they had enjoyed for several decades. When they refused to agree, an altercation between them and officials culminated in firings and the death of several villagers. Ironically, scientific studies now suggest that grazing was not adversely affecting bird life in the sanctuary; on the contrary, it was essential for keeping down excessive growth of the *paspalum* grass, which otherwise choked the shallow marshes, rendering them unsuitable for the migratory species of waterfowl which are one of the sanctuary's main attractions (Vijayan 1987).

The Changing Profile of Forest Conflicts

It would be appropriate to conclude this chapter with a brief comparison with the colonial period. While the framework of forest management introduced by the British is very much in place, the much higher rates of industrial growth have informed radical modifications in the systems of forest working. Simultaneously, the pressures of demographic expansion and ecological decline have forced many forest-dependent communities to look for alternative modes of subsistence. With respect both to the hardware and software of forest resource use, therefore, the post-colonial period is marked by both change and continuity. How is this reflected in the patterns of social conflict over living resources?

Table 7.1 summarizes what appear to be the salient features of this process. We can draw four major conclusions from the table.

First, there has been a diminution in the scale and spread of some conflicts, notably nos. 1, 2, and 3. However, this does not mean that these conflicts have been *resolved*. On the contrary, one party has been forced to accept defeat, and even in some cases (for example hunter-gatherers) virtual extinction.

Second, there has been the intensification of some conflicts (nos. 4 and 5) as well as the emergence of forms of conflict almost wholly absent in the colonial period (nos. 7 and 8). Conflict 7 is the consequence of the greater exploitation of forest resources to keep pace with a growing market demand. Conflict 8, on the other hand, is the result of schemes (however narrowly conceived) to *protect* certain habitats in their pristine state.

TABLE 7.1

CHANGE IN INTENSITY OF DIFFERENT FORMS OF RESOURCE-
RELATED CONFLICT BEFORE AND AFTER INDEPENDENCE

No.	Form of conflict	Comparative intensity (post-47 / pre-47)
1.	Hunter-gatherers *vs* the state	Sharply reduced on the mainland; intensifying in areas like the Andamans
2.	*Jhumiyas vs* the state	Reduced in peninsular India; intensifying in the north-east
3.	Settled cultivators *vs* the State	Reduced in some areas (where forests are no longer important), constant in other areas (Himalaya, Western Ghats)
4.	Conflicts within village society (decline of CPRs)	Sharply increased
5.	Cultivators *vs* nomads	Sharply increased
6.	Artisans *vs* the state	Diminished for some categories (charcoal makers), increased or constant for others (basket weavers)
7.	Labourers *vs* contractors	Sharply increased
8.	Wildlife *vs* villagers	Largely new conflict

Third, the state, as one party to conflicts 1, 2, 3 and 6, is really acting as a proxy for the commercial–industrial sector. All these conflicts have the same underlying cause—the preference shown in forest management to commercial, profit-oriented uses at the expense of small-scale, subsistence-oriented uses.

Finally, conflicts 4 and 5 point to perhaps the most disturbing consequence of these processes—increasing conflicts between different sections of the agrarian population.

As in other former European colonies like Indonesia (see Peluso 1989), popular resistance to state forest management cuts across four axes: those of land control, labour control, species control, and ideological control. Thefts and conflicts with forest officials challenge the state's control over non-cultivated land; recent years have seen a growing militancy among forest labourers concerning their terms and conditions of work; efforts to manipulate the forest in favour of commercially valued species have been bitterly resisted by local populations, and the option of decentralized, community-based management has been put forward as an alternative to the ideology of state control. In 1913, the government of the Madras Presidency had bracketed the forest department with the salt department as the most unpopular among state agencies. Sixty years after Gandhi's Dandi march hastened the abolition of the state monopoly over salt, the forest department remains a largely unwelcome presence in the Indian countryside.

CHAPTER EIGHT

Cultures in Conflict

This book has traced the broad contours of eco-cultural evolution in India, moving from the hunter-gatherer mode through the peasant mode and finally to the continuing attempt by the industrial mode to impose its definitive stamp on the ecological history of the subcontinent. The Indian experience is decisively marked by the colonial encounter; in this sense it differs from the paths traced by the two other Asian giants, Japan and China. Fortuitously escaping European colonialism, ecological change within Japan followed a more or less autonomous path, and it is as yet the only major Asian country to make a successful transition to industrial society. The Chinese experience is no less interesting: although the pace of industrialization has been noticeably slower, the dominantly socialist character of the state and existing property relations give its ecological history a distinctive twist. While Japan draws heavily on the natural resources of South East Asia and South America, China, like India, has to largely rely on its own resources in its industrialization strategy.

The ecological histories of Japan and China are finding their chroniclers (for sample writings in English, see Totman 1985 and 1989; Menezies, in press) and will doubtless display some interesting comparisons with the Indian case. We are more concerned here with the lessons that can be drawn from the two processes of eco-cultural change most extensively studied by historians—the European 'miracle' of successful industrialization and the imposition of Neo-Europes in the New World. While the environmental impacts of the neolithic revolution in Europe may have been relatively neglected by historians, many impressive volumes have been written on the socio-ecological dimensions of the clash between the peasant and industrial modes in that continent. To summarize a well-known story, it seems this conflict was resolved in two major ways:

1. By the discovery of new (chiefly inanimate) sources of energy, which when combined with the revolution in science and technology fuelled an unprecedented expansion in productive forces. Thus industrial expansion was able to absorb much of the surplus population from the countryside. The celebration of these European achievements in science and technology has, however, tended to obscure the critical role played in this transition by the substitution of plant by non-plant materials. The discovery of more efficient ways of using coal in the early eighteenth century led to coal quickly replacing wood in the critical industry of iron smelting. And as fodder became scarce for horses, the chief locomotory force till then, the steam engine was invented. Finally, iron replaced timber as building material as well as for textile machinery (i.e. in the leading industry). As a French observer put it in 1817, 'this continuous substitution of wood by iron is not at all the result of a craze or a passing fancy: it stems from a comparison of the low price for this metal with the dearness of timber which is excessive throughout Britain' (quoted in von Tunzelman 1981, p. 162). Having devastated its own forests and those of its Irish colony by 1700, England was saved by the timely discovery of non-wood substitutes.

2. By colonial expansion, involving (a) the extraction of raw materials, and (b) the settling of surplus population in

newly-conquered territories. Especially in its early stages, colonization was closely linked to the requirements of the domestic economy. As Karl Polanyi (1957, p. 179) observed many years ago, colonialism, following upon the commercialization of the soil and the increases in food production to meet the needs of a growing domestic population, was the third and final stage in the subordination of the resources of the planet to the imperatives of European industrialization. In time, however, the fabulous natural resources of these lands and the enterprise of the settlers worked synergistically to create an autonomous process of industrialization through much of the New World.

New World colonialism therefore provides an organic link between these two patterns of eco-cultural change. Fundamental to the making of the modern world, both processes have been strikingly successful when judged on their own terms: indeed, they are frequently held aloft as models for other cultures to emulate. This is not to say they were harmonious. New World colonization led to the extermination of indigenous cultures and populations, while the Industrial Revolution was not exactly a painless process either. Whatever these costs, however, both processes have ultimately resulted in the establishment of prosperous, relatively egalitarian and harmonious societies. Moreover, none of these societies are faced with the prospect of impending ecological collapse. Of course, outside their borders their behaviour is not always characterized by ecological restraint, as witness the large-scale logging of virgin forests by Japanese multinationals in Papua New Guinea and Kalimantan, and the equally notorious 'hamburger connection', wherein millions of acres of Amazonian rain forest are being destroyed to raise beef for the American market. Within their borders, however, many (though not all—as the case of acid rain in Europe testifies) industrial societies are doing a good job of protecting their forests. In some parts, for example north-eastern United States and Japan, vigorous tree growth has actually colonized land deforested for centuries.

The theme of this work bears a curious relation to the two

processes outlined above. For India is akin to Europe in having had for centuries a complex agrarian civilization, yet more like the New World in having been subjected to the ravages of European colonialism. Sidestepping for the most part the question of the extent to which the colonization of India actually enabled the European 'miracle', we have tried to document the other side of the coin, namely the impact it had *within* the subcontinent. British imperialism could not wipe out the population of India—ironically, it set in motion a process of demographic expansion—but it did certainly disrupt, perhaps irrevocably, the ecological and cultural fabric of its society. And after it formally left Indian shores, the tasks it had left unfinished were enthusiastically taken up by the incoming nationalist elites, whose unswerving commitment to a resource-intensive pattern of industrialization has only intensified the processes of ecological and social disturbance initiated by the British.

From an ecological perspective, the clash of pre-industrial and industrial cultures in India may be represented in terms of the closure and creation of niches. In India, as elsewhere, the British usurped the ecological niches occupied by the hunter-gatherers, many of whom also practised shifting cultivation, and diminished substantially the niche space occupied by food producers, by alienating them from access to non-cultivated lands. The resource processors and transporters of European civilization had by the nineteenth century a tremendously greater access to resources, largely because of their technological ability to tap additional sources of energy and materials. They out-competed and usurped the niche space of Indian handicraft workers and artisans, as well as of itinerant traders. This tremendous shrinkage of the niche space available to the Indian population was only marginally compensated by new niches which opened up to collaborators of the British, in the usurpation and transport of resources, as their clerks and trading partners.

The literate castes of pre-British India, involved in priesthood and administration, filled the clerical jobs, with merchants and shopkeepers in the role of trading partners. These groups prospered as time went by, and moved into the modern resource-processing industry. But the others—hunter-gatherers, peasants, artisans, and pastoral and non-pastoral nomads—had all to squeeze into the already diminishing niche space for food production. And they, we have seen, suffered great impoverishment.

While the British ruled India, they discouraged Indians from taking up resource-processing and transport on the basis of modern technology and with access to fossil fuel and other modern energy sources. With time, however, this resistance was broken down, and India began to industrialize. The emerging Indian capitalist class, in fact, provided financial support to the national movement, aware that in an independent country they would face less competition. Following independence, industrialists were able to steer the course of development on a path beneficial to them, namely as an all-out state-subsidized effort to intensify the use of resources such as land, water, vegetation, minerals, and energy.

Such an effort has to function within severe constraints, for unlike the Europeans who gained access to the resources of new lands in a comparable phase of industrial development, Indians are confined to a land already suffering from many kinds of resource depletion. Further, it is once again the Western world which has access to newer and newer resources as technological advances render useful various forms of energy and materials that were earlier of little value. India finds itself falling ever further behind in this race for technological substitution and resource creation. This disadvantage is reflected in the net outflow of resources from India to the West, be it fish, iron ore or scientifically trained manpower.

Within the country, meanwhile, efforts at the intensification of resource use have further stepped up the outflows of resources from cultivated as well as non-cultivated land to resource processors—industry, and the urban agglomerations built around it. Existing levels in the disruption of energy and material cycles, which ultimately must be closed, cannot be sustained indefinitely. They are in fact leading to a continuous depression of the productive potential of cultivated and non-cultivated land (cf. CSE 1985). The situation has been saved from serious disaster by an inflow of irrigation water, agro-chemicals and high-yielding varieties to the agricultural sector. This inflow is restricted to only 20 per cent of the land under cultivation. Nevertheless, it has succeeded in enhancing food production to a level adequate for subsistence by the entire population—though serious disparities in the availability of food for different social classes remain.

There has thus been a significant expansion in the niche space of food production in tracts of intensive agriculture. There has also been expansion of niche space for resource processing and transport, information processing and resource usurpation. However, these have been more than offset by the continuing contraction of niche space in tracts of subsistence agriculture, and for those dependent on foraging for resources—landless and small peasants, fishermen, and traditional resource processors (artisans and nomads). These difficulties are compounded by the overall growth in numbers of people. The consequence has been a scramble for resources and intense conflict, in the countryside and in the cities where people who have been driven out from elsewhere are flocking. While traditional relationships based on low levels of niche overlap between different endogamous groups have broken down, the barriers of endogamy persist. Endogamous caste groups therefore remain cultural entities, but have no common belief system to hold them together. No longer functional entities in the present scenario of shrinking niche space, castes and communities are set up against each other, with frighteningly high levels of communal and caste violence being the result.

In India the ongoing struggle between the peasant and industrial modes of resource use has come in two stages: colonial and post-colonial. It has left in its wake a fissured land, ecologically and socially fragmented beyond belief and, to some observers, beyond repair. Where do we go from here? There seems no realistic hope of emulating European or New World modes of industrial development. There is no longer a 'frontier' available with which to easily dispose of our population. Nor are there readily available substitutes for energy or construction material, enabling us to prevent our forest resources getting depleted. On both these counts the Western world has pre-empted the two-thirds of humanity which is lumped under the label 'Third World'. Through most of the Third World, the transition from the peasant to the industrial mode is very incomplete and, indeed, likely to remain incomplete for a very long time to come.

Not surprisingly, the Indian environmental debate has taken an altogether different track from its Western counterpart. Western environmentalists, contemplating the arrival of the 'post-industrial' economy and for the most part unaware of the damage its industrial economy is doing to other parts of the globe, are moving towards a 'post-materialist' perspective in which the forest is not central to economic production but rather to the enhancement of the 'quality of life'. In India, by contrast, the debate around the forest, and the environment debate more generally, is firmly rooted in questions of production and use. The issues in contention include the relative claims of the industrial and agrarian sector over natural resources (and within each, the claims of large *versus* small units), the uses of nature for subsistence or for profit, the respective proprietary claims of individuals, communities, and the state, and finally the role of natural resource management in an alternative development strategy.

But whether these debates will result in a new mode of resource use and a new belief system to hold our society together, it is too early to say.

Bibliography

Aatre, T.N., 1915. *Gaon-Gada—Notes on Rural Sociology and Village Problems* (in Marathi). Mote Publishers, Bombay.

Adas, M., 1981. 'From avoidance to confrontation: Peasant protest in precolonial and colonial southeast Asia'. *Comp. Stud. Soc. Hist.*, 23.

Agarwal, A., 1986. 'Human-Nature interactions in a third world country'. *The Environmentalist*, 6.

Agarwal, D.P. and Sood, R.K., 1982. 'Ecological factors and the Harappan civilization'. G.L. Possehl (ed.), *Harappan Civilization*. Oxford and IBH, New Delhi.

Agulhon, M., 1982. *The Republic in the Village*. Cambridge University Press, Cambridge.

Aiyappan, A., 1948. *Report on the Socio-economic Conditions of the Aboriginal Tribes of the Province of Madras*. Madras Government Press, Madras.

Albion, R.G., 1926. *Forests and Sea Power*. Harvard University Press, Cambridge, Massachussets.

Allchin, B. and Allchin, F.R., 1968. *The Birth of Indian Civilization*. Penguin, Harmondsworth.

Allchin, F.R., 1963. *Neolithic Cattle Keepers of South India*. Cambridge University Press, Cambridge.

Ambedkar, B.R., 1948. *The Untouchables*. Amit Book Co., New Delhi.

Amery, C.F., 1875. 'On Forest Rights in India'. D. Brandis and A. Symthies (ed), *Report on the Proceedings of the Forest Conference held at Simla*, October. Government Press, Calcutta.

Anderson, R. and Hubner, W., 1988. *The Hour of the Fox*. Vistar Publications, New Delhi.

Anonymous, 1906. *A Manual of Forest Law Compiled for the Use of the Students at the Imperial Forest College, Dehra Dun*, Government Press, Calcutta.

Anonymous, 1913. *Report of the Forest Committee, Vol. I*. Government Press, Madras.

Anonymous, 1920. *Report of the Imperial Economic Committee : Tenth Report : Timber*. HMSO, London.

Anonymous, 1927. *Report of the Royal Commission of Agriculture*. HMSO, London.

Arnold, D., 1982. 'Rebellious Hillmen : The Gudem Rampa Rebellions (1829-1914)'. Ranajit Guha (ed.), *Subaltern Studies I*. Oxford University Press, Delhi.

Avchat, A., 1981. *Manase* (in Marathi). Granthali Publishers, Pune.

Ayers, R.V., 1978. *Resources, Environment and Economics. Applications of the Materials / Energy Balance Principle*. John Wiley and Sons, New York.

Badam, G.L., 1978. 'The quarternary fauna of Inamgaon'. V.N. Misra and P. Bellwood (ed.), *Proceedings of the International Symposium on Recent Advances in Indo-Pacific Prehistory*. Croom Helm, London.

Baden-Powell, B.H., 1874. *The Forest System of British Burma*. Government Press, Calcutta.

——, 1875. 'On the defects of the existing Forest Law (Act VII of 1865) and Proposals for a New Forest Act'. B.H. Baden-Powell and J.S. Gamble (ed.), *Report of the Proceedings of the Forest Conference, 1873-74*. Government Press, Calcutta.

——, 1882. *A Manual of Jurisprudence for Forest Officers*. Government Press, Calcutta.

——, 1892. *Memorandum on Forest Settlements in India*. Government Press, Calcutta.

Badgeley, C., Kelly, J., Pilbean, D. and Ward, S., 1984. 'The Palaeobiology of South Asian miocene hominoids'. J.R. Lukacs (ed.) *The People of South Asia*. Plenum Press, New York.

Bahro, R., 1984. *From Red to Green*. Verso Books, London.

Baker, C.J., 1984. *An Indian Rural Economy, 1880-1955*. Oxford University Press, Delhi.

Baker, D.E.U., 1984. 'A serious time : Forest satyagraha in Madhya Pradesh, 1930'. *Indian Econ. and Social Hist. Rev.*, 21.

Beckerman, W., 1972. 'Economists, scientists and environmental catastrophe'. *Oxford Economic Papers*, 24.

Beddington, J.R. and May, R.M., 1982. 'The harvesting of interacting species in a natural ecosystem'. *Scientific American*, 247.

Bennet, S., 1984. 'Shikar and the Raj'. *South Asia N.S.*, 7.

Berkes, F. (ed.), 1989. *Common Property Resources : Ecology and Community-Based Sustainable Development*. Belhaven Press, London.

Berkes, F. and Kence, A., 1987. 'Fisheries and the prisoners dilemma game : Conditions for the evolution of cooperation among users of common property resources'. *Metu Journal of Pure and Applied Sciences*, 20 (2).

Berlin, B., 1973. 'Folk systematics in relation to biological classification and nomenclature'. *Annual Review of Ecology and Systematics*, 4.

Best, J.W., 1935. *Forest Life in India*. John Murray, London.

Bhattacharya, S., 1972. 'Iron smelters and the indigenous iron and steel industry of India : From stagnation to atrophy'. S. Sinha (ed.), *Aspects of Indian Culture and Society*. Indian Anthropological Society, Calcutta.

Birrel, J., 1987. 'Common rights in the medieval forest'. *Past and Present*, no. 117.

Blanford, H.R., 1925. 'Regeneration with the assistance of Taungya in Burma'. *Indian Forest Records*, 11, part 3.

Blair, H., 1986. 'Social Forestry in India : Time to Modify Goals'. *Economic and Political Weekly*, 21 July.

Bloch, M., 1978. *French Rural History : An Essay on its Essential Characteristics* (1931 reprint). Routledge and Kegan Paul, London.

Borgerhoff Mulder, M., 1988. 'Behavioural Ecology in Traditional Societies'. *Trends in Ecology and Evolution*, 3 (10).

Brahme, S. and Upadhya, A., 1979. 'A Critical Analysis of the Social Formation of and Peasant Resistance in Maharashtra'. *Mimeo*, three volumes. Gokhale Institute of Politics and Economics, Pune.

Brandis, D., 1873. *The Distribution of Forests in India*. McFarlane and Erskine, Edinburgh.

——, 1875. *Memorandum on the Forest Legislation Proposed for British India (other than the Presidencies of Madras and Bombay)*. Government Press, Simla.

——, 1876. *Suggestions Regarding Forest Administration in the Central Provinces*. Government Press, Calcutta.

——, 1882. *Suggestions Regarding Forest Administration in the North-western Provinces and Oudh*. Government Press, Calcutta.

——, 1884. *Progress of Forestry in India*. McFarlane and Erskine, Edinburgh.

——, 1897. *Indian Forestry*. Oriental Institute, Woking.

Brara, R., 1987. 'Shifting Sands : A Study of Rights in Common Pastures'. *Mimeo*. Institute of Development Studies, Jaipur.

Brenner, R., 1976. 'Agrarian class structure and economic development in pre-industrial Europe'. *Past and Present*, 70.

——, 1978. 'Dobb on the transition from feudalism to capitalism'. *Cambridge Journal of Economics*, 2 (2).

Calman, L., 1985. *Protest in Democratic India*. Westview Press, Boulder.

Campbell, 1883. *Bombay Gazetteer : Kanara*. Government Central Press, Bombay.

Centre for Science and Environment, 1985. *The State of India's Environment 1984-85 : A Second Citizens' Report*. Centre for Science and Environment, New Delhi.

Champion, H.G. and Osmaston, F.C., (ed.), 1962. *E.P. Stebbing's The Forests of India*, Vol. IV. Oxford University Press, Oxford.

Champion, H.G. and Seth, S.K., 1968. *General Silviculture for India*. Manager of Publications, Delhi.

Chandra, G.S. and Srivastava, S.S., 1968. 'Forestry economics in India, some areas of research'. *Arthavijnana*, 10.

Chandrasekhar, D.M., Krishnamurthy, B.V. and Ramaswamy, S.R., 1987. 'Social forestry in Karnataka : An impact analysis'. *Economic and Political Weekly*, 29 September.

Chatterjee, P., 1983. 'More on modes of power and the peasantry'. Ranajit Guha (ed.), *Subaltern Studies II*. Oxford University Press, Delhi.

———, 1984. 'Gandhi and the critique of civil society'. Ranajit Guha (ed.), *Subaltern Studies III.* Oxford University Press, Delhi.

Chattopadhyay, R., 1985. 'The Idea of Planning in India 1930-51'. Unpublished D. Phil thesis, Australian National University, Canberra.

Chaudhuri, K.A., 1977. *Ancient Agriculture and Forestry in Northern India.* Bombay.

Choudhury, L., Personal Communication.

Clark, C.W., 1985. *Bioeconomic Modelling and Fisheries Management.* John Wiley and Sons, New York.

Cleghorn, H., 1860. *Forests and Gardens of South India.* W.H. Allen, London.

Conklin, H., 1969. 'An ethno-ecological approach to shifting agriculture'. A.P. Vayda (ed.), *Environment and Cultural Behaviour.* Academic Press, New York.

Coward, M.P., Bulter, R.W.H., Chambers, A.F., Graham, R.H., Izatt, C.N., Khan, M.A., Knipe, R.J., Prior, D.J., Treloar, P.J. and Williams, M.P., 1988. 'Folding and imbrication of the Indian crust during Himalayan collision'. *Phil. Trans. Royal Society, London,* A 326.

Cronon, W., 1983. *Changes in the Land : Indians, Colonists and the Ecology of New England.* Hill and Wang, New York.

Crosby, A., 1986. *Ecological Imperialism : The Biological Expansion of Europe.* Cambridge University Press, Cambridge.

D'Arcy, W.E., 1910. *Preparation of Forest Working Plans in India.* Government Press, Calcutta.

Dasgupta, P., 1982. *The Control of Resources.* Oxford University Press, Delhi.

Dasgupta, S., 1980. 'Local Politics in Bengal : Midnapur District 1907-1923'. Unpublished thesis, School of Oriental and African Studies, University of London.

Dasmann, R., 1988. 'Towards a biosphere consciousness'. Worster, D., *The Ends of the Earth : Perspectives on Modern Environmental History.* Cambridge University Press, Cambridge.

Dharampal, 1986. 'Some aspects of earlier Indian society and polity and their relevance to the present'. *New Quest,* 57.

Dhareshwar, S.S., 1941. 'The denuded condition of the minor forest in Kanara coastal tract : Its history and a scheme for its regeneration'. *Indian Forester,* 67.

Dhavalikar, M.K., 1988. *The First Farmers of the Deccan.* Deccan College, Pune.

Digby, S., 1971. *War Horse and Elephant in the Delhi Sultanate.* Clarendon Press, Oxford.

Draz, O., 1985. 'The Hema system of range reserves in the Arabian peninsula : Its possibilities in range improvement and conservation projects in the near east'. J.A. McNeely and D. Pitt (ed.), *Culture and Conservation : The Human Dimension in Environmental Planning.* Croom Helm, Dublin.

Dumont, L., 1970. *Homo Hierarchicus : The Caste System and its Implications* (translated by M. Sainbury). Weidenfeld and Nicolson, London.

Eaton, P., 1985. 'Customary land tenure and conservation in Papua New Guinea'. J.A. NcNeely and D. Pitt (ed.), *Culture and Conservation : The Human Dimension in Environmental Planning.* Croom Helm, Dublin.

Edye, J., 1835. 'Description of the sea-ports of the coast of Malabar, of the facilities they afford for building vessels of different descriptions, and of the produce of the adjacent forests'. *Journal of the Royal Asiatic Society,* 11.

Ehrenfeld, U.R., 1952. *The Kadar of Cochin.* Madras University, Madras.

Elliott, J.G., 1973. *Field Sports in India, 1800-1947.* Gentry Books, London.

Elwin, V., 1939. *The Baiga.* John Murray, London.

——, 1942. *The Agaria.* Oxford University Press, Calcutta.

——, 1943. 'The Aboriginals'. *Oxford Pamphlets on Indian Affairs,* no. 14.

——, 1945. 'Saora Fituris'. *Man in India,* 25.

——, 1958. *Leaves from the Jungle* (1936 reprint). Oxford University Press, London.

——, 1960. *A Philosophy for NEFA.* Government Press, Shillong.

Engels, F., 1956. *The Peasant War in Germany.* Progress Publishers, Moscow.

Faith, R., 1984. 'The great rumour of 1377 and peasant ideology'.

R.H. Hilton and T.H. Ashton (eds.), *The English Rising of 1381*. Cambridge University Press, Cambridge.

Feldman, M.W. and Thomas, E.A.C., 1986. *Behaviour—dependent contexts for repeated plays of the prisoner's dilemma II : Dynamical aspects of the evolution of cooperation*. Working Paper Series : Paper no. 0002. Stanford University, U.S.A.

Fernandes, W. and Menon, G., 1987. *Tribal Women and Forest Economy : Deforestation, Exploitation and Status Change*. Indian Social Institute, New Delhi.

Fernandes, W., Menon, G. and Viegas, P., 1988. *Forests, Environment and Tribal Economy : Deforestation, Impoverishnent and Marginalization in Orissa*. Indian Social Institute, New Delhi.

Fernow, B.E., 1907. *A History of Forestry*. Toronto University Press, Toronto.

Fisher, R.A., 1958. *Genetical Theory of Natural Selection*. Dover Publications, Inc., New York.

Food and Agricultural Organization, United Nations 1984 (FAO 1984), 'Intensive Multiple-Use Forest Management in Kerala'. *FAO Forestry Paper* 53, FAO, Rome.

Forde, C.D., 1963. *Habitat, Economy and Society : A Geographical Introduction to Ethology*. Dutton, New York.

Ford Robertson, F.C., 1936. *Our Forests*. Government Press, Allahabad.

Fortmann, L.P. And Fairfax, S.K., 1989. 'American forestry professionalism in the Third World—some preliminary observations'. *Economic and Political Weekly*, 12 August.

Freeman, M.M.R., 1989. 'Graphs and gaffs : A cautionary tale in the common property resources debate'. F. Berkes (ed.), *Common Property Resources : Ecology and Community-Based Sustainable Development*. Belhaven Press, London.

Gadgil, M., 1985a. 'Social Restraints on Resource Utilization : The Indian Experience'. J.A. McNeely and D. Pitt (ed.), *Culture and Conservation : The Human Dimension in Environmental Planning*. Croom Helm, Dublin.

——, 1985b. 'Cultural Evolution of Ecological Prudence'. *Landscape Planning*, 12.

——, 1987. 'Diversity : Cultural and Biological'. *Trends in Ecology and Evolution*, 2(2).

——, 1989. 'The Indian heritage of a conservation ethic'. B. Allchin, E.R. Allchin and B.K. Thapar (ed.), *Conservation of the Indian Heritage*. Cosmo Publications, New Delhi.

——, 1991. 'Conserving India's biodiversity : The societal context'. *Evolutionary Trends in Plants*, in press.

Gadgil, M. and Berkes, F., 1991. 'Traditional resource management systems'. *Resource Management and Optimization*. In press.

Gadgil, M., Hegde, K.M. and Bhoja Shetty, K.A., 1986. 'Uttara Kannada : A case study in hill area development'. C.J. Saldanha (ed.), *Karnataka State of Environment Report 1985-86*. Centre for Taxonomic Studies, Bangalore.

Gadgil, M. and Iyer, P., 1989. 'On the diversification of common property resource use by Indian society'. F. Berkes (ed.), *Common Property Resources : Ecology and Community-Based Sustainable Development*. Belhaven Press, London.

Gadgil, M. and Malhotra, K.C., 1982. 'Ecology of a pastoral caste : The Gavli Dhangar of Peninsular India'. *Human Ecology*, 10.

Gadgil, M. and Prasad, S.N., 1978. 'Vanishing Bamboo Stocks'. *Commerce*, 136 (3497), 17 June.

Gadgil, M., Prasad, S.N. and Ali, R., 1983. 'Forest management and forest policy in India : A critical review'. *Social Action*, 33.

Gadgil, M. and Sinha, M., 1985. 'The biomass budget of Karnataka'. C.J. Saldanha (ed.), *Karnataka State of Environment Report 1984-85*. Centre for Taxonomic Studies, Bangalore.

Gadgil, M. and Subash Chandran, 1989. 'Environmental impact of forest-based industries on the evergreen forests of Uttara Kannada district : A case study. Final report', submitted to Department of Ecology and Environment. Government of Karnataka.

Gadgil, M. and Vartak, V.D., 1976. 'Sacred Groves of Western Ghats of India'. *Economic Botany*, 30.

Gause, G.F., 1969. *The Struggle for Existence*. Hafner Publishing Company, New York.

Geertz, C., 1963. *Agricultural Involution*. University of California Press, Berkeley.

Goldschmidt, W., 1979. 'A general model for pastoral social systems'. *Pastoral Production and Society*. Cambridge University Press, Cambridge.

Government of India (GOI), 1929. *Report of the Forestry Committee.* Government Press, Simla.

———, 1948. *India's Forests and the War.* Ministry of Agriculture, New Delhi.

———, 1952. *The National Forest Policy.* Government Press, Delhi.

———, 1956. *The Second Five Year Plan.* Planning Commission, Delhi.

———, 1961. *Report of the Scheduled Areas and Scheduled Tribes Commission,* Volume I, 1960-61. Manager of Publications, Delhi.

———, 1964. *History of Indian Railways.* Government Press, Delhi.

———, 1967. *Report of the Committee on Tribal Economy in Forest Areas.* Department of Social Welfare, Delhi.

———, 1980. *Task Force Report on Taking Forestry to the People.* Ministry of Agriculture, Delhi.

Grigg, D.B., 1980. *The Agricultural Systems of the World : An Evolutionary Approach.* Cambridge University Press, Cambridge.

Grigson, W.V., 1938. *The Maria Gonds of Bastar.* Oxford University Press, London.

Grove, R., 1990. 'Colonial conservation, ecological hegemony and popular resistance : Towards a global synthesis'. J.M. Mackenzie (ed.), *Imperialism and the Natural World.* Manchester University Press, Manchester.

Guha, Ramachandra, 1983. 'Forestry in British and post-British India : A historical analysis'. *Economic and Political Weekly,* 29 October and 5-12 November.

———, 1989a. *The Unquiet Woods : Ecological Change and Peasant Resistance in the Himalaya.* Oxford University Press, Delhi and University of California Press, Berkeley.

———, 1989b. 'Radical American environmentalism and wilderness preservation : a Third World critique'. *Environmental Ethics,* Spring.

Guha, S.R.D., 1989. Personal Communication.

Gupta, R., Bannerji, P. and Guleria, A., 1981. *Tribal Unrest and Forestry Management in Bihar.* Indian Institute of Management, Ahmedabad.

Gupta, T. and Sambrani, S., 1978. 'Control of shifting cultivation : The need for an integrative approach and systematic appraisal'. *Indian Journal of Agricultural Economics,* 31.

Hahn, S., 1982. 'Hunting, fishing and foraging : Common rights and class relations in the post-bellum South'. *Radical History Review*, 26.

Halappa, G.S., 1964. *History of Freedom Movement in Karnataka*, vol. II. Government Press, Bangalore.

Hardin, G., 1968. 'The tragedy of the commons'. *Science*, 162, 1243-8.

Harris, M., 1980. *Culture, People and Nature : An Introduction to General Anthropology*. Harper and Row, New York.

Hawley, A.H., 1986. *Human Ecology : A Theoretical Essay*. Chicago University Press, Chicago.

Hay, D. *et al.*, 1975. *Albion's Fatal Tree*. Penguin, Harmondsworth.

Hays, S.P., 1958. *Conservation and the Gospel of Efficiency : The Progressive Conservation Movement 1880-1920*. Harvard University Press, Cambridge, Mass.

——, 1987. *Beauty, Health and Permanence : Environmental Politics in the United States, 1955-85*. Cambridge University Press, Cambridge.

Hearle, N., 1888. *Working Plan of the Tehri Garhwal Leased Forests. Jaunsar Forest Division*. Government Press, Allahabad.

——, 1889. *Working Plan of the Deoban Range, Jaunsar Forest Division, Northwestern Provinces*. Government Press, Allahabad.

Heske, F., 1937. *German Forestry*. Yale University Press, New Haven.

Hivale, S. and Elwin, V., 1935. *Songs of the Forest : The Folk Poetry of the Gonds*. Allen and Unwin, London.

Hutchinson, J., Clark, G., Jope, E.M. and Riley, R., 1977. *Early History of Agriculture*. Oxford University Press, Oxford.

International Institute for Environment and Development and World Resources Institute 1987 (IIED and WRI). *World Resources, 1987*. Basic Books, New York.

Jarrige, J.F. and Meadow, R.H., 1980. 'The Antecedents of Civilization in the Indus Valley'. *Scientific American*, 243.

Jodha, N.S., 1986. 'Common property resources and rural poor in dry regions of India'. *Economic and Political Weekly*, 5 July.

Johannes, R.E., 1978. 'Traditional marine conservation methods in Oceania and their demise'. *Annual Review of Ecology and Systematics*, 9.

Jones, E.L., 1979. 'The environment and the economy'. Peter Burke (ed.), *The New Cambridge Modern History*, vol. XIII. Cambridge University Press, Cambridge.

Joshi, N.V., 1987. 'Evolution of cooperation by reciprocation within structured demes'. *Journal of Genetics*, 66 (1).

Joshi, N.V. and Gadgil, M., 1991. 'On the role of refugia in promoting prudent use of biological resources'. *Theoretical Population Biology*. In press.

Kajale, M.D., 1988. 'Plant economy'. M.K. Dhavalikar, H.D. Sankhalia and Z.D. Ansari (ed.), *Excavations at Inamgaon*, vol. 1, part ii. Deccan College, Pune.

Kangle, R.P., 1969. *Arthasasthra*. University of Bombay, Bombay.

Karve, I., 1961. *Hindu Society : An Interpretation*. Deccan College, Poona.

——, 1974. *Yuganta. The End of an Epoch*. Sangam Books, Poona, and Orient Longman Ltd., New Delhi.

Karve, I., and Malhotra, K.C., 1968. 'A biological comparison of eight endogamous groups of the same rank'. *Current Anthropology*, 9.

Keer, D. and Malshe, S.G., 1969. 'Jotirau Phule, Shetkarya Asud : The Whipcord of the Farmer (1882-3)'. *The Collected Works of Mahatma Phule* (in Marathi). Maharashtra Sahitya and Sanskriti Mandal, Pune.

Khazanov, A.V., 1984. *Nomads and the Outside World*. Cambridge University Press, Cambridge.

Kjekshus, H., 1977. *Ecology Control and Economic Development in East African History*. University of California Press, Berkeley.

Kosambi, D.D., 1970. *The Culture and Civilization of Ancient India in Historical Outline*. Vikas Publishing House Pvt. Ltd., Delhi.

Kothari, A., Pande, P., Singh, S. and Variava, D., 1989. *Management of National Parks and Sanctuaries in India : A Status Report*. Indian Institute of Public Administration, New Delhi.

Krishnakutty, C.N. and Chundamannil, M., 1986. 'Are eucalyptus plantations fulfilling the goals in Kerala?'. *Eucalyptus in India : Past, Present and Future*. Kerala Forest Research Institute, Peechi.

Kumar, D. (ed.), 1983. *The Cambridge Economic History of India*, vol. 2. Cambridge University Press, Cambridge.

Ladurie, Le Roy, E., 1980. *Carnival in Romans*. George Brazillier, New York.

Lal, M., 1984. *Settlement History and the Rise of Civilization in the*

Ganga-Yamuna Doab from 1500 B.C. – A.D. 300. B.R. Publishing, Delhi.

Laptev, I., 1977. *The Planet of Reason.* Progress Publishers, Moscow.

Leakey, R.E., 1981. *The Making of Mankind.* Abacus, New York.

Leathart, S., 1982. 'Review of N.D.G. James, A History of English Forestry'. *Times Literary Supplement*, 8 January.

Leeds, A. and Vayda, A.P., 1965. *Man, Culture and Animals : The Role of Animals in Human Ecological Adjustments.* American Association for the Advancement of Science, Washington D.C.

Lefebvre, G., 1982. *The Great Fear* (1932 reprint). Princeton University Press, Princeton.

Lenski, G. and Lenski, J., 1978. *Human Societies : An Introduction to Macrosociology.* McGraw-Hill, New York.

Lewis, O., 1964. *Pedro Martinez.* Alfred Knopf, New York.

Linebaugh, P., 1976. 'Karl Marx, the theft of wood, and working class composition : A contribution to the current debate'. *Crime and Social Justice* n.s. no. 6.

Macleod, W.C., 1936. 'Conservation among primitive hunting peoples'. *The Scientific Monthly*, December.

Mahalanobis, P.C., 1963. *The Approach of Operational Research to Planning.* Indian Statistical Institute, Calcutta.

Malhotra, K.C. 1974. 'Socio-biological investigations among the Nandiwallas of Maharashtra'. *Bulletin of the Urgent Anthropological and Ethnological Sciences* (Austria), 16.

Malhotra, K.C., 1982. 'Nomads'. *The State of India's Environment, 1982-83 : A Citizens' Report.* Centre for Science and Environment, New Delhi.

Malhotra, K.C. and Gadgil, M., 1981. 'The ecological basis of the geographical distribution of the Dhangars : A pastoral caste-cluster of Maharashtra'. *South Asian Anthropologist*, 2.

Malhotra, K.C., Hulbe, S.K., Khomne, S.B. and Kolte, S.B., 1983. 'Economic organization of a nomadic community, the Nandiwallas'. P.K. Misra and K.C. Malhotra (ed.), *Nomads in India.* Anthropological Survey of India, Calcutta.

Malhotra, K.C. and Khomne, S.B., 1978. 'Social stratification and caste ranking among the Nandiwallas of Maharashtra'. *Proceedings of the Seminar on Nomads in India*, Mysore.

Malhotra, K.C., Khomne, S.B. and Gadgil, M., 1983. 'On the role of hunting in the nutrition and economy of certain nomadic populations of Maharashtra'. *Man in India*, 63.

Mani, A., 1984. 'Social Intervention in the Management of Forest Resources : A Report on the Appiko Movement'. *Mimeo*. Indian Institute of Management, Bangalore.

Martin, C., 1978. *Keepers of the Game : Indian-Animal Relationships and the Fur Trade*. University of California Press, Berkeley.

May, R.M. (ed.), 1984. *Exploitation of Marine Communities*. Life Sciences Research Report 32. Springer Verlag, Berlin.

McEvoy, A.E., 1988. 'Towards an interactive theory of nature and culture : Ecology, production and cognition in the California fishing industry'. Worster, D., *The Ends of the Earth : Perspectives on Modern Environmental History*. Cambridge University Press, Cambridge.

McNeely, J.A. and Pitt, D. (eds.), 1985. *Culture and Conservation : The Human Dimension in Environmental Planning*. Croom Helm, London.

Meher-Homji, V.M., 1989. 'History of Vegetation of Peninsular India'. *Man and Environment*, 13.

Mehra, K.L. and Arora, R.K., 1985. 'Some considerations on the domestication of plants in India'. V.N. Misra and P. Bellwood (ed.), *Recent Advances in Indo-Pacific Prehistory*. Oxford and IBH, New Delhi.

Menant, J.C., Barbault, R., Lavelle, P. and Lepage, M., 1985. 'African savannas : Biological systems of humification and mineralization'. J.C. Tothill and J.J. Mott (ed.), *Ecology and Management of the World's Savannas*. Australian Academy of Sciences, Canberra.

Menezies, N., (in press). 'A History of Forestry in China'. J. Needham (ed.), *Science and Civilization in China*. Cambridge University Press, Cambridge.

Merriman, J., 1975. 'The Demoiselles of the Ariege, 1829-31'. Merriman (ed.), *1830 in France*. New Viewpoints, New York.

Misra, P.K., 1977. 'The Jenu Kurubas'. Surajit Sinha and B.D. Sharma (ed.), *Primitive Tribes : The First Step*. Manager of Publications, New Delhi.

Misra, V.N., 1973. 'Ecological Adaptations during Stone-age in

Western and Central India'. K.R.A. Kennedy and G.L. Possehl (ed.), *Ecological Background of South Asian Prehistory*. South Asia Occasional Papers and Theses. Cornell University Press, Ithaca.

Mooser, J., 1986. 'Property and wood theft : Agrarian capitalism and social conflict in rural society, 1800-1850. A Westphalian case study'. R.G. Moeller, (ed.), *Peasants and Lords in Modern Germany*. Allen and Unwin, London.

Moosvi, S., 1987. *The Economy of the Mughal Empire c. 1595. A Statistical Study*. Oxford University Press, Delhi.

Morris, M., 1982. *Forest Traders : A Socio-Economic Study of the Hill Pandaram*. The Athlone Press, London.

Mukerjee, R.K., 1916. *The Foundations of Indian Economics*. Longman, Green and Co., London.

——, 1926. *Regional Sociology*. The Century Co., New York.

Muranjan, S.W., 1974. 'Exploitation of forests through forest labour cooperatives'. *Artha Vijnana*, 16(2).

——, 1980. 'Impact of some policies of the Forest Development Corporation on the working of the Forest Labourers Cooperatives'. *Artha Vijnana*, 22 (4).

Nair, K.K., 1967. 'Forestry Development in India'. *Indian Journal of Agricultural Economics*, 22.

Nandy, A., 1980. *At the Edge of Psychology and Other Essays*. Oxford University Press, Delhi.

Nash, R., 1982. *Wilderness and the American Mind*. Yale University Press, New Haven.

National Commission of Agriculture, 1976. *Report of the National Commission of Agriculture*. vol. IX. Ministry of Agriculture, Delhi.

National Council of Applied Economic Research, 1963. *Socio-Economic Survey of Primitive Tribes in Madhya Pradesh*. National Council of Applied Economic Research, New Delhi.

Nietschmann, B., 1985. 'Torres Strait islander sea resource management and sea rights'. K. Ruddle and R.E. Johannes (ed.), *The Traditional Knowledge and Management of Coastal Systems in Asia and the Pacific*. UNESCO, Indonesia.

Pandian, M.S.S., 1985. 'Political Economy of Agrarian Change in Nanchilnadu : The Late Nineteenth Century to 1939'. University of Madras, Unpublished Ph. D. thesis.

Pant, G.B. and Maliekel, J.A., 1987. 'Holocene climatic changes over north west India : An appraisal'. *Climatic Change*, 10.

Parulekar, G., 1976. *Adivasis Revolt*. National Book Agency, Calcutta.

Paul, G.P., 1871. *Felling Timber in the Himalaya*. Punjab Printing Co., Lahore.

Pearson, G.F., 1870. 'Deodar forests of Jaunsar Bawar'. *Selections from the Records of the Government of the Northwestern Provinces*, 2nd series, vol. II, Allahabad.

Peluso, N., 1989. 'Rich Forests, Poor People and Development'. Unpublished Ph. D. thesis, Department of Rural Sociology, Cornell University.

Peoples Union for Democratic Rights, 1982. *Undeclared Civil War : A Critique of the Forest Policy*. Peoples Union for Democratic Rights, Delhi.

Pimentel, D. and Pimentel, M., 1979. *Food, Energy and Society*. Arnold, London.

Pimm, S.L., 1986. 'Community stability and structure'. M.E. Soule (ed.), *Conservation Biology : The Science of Scarcity and Diversity*. Sinauer, Sunderland, Mass.

Pingle, U., Raja Reddy, N.V. and von Fürer Haimendorf, 1982. 'Should shifting cultivation be banned?'. *Science Today*, April.

Polanyi, K., 1957 (1944). *The Great Transformation*. Beacon Press, Boston.

Possehl, G.L., 1982. *Harappan Civilization : A Contemporary Perspective*. Oxford and IBH, New Delhi.

Prasad, S.N., Personal Communication.

Prasad, S.N. and Gadgil, M., 1981. 'Conservation of Bamboo Resources in Karnataka'. *Mimeo*. Karnataka State Council of Science and Technology, Bangalore.

Pressler, F.A., 1987. 'Panchayat Forests in Madras 1913-1952'. Unpublished Paper, Department of Political Science, Kalamazoo College.

Prucha, F.P., 1985. *The Indians in American Society : From the Revolutionary War to the Present*. University of California Press, Berkeley.

Rai, S.N., 1981. 'Protection forestry with a reference to ecological balance in the tropical forests of Western Ghats of Karnataka'. National Seminar on Forests and Environment, 2-3 Dec. 1981. Karnataka Forest Department.

Rajaguru, S.N., Badam, G.L. and Abhyankar, H., 1984. 'Late Pleistocene Climatic Change in India'. *Proc. Symp. Episodes.* Dept. Geol. M.S.University, Baroda.

Rana, S., 1983. 'Vanishing Forests'. *Frontier*, 16 (6).

Randhawa, M.S., 1949. 'Nature conservation, national parks and bio-aesthetic planning in India'. Presidential Address, Botany Section, 36th Indian Science Congress, Allahabad.

Rappaport, R.A., 1984. *Pigs for the Ancestors : Ritual in the Ecology of a New Guinea People.* Yale University Press, New Haven.

Raumolin, J. 1986. 'The Impact of Technological Change on Rural and Regional Forestry in Finland'. *Mimeo.* World Institute of Development Economics Research, Helsinki.

Rendell, H. and Dennell, R.W., 1985. 'Dated lower palaeolithic artefacts from northern Pakistan'. *Current Anthropology*, 26 (3).

Richards, J.F., 1986. 'World environmental history and economic development'. W.C. Clark and R.E. Munn (ed.), *Sustainable Development of the Biosphere.* Cambridge University Press, Cambridge.

Ribbentrop, B., 1900. *Forestry in British India.* Government Press, Calcutta.

Roy, S.L., 1925. *The Birhors : A Little Known Jungle Tribe of Chota Nagpur.* K.E.M. Mission Press, Ranchi.

Ruddle, K. and Johannes, R.E. (ed.), 1985. *The Traditional Knowledge and Management of Coastal Systems in Asia and the Pacific.* UNESCO, Indonesia.

Sagreya, K.P., 1979. *Forests and Forestry.* National Book Trust, Delhi.

Sahlins, M., 1971. *Stone Age Economics.* Aldine Publishers, Chicago.

Saldanha, C.J., 1989. *Andaman, Nicobar and Lakshadweep, An Environmental Impact Assessment.* Oxford and IBH Publishing Co. Pvt. Ltd., New Delhi.

Sankhala, K.S. and Jackson, P., 1985. 'People, trees and antelopes in the Indian desert'. J.A. McNeely and D. Pitt (ed.), *Culture and Conservation : The Human Dimensions in Environmental Planning.* Croom Helm, Dublin.

Sarkar, S., 1980. 'Primitive rebellion and modern nationalism : A note on forest satyagraha in the non-cooperation and civil disobedience movements'. K.N. Panikar (ed.), *National and Left Movements in India.* Vikas, New Delhi.

Sarkar, S., 1983. *Modern India, 1885-1947*. Macmillan, New Delhi.

——, 1984. 'The conditions and nature of Subaltern militancy : Bengal from Swadeshi to non-cooperation'. R. Guha (ed.), *Subaltern Studies III*. Oxford University Press, New Delhi.

Savyasachi, 1986. 'Agriculture and social structure : The hill Maria of Bastar'. *Mimeo*. World Institute of Development Economics Research, Helsinki, January.

Scott, J.C., 1976. *The Moral Economy of the Peasant*. Yale University Press, New Haven.

——, 1986. *Weapons of the Weak : Everyday Forms of Peasant Resistance*. Yale University Press, New Haven.

——, 1987. 'Resistance Without Protest and Without Organization : Peasant Opposition to the Islamic Zakat and the Christian Tithe'. *Comp. Studies in Soc. and Hist.*, 29.

Sengupta, N., 1980. 'The indigenous irrigation organization of South Bihar'. *Indian Econ. and Social Hist. Rev.*, 17.

——(ed.), 1982. *Jharkhand : Fourth World Dynamics*. Authors' Guild, Delhi.

Service, E.R., 1975. *Origins of the State and Civilization : The Process of Cultural Evolution*. W.W. Norton and Company, New York, London.

Shanin, T., 1986. *The Roots of Otherness : Russia's Turn of Century*, volumes I and II. Macmillan, London.

Sharma, G.R., 1980. *The Beginnings of Agriculture*. Allahabad.

Sharma, R.S., 1987. *Urban Decay in India*. New Delhi.

Shepard, P., 1982. *Nature and Madness*. Sierra Books, San Francisco.

Shiva, V., Sharatchandra, H.C. and Bandopadhyay, J., 1982. 'Social forestry : No solution within the market place'. *The Ecologist* 12.

Singh, K.S. (ed.), 1983. *Tribal Movements in India*, volume II. Manohar, New Delhi.

Sinha, A.C., 1986. 'Social Frame of Forest History'. *Social Science Probings* 3 (2).

Sinha, D.P., 1972. 'The "Birhors"'. M.G. Bicchieri (ed.), *Hunters and Gatherers Today*. Holt, Reinhart and Winston, New York.

Slobodkin, L.B., 1968. 'How to be a predator?'. *American Zoologist*, 8.

Smith, E.A., 1983. 'Anthropological applications of optimal foraging theory : A critical review'. *Current Anthropology*, 24.

Smythies, E.A., 1925. *India's Forest Wealth*. Humphrey Milford, London.

Smythies, A. and Dansey, E. (eds.), 1887. *A Report on the Proceedings of the Forest Conference held at Dehra Dun in October 1886*. Govt. Press, Simla.

Soule, M.E. (ed.), 1986. *Conservation Biology : The Science of Scarcity and Diversity*. Sinauer, Sunderland, Massachusetts.

Srinivas, M.N., 1962. *Caste in Modern India and Other Essays*. Asia Publishing House, Calcutta.

Stanhill, G. (ed.), 1984. *Energy and Agriculture*. Springer Verlag, Berlin.

Stebbing, E.P., 1922-27. *The Forests of India*, vols. I, II, III. John Lane, London.

Sukumar, R., 1989. *The Asian Elephant : Ecology and Management*. Cambridge University Press, Cambridge.

Terborgh, J., 1986. 'Keystone plant resources in the tropical forest'. M.E. Soule (ed.), *Conservation Biology—The Science of Scarcity and Diversity*. Sinauer Associates, Sunderland, Mass.

Tewari, K.M., 1981. 'Research Needs of Social Forestry'. *Indian Forester*, 107.

Thakurdas, P., *et al.*, 1944. *Memorandum Outlining a Plan of Economic Development for India*. Penguin, London.

Thapar, R., 1966. *A History of India—Vol. 1*. Penguin Books, Harmondsworth.

———, 1984. *From Lineage to State*. Oxford University Press, Bombay.

Thompson, E.P., 1970-1. 'The moral economy of the English crowd in the eighteenth century'. *Past and Present*, no. 50.

———, 1975. *Whigs and Hunters*. Penguin, Harmondsworth.

Totman, C., 1985. *The Origins of Modern Japan's Forests : The Case of Akita*. University of Hawaii Press, Honolulu.

———, 1989. *The Green Archipelago : Forestry in Preindustrial Japan*. University of California Press, Berkeley.

Trautmann, T.R., 1982. 'Elephants and the Mauryas'. S.N. Mukherjee (ed.), *India : History and Thought. Essays in Honour of A.L. Basham*. Subarnarekha, Calcutta.

Trevor, C.G. and Smythies, E.A., 1923. *Practical Forest Management*. Government Press, Allahabad.

Tucker, R.P., 1979. 'Forest management and imperial politics : Thana district, Bombay, 1823-1887'. *Indian Economic and Social History Review*, 16.

———, 1988. 'The depletion of India's forests under British imperialism'. D. Worster, (ed.), *The Ends of the Earth : Perspectives on Modern Environmental History*. Cambridge University Press, New York.

Tucker, R.P. and Richards, J.F. (eds.), 1983. *Deforestation and the Nineteenth Century World Economy*. Duke University Press, Durham.

USAID, 1970. *A Survey of India's Export Potential of Wood and Wood Products*, vol. I. United States Agency for International Development, Delhi.

Vail, D., 1987. 'Contract Logging, Clear Cuts and Chainsaws'. *Mimeo*. World Institute of Development Economic Research, Helsinki.

Vayda, A.P., 1974. 'Warfare in ecological perspective'. *Annual Review of Ecology and Systematics*, 5.

Vijayan, V.S., 1987. 'Keoladeo national park ecology study'. *Bombay Natural History Society, Annual Report 1987*.

Visveswaraya, M., 1920. *Reconstructing India*. P.S. King, London.

Voelcker, J.A., 1893. *Report on the Improvement of Indian Agriculture*. Government Press, Calcutta.

von Fürer Haimendorf, C., 1943a. *The Chenchus : Jungle Folk of the Deccan*. Macmillan, London.

———, 1943b. *The Reddis of the Bison Hills : A Study in Acculturation*. Macmillan, London.

———, 1945a. *Tribal Hyderabad : Four Reports*, Government Press, Hyderabad.

———, 1945b. 'Aboriginal rebellions in the Deccan'. *Man in India*, 25.

von Monroy, J.A., 1960. *Report to the Government of India on Integration of Forests and Forest Industries*. Food and Agricultural Organization, Rome.

von Tunzelman, G.N., 1981. 'Technical progress during the industrial revolution'. R. Floud and D. McCloskey (eds.), *The Economic History of Britain Since 1700*, vol. 1 : 1700-1860. Cambridge University Press, Cambridge.

Wade, R., 1988. *Village Republics : Economic Conditions for Collective Action in South India*. Cambridge University Press, Cambridge.

Wallerstein, I., 1974. *The Modern World System*. Academic Press, New York.

Walton, H.G., 1910. *British Garhwal : A Gazetteer*. Government Press, Allahabad.

Ward, H.C., 1870. *Report of the Land Revenue Settlement of the Mundlah District of the Central Provinces (1868-9)*. Government Press, Bombay.

Webb, W.P., 1964. *The Great Frontier*. University of Texas Press, Austin.

Webber, T.W., 1902. *The Forests of Upper India and Their Inhabitants*. Edward Arnold, London.

Whitcombe, E., 1971. *Agrarian Conditions in Northern India, Volume I : The United Provinces Under British Rule, 1860-1900*. University of California Press, Berkeley.

White, L., 1967. 'The historical roots of our ecological crisis'. *Science*, 155, 1203-5.

Wilkinson, R.G., 1988. 'The English industrial revolution'. Worster, D., *The Ends of the Earth : Perspectives on Modern Environmental History*. Cambridge University Press, Cambridge.

Womack, J., 1969. *Zapata and the Mexican Revolution*. Alfred Knopf, New York.

World Commission on Environment and Development, 1987 (WCED), *Our Common Future*. Oxford University Press, New Delhi.

World Resources Institute, 1987.

Worster, D. (ed.), 1988. *The Ends of the Earth : Perspectives on Modern Environmental History*. Cambridge University Press, Cambridge.

Index

agriculture. *See* settled cultivators; shifting cultivation
Alluri Sita Rama Raju, 155
Appiko movement, 224–5
Arnold, David, 155
artisans, 83, 94, 97–8, 102, 104, 113, 171–3, 176–7, 185, 199, 216, 228–9, 242, 243, 244

Baden-Powell, B.H., 124–30, 133
Bahuguna, Sunderlal, 224
bamboo species, 136, 138, 171–2, 186, 198–200, 228
Bhatt, Chandi Prasad, 224
biological diversity, 15, 18, 25–6, 47, 50–1, 56, 96, 105, 109, 135, 174, 208–9, 212, 235–6
decline of, 142, 187–8, 190, 197–8. *See also* sacred groves; species extinction
Bloch, Marc, 7
Brahminism. *See* Hinduism

Brandis, Dietrich, 122–4, 127–33, 141, 143, 172, 173, 212
Brenner, Robert, 12
British colonialism, 123, 126, 129
and ecological change, 5, 116–8, 142–7
in India, 5–6, 133, 136, 137, 148, 171, 172, 179–80, 183, 239
revenue orientation of, 119–20, 138, 141, 157, 168, 176
broad-leaved species. *See* oak species
Buddha, 82, 84, 88, 105
Buddhism, 84, 103
and prudent resource use, 81–2, 87–90, 91
Burma, 119, 122

capitalism, 11, 14, 45, 54, 58–9, 116, 122, 137, 182, 184–5, 229
caste, 5, 83–84, 89, 93–94, 113,

158, 221, 242–3
and prudent resource use, 94–
  106
and resource use diversification, 95–100, 109–10, 244
chemical agriculture, 30–1, 222–
  3, 244
Chipko movement, 223–5
Christianity, 29, 75–6, 110, 113,
  115, 116
Cleghorn, Henry, 119, 121
climate change, 27, 36, 52, 72,
  73, 74–5, 76, 78
colonialism, 36, 41, 43, 54–5
  in the New World, 5, 43, 53,
    109, 117–8, 240–2. *See also*
    British colonialsim
common lands. *See* common
  property; community forestry
common property, 2, 28, 44–5,
  54, 115, 124, 127, 128, 131,
  165–6, 201, 216, 225–6. *See
  also* community forestry
community forestry, 2, 3, 32, 34,
  35, 38, 47, 76, 94–5, 106, 123,
  124, 131, 132–3, 134, 143–4,
  145, 147, 159, 163, 189
conservation. *See* prudent
  resource use
cooperative behavior, 18, 24–5,
  28, 32, 36, 38, 115–6
Congress Party, 161, 162–3, 164,
  179, 181–3, 222, 230
conifers. *See* pine species.
contractor system, 229–32
Crosby, Alfred, 117–8
cultural diversity, 1, 4–5, 96–7,
  105, 109–10

deforestation, 3, 6, 38-9, 47, 52,
  56, 79, 81, 87, 88–9, 120–2,
  139, 225, 241
  by the British, 118–21, 139,
    143, 198, 240
  in independent India, 187,
    189, 192, 196–7, 201, 210–
    11, 213, 222. *See also* sequen-
    tial exploitation; sustained
    yield forestry
deodar, 122, 137, 147, 167, 175,
  197
disease, 75, 92, 109–10, 117, 189,
  217
division of labour, 23, 34, 43–4
  and caste, 83–4
  by gender, 16, 23, 28, 32, 34,
    44
domestication of plants and
  animals, 27, 30, 76–7, 107

Eastern Ghats, 75, 82, 92
ecological history, 3–7, 67
  in comparative perspective,
    3, 54–5, 109–10, 116–8, 127–
    30, 132, 169, 237–8, 239–43,
    245
  neglect of, 5–7, 12–3, 145
ecological imperialism. *See*
  British colonialism;
  colonialism
ecological niches, 115
  and caste, 105–6, 110
  in contemporary India, 242–
    44
  of hunter-gatherers, 72–3. *See
    also* territoriality.
elephants, 35, 86–7, 108, 142–3,

217, 233–4

Elwin, Verrier, 149–50, 152, 154, 172, 176, 220

endogamy, 16, 82–4, 93–4, 96–8, 100, 103, 104–5. *See also* caste

energy, forms of, 15, 27, 31, 32, 40, 41, 114, 222, 240, 243, 244, 245. *See also* fuelwood.

environmental debate, 46, 55–6, 245

environmental degradation, 2–3, 17, 26, 29–30, 41, 43, 45–6, 51, 56, 91–2, 109, 117–8, 121, 143, 144, 190, 191, 225, 226, 230, 232–3, 241, 243–4. *See also* deforestation; profligate resource use

eucalyptus species, 188–92, 200–01, 207, 227

farm forestry, 189–92, 200, 204, 207

fertilizers, 30–1, 35, 36, 37, 55, 127, 159, 222

ficus spp, 20, 22, 24, 47, 104

fire, 26, 78–9, 81, 85, 87–8, 104, 118–9, 129, 142, 163, 169–70, 186

firewood. *See* fuelwood

fishing, 18, 21, 23, 24, 47, 92, 94, 96, 97, 107, 109, 161, 173, 244

fodder, 29, 32, 36, 37, 47, 138, 141, 159, 167, 171, 189, 191, 226, 227, 240

forest based industries, 2, 136, 171, 185, 193, 196–9, 205, 215–7, 223
  subsidies to, 185–7, 189, 191,

192, 197, 199–201. *See also* forest policy; sustained yield forestry

forest labour, 153, 155, 158, 161, 167, 196, 221, 223, 229–32

forest labour cooperatives, 223–4, 230–2

forest laws, 44, 57, 157
  in India, 122–35, 138, 140, 144, 148, 159, 161–2, 167, 169, 171, 173, 174, 178–80, 194, 215, 219

forest policy
  and railways, 120–2, 136–7, 138, 165, 168, 186
  and Royal Navy, 119
  commercial orientation of, 135–44, 148, 149, 151, 166, 173, 174–5, 188, 195–6, 209, 214, 218, 223, 231, 237
  in British India, 127, 130–1, 132, 134, 136–7, 141, 146, 153, 160, 167, 174, 177–9, 210
  in independent India, 185–97, 215–7
  industrial bias of, 171, 172, 186–93, 215–6. *See also* social conflict; sustained yield forestry

forest privileges, 125, 126, 133–4

forest rights, 125–35, 137, 147, 165

fossil fuels. *See* energy, forms of

fuelwood, 32, 37, 40, 47, 92, 108, 114, 120, 125, 127, 134, 135, 136, 141, 143, 159, 160, 165, 167, 172, 189, 191, 226, 227

Gandhi, Mahatma, 162, 179, 181–3, 222, 238
Ganges River, 78, 92
Gangetic plain, 72, 76, 85, 103
gatherers. *See* hunter-gatherers.
Gause, G.F., 24
grass. *See* fodder
graziers. *See* pastoralists
grazing, 1, 2, 30, 49, 54, 55, 92, 95, 102, 124, 125, 127, 128, 129, 133, 134, 141, 159–60, 162, 165, 167, 174, 186, 190, 225–8, 235–6. *See* also pastoralists

Himalaya, 71–2, 78, 82, 92, 120, 122, 136, 137, 139, 150, 174, 186
Hinduism, 78–82, 88, 103–4, 107, 110, 149.
See also caste
hunter-gatherers, 2, 34, 39, 44, 54, 55, 57, 59, 67, 109
  ecological impact of, 26–7
  economy of, 17–8, 19
  ideologies of nature among, 18
  in India, 72, 77, 79–81, 82–3, 86–7, 93, 110, 146, 148–50, 180, 216, 217–8, 242, 243
  knowledge base of, 15, 18, 25, 26, 217
  social organization of, 16–7
  technologies of resource use in, 15–6. *See also* profligate resource use; prudent resource use; social conflict

hunting, 22, 39, 49, 54–5, 92, 96, 97, 98–100, 104–5, 109, 142–3, 148, 149–50, 232–4
hunting preserves, 35, 55, 58, 86–7, 107–8, 128
individualism, 44, 115–6
Industrial Revolution, 17, 114–6
industrial society, 32, 55–6, 58–9, 68, 176, 239
  ecological impact of, 40, 41, 51–3, 184–5
  economy of, 41–3
  ideology of nature in, 45–6
  in India, 184–5, 241–5
  social organization of, 43–5
  technologies of resource use in, 39–41. *See also* profligate resource use; prudent resource use; social conflict.
International Whaling Commission, 47, 50
irrigation, 31, 36, 37, 39, 55, 78, 85–6, 92, 106–7, 120, 145, 244
Islam, 29, 110, 113

Jainism, 84
  and ecological prudence, 81–2, 87–90, 91, 103
jhum. See shifting cultivation.
Judaism, 29

k-strategists, 18, 36, 81
Kumra Bhimu, 157
Madras government: and forest legislation, 126–7, 129–31, 143, 180
Mahabharata, 48, 53, 79, 81
manure. *See* fertilizers

Marx, Karl, 40
Marxism, 11–3, 59
Mauryas, 85–7, 88–9
minor forest produce, 137, 138, 147, 148, 154, 159, 186, 217–8, 223, 229, 231–2
modes of production, 4, 11–3
modes of resource use, 4, 15, 52, 60–6, 114, 245
and population growth, 67–8
compared to modes of production, 4, 13–4, 59
defined, 13–5. *See also* hunter-gatherers; pastoralists; settled cultivators; shifting cultivation; social conflict; industrial society.
Mughals, 107–8 113

natural resource conflict. *See* social conflict
nature worship. *See* religion; sacred groves
Nehru, Jawaharlal, 183
niches. *See* ecological niches
nomads. *See* pastoralists
non-wood forest produce. *See* minor forest produce

oak species, 119, 142, 147, 167, 175, 195, 211, 223

panchayat forests, *See* community forestry
pastoralists, 38, 55, 67, 109, 185
ecological impact of, 29–30
economy of, 27–8
ideology of nature in, 28–9
in India, 77, 78, 82–4, 93–4, 102–3, 159, 167–8, 174, 178, 228, 242
social organization of, 28
technologies of resource use in, 27
pasturage. *See* grazing
peasant resistance. *See* protest, mechanisms of; social conflict
peasants. *See* settled cultivators
Phadke, Vasudev Balwant, 151
Phule, Jotirau, 146
Pine species, 50, 136, 137, 139, 142, 147, 163, 169, 175, 186, 188, 195, 197, 207, 212, 213, 221, 223
plantation forestry, 118, 166, 187–92, 201, 205, 207, 214, 220–1, 224, 227
Polanyi, Karl, 241
population decline, 68, 117–8, 149, 157, 241
population density, 75, 95, 109–10, 117, 148
population growth, 36, 58, 67–8, 81, 92, 132, 158, 178, 218–9, 236, 241, 242
princely states, 137–8, 150, 153, 155–7, 163–4
private property, 16, 28, 33–4, 44–5, 59, 115, 126, 131, 189, 191, 200, 226
profligate resource use, 3, 4, 20, 51, 81, 184
and hunter-gatherers, 26
and industrial society, 46–7, 116

and settled cultivators, 37, 39
in India, 79, 81, 87, 196–7,
199–200, 205, 210–1. *See
also* deforestation; environmental degradation;
religion; resource consumption; sequential exploitation; species extinction; sustained yield forestry
protest, mechanisms of, 174–9
and violence, 54, 153, 155,
156, 157, 160, 162, 164, 178,
arson, 163, 169–70, 175, 234
attacks on state property and
officials, 155, 156, 160, 161,
163, 234
forest 'crime', 54, 58, 150, 156,
159, 161–4, 169–71, 172,
175, 177, 220
forest invasions, 58, 154, 157,
161, 221, 224, 227
migration, 153, 157, 164, 172,
177
petitions, 153, 157, 164, 165,
168, 178
strikes, 160, 161, 164, 231. *See
also* social conflict
prudent resource use, 3, 4, 20,
51, 76, 92–3, 163, 184, 218–9
and hunter-gatherers, 20, 25,
26, 73, 148
and industrial society, 46–7
and pastoralists, 29
and settled cultivators, 37–8
decline of, 143–4, 207, 210–1
different forms of, 21–3
in India, 82–4, 94–106, 113
rule-of-thumb prescriptions

for, 23–5. *See also* community forestry; profligate
resource use; sacred
groves; religion; scientific
conservation; territoriality
r-strategists, 17–8, 28, 36, 45, 81
religion, 29, 150, 151
and profligate resource use,
29, 78–9, 81
and prudent resource use, 18,
20, 38, 45, 56–7, 87–90, 103–
4, 108
and protest, 150, 162, 169–70,
175–7, 224. *See also* Buddhism; Christianity; Hin-
duism; Islam; Jainism;
Judaism; sacred groves
reserved forests, 134, 135, 150,
154, 156, 162, 172, 174, 200,
210–1, 216, 218, 219. *See also*
forest policy; state forestry
resource conservation. *See* prudent resource use
resource consumption, 15, 31,
40–1, 51, 68, 114–6, 184, 198
resource destruction. *See*
profligate resource use
resource flows, 15, 17, 19, 27–8,
31–6, 40–3, 114–5, 243–4
resource substitution, 3, 41, 240,
243

sacred groves, 23, 24, 38, 76, 88,
104, 106, 108, 132, 207, 209,
235
sacred ponds, 2, 47, 106, 207
sal, 122, 136, 138, 139, 175, 195,
197, 221

sandalwood, 123n, 125, 127, 162
scientific conservation, 46–51.
  See also sustained yield
  forestry
scientific forestry. *See* sustained
  yield forestry
Scott, James, 164
sequential exploitation, 121,
  197–207, 210–1. *See also* sustained yield forestry
settled cultivators, 1, 2, 44, 53–
  4, 55, 57–8, 59, 67–8, 109
  ecological impact of, 38–9
  economy of, 31–3
  ideology of nature in, 37
  in India, 76–7, 78–82, 86–7,
    89, 95, 96, 107–8, 110, 113,
    120, 140, 141, 145, 147, 152–
    3, 158–71, 176, 177–8, 180,
    185, 188, 194, 216, 221–9,
    242, 243, 244–5
  social organization of, 32, 34–
    7
  technologies of resource use
    in, 30–1. *See also* profligate
    resource use; prudent
    resource use; social conflict
shifting cultivation, 2, 15, 30,
  75, 77, 93, 95, 104, 109, 130,
  141, 146, 150–8, 171, 176, 177–
  8, 216, 218–21, 242. *See also* social conflict
shilkar. *See* hunting
silviculture. *See* sustained yield
  forestry
social conflict, 2, 3, 4, 6, 16, 28,
  132, 133, 146–80, 215–38
  between hunter-gatherers

    and the state, 148–50, 180,
    217–8
  between modes of resource
    use, 28, 29, 36, 37, 41–2, 53–
    7, 78–81, 85–6, 109, 115–6,
    171–2, 174, 194–6, 228–9,
    240–1, 244–5
  between settled cultivators
    and the state, 108, 158–71,
    221–9
  between shifting cultivators
    and the state, 150–8, 218–21
  within modes of resource
    use, 16–7, 26, 35, 57–9. *See*
    also modes of resource use;
    protest, mechanisms of
socialism, 14, 45, 239
species extinction, 26, 39, 49, 52,
  75, 108, 143, 171, 233
state forestry, 2, 5–6, 35, 54, 59,
  128–30, 171, 178, 217, 228
  in British India, 122–3, 131,
    144, 147, 148–9
  in independent India, 185,
    193–4, 210, 216
  in precolonial India, 86–7,
    107–8. *See also* forest policy;
    reserved forests
sustained yield forestry, 46, 47,
  48, 50, 142, 167, 186, 229
  ecological insensitivity of,
    198, 212–3
  failures of, 50, 139, 186–7,
    194–5, 197–214, 230
  insufficient data base of, 198,
    211–4
state property, 44–5, 54, 115,
  124–6, 128, 130, 131, 134, 135,

145, 165–6, 169, 175, 184, 189, 193–4, 200, 209. *See also* forest policy; state forestry
sustainability. *See* profligate resource use; prudent resource use
swidden cultivation. shifting cultivation.
teak, 43, 118, 119, 122, 123n, 127, 137, 138, 142, 147, 162, 173, 175, 188, 195, 197, 201, 221, 224, 231
territoriality, 2, 93, 114, 160
    among hunter-gatherers, 16–7, 18, 57, 67, 72
    in caste society, 100–3.
Thompson, E.P., 175
timber harvesting, 1, 39, 40, 45, 47, 50, 51, 59, 92, 108, 129, 135, 137, 138, 139, 147,

168,186–9, 223–4. *See also* deforestation; sustained yield forestry
tree felling. *See* deforestation; timber harvesting; sustained yield forestry
tribal revolts. *See* protest, mechanisms of; social conflict

Untouchables, 83, 88, 94–5.

vegetarianism, 89, 96
Visveswaraya, M., 183–4

Western Ghats, 72, 82, 92, 95, 96, 139, 151, 189, 211
wildlife conservation, 48–9, 50–1, 217, 232–6. *See also* biological diversity; species extinction